YELLOW OVER
THE BLUEGRASS

STREETCARS AND INTERURBANS OF KENTUCKY

VOLUME ONE

CHARLES H. BOGART

Front cover drawing
MAIN STREET TROLLEY
by
Paul Sawyier
Used with the permission of
Bill Coffey
and
Paul Sawyier Gallery
Frankfort, Kentucky
www.Paulsawyiergalleries.com

TABLE OF CONTENTS

VOLUME ONE

VOLUME TWO

FOREWORD

As a child growing up in Newport, Kentucky, from our house I could watch the Green Line's Fort Thomas streetcar run its route alongside Tenth Street. While attending St. Stephen School on Washington Street, the #11 Line's streetcars ran past my classroom. On a hot July or August afternoon, with no air conditioning at home, Mom would at times take my sister and me for a ride out to the Fort Thomas military post. Then every other Sunday, after church, we would visit my Dad's mother who lived in Cincinnati, Ohio. We would board a #11 Line streetcar at Seventh and Washington and ride to Dixie Terminal. It was then walk to Government Square to catch a Cincinnati Street Railway streetcar out to Grandma's apartment. At least once a month my Grandma Nobbe would travel to Mount Adams, in Cincinnati, to meet with her sisters. Often I went with her, not only riding streetcars, but traveling via the incline to the top of Mt. Adams. Thus, streetcars are part of my fondest childhood memories.

I later studied history at Thomas More College and urban planning at Ohio State University. Within my studies in both of these fields, I came to realize that transportation is a shaper of a nation's economic well being. It was the availability or non-availability of cheap and dependable transportation that has shaped today's Commonwealth of Kentucky by confirming economic supremacy on this or that city and withholding it from others. In fact, I came to realize during my 40-years of employment with the Commonwealth of Kentucky that many of the problems it faced revolved around transportation. Among the transportation systems that affected Kentucky was the street railway in its many shapes and forms: horsecar, trolley, streetcar, and interurban. Hopefully, within the following pages I will have provided an introductory look into what was, at its time, a revolutionary change in the way people traveled, the use of the electric traction motor to power vehicles riding on steel rails lying within the streets of a city.

This book would not have been possible without the knowledge shared with me by members of Doc Blackburn's Hoosier Traction Meet and the Cincinnati Railbuffs. I also wish to extend my thanks to the staff of the many city, county, university, museum, and historical societies' libraries I visited. They all went an extra step to help me.

I also need to thank the Kentucky Historical Society and Kentucky Explorer Magazine. Both organizations provided me with encouragement in undertaking this research and, as a result, some of the chapters within these two volumes first saw light in their publications.

Finally I must recognize the support and encouragement my wife, Mary Ann, provided during this long term endeavor.

Please notify the author of any errors or omissions found with in the text, or the availability of any documentation I overlooked in researching this book at frankfortrail@fewpb.net.

"There are three things that make a nation great and prosperous – a fertile soil, busy work shops, and easy conveyance of men and animals from place to place."
Lord Bacon (1521-1626)

INTRODUCTION
TRANSPORTATION IN KENTUCKY

During the 200 years that the Commonwealth of Kentucky has been part of the United States, its citizens have enjoyed numerous forms of private and public transportation systems. They used these systems to move themselves and their goods both within and beyond the Commonwealth's borders. Included among the transportation systems used by Kentuckians during these first 200 years of statehood were walking, riding on or behind an animal, and boats that used human, animal, wind, and mechanical power to move. In addition, roller and ice skates, skis and sleds, bicycles of all types, and powered scooters and motorcycles were used. Last of all, citizens of the Commonwealth used steam, gasoline, diesel and electrical powered automobiles, trucks, and buses, powered and un-powered aircraft, blimps, balloons, and steam, gasoline, diesel, and electrical powered rail cars.

Interestingly, during the countdown for the 220 years of statehood in 2013, one of these forms of transportation is no longer available in Kentucky. Electrical powered cars running on rails, in particular the interurban, the trolley, and the streetcar powered by overhead electrical wires, have disappeared. (#1) At one time, 20 of Kentucky's 120 counties, Bell, Boyd, Bourbon, Campbell, Clark, Daviess, Fayette, Franklin, Henderson, Jefferson, Jessamine, Kenton, Mason, McCracken, Oldham, Pulaski, Scott, Shelby, Warren, and Woodford had access to interurban, trolley, or streetcar service powered by electric traction motors. In addition, two counties, Knox and Madison, enjoyed horsecar service while two other counties, Kenton and Jefferson, had trolley bus service. With the start of the 21st century, no county in Kentucky can boast an interurban, trolley, streetcar, trolley bus, or horsecar line.

The following is an account of the first and last horsecar, trolley, streetcar, and interurban lines within Kentucky. The Commonwealth's first horsecar line opened in 1844 in Louisville (Jefferson Co.), and the last horsecar line closed in 1919 in Barbourville (Knox Co).(#2) The first electric powered trolley line opened in 1882 in Middlesborough (Bell Co.), and the last closed in 1950 in Covington (Kenton Co.). The first electric overhead wire powered streetcar line opened in 1890 in Paducah (McCracken Co.) (#3), and the last closed in Ft. Mitchell (Kenton Co.) in 1950. The first interurban line in Kentucky started running from Louisville (Jefferson Co.) in 1901, and the last interurban operation within Kentucky ended here in 1939. Trolley bus service started in 1936 in Louisville (Jefferson Co.) and ended in 1958 in Covington (Kenton Co.). Electric powered cars pulling trailers were first used in 1882 in Middlesborough (Bell Co.), and the last was used in 1948 in Louisville (Jefferson Co.).

The question is often raised as to why Kentucky's streetcar, trolley, and interurban companies disappeared. The easy answer is that a conspiracy by the automobile, gasoline, and tire industries drove them out of business. The real answer is more complicated, involving actions and inactions by local, state, and federal governments. Local and state taxes favored the bus over rail transportation. Rail transportation had to pay real estate taxes on its tracks and overhead wires. With the signing of the Federal Highway Act of 1921, the Federal Government directed governmental and private funds away from rail transportation to road transportation. The Public Utility Holding Company Act of 1935, while designed to break up the concentration of monopolies controlling the electrical utilities, had the unintended effect of forcing utilities to divest themselves of cross-subsidized electric trolley, streetcar, and interurban services. Then governments at all levels refused to offer the subsidies the trolleys, streetcars, and interurbans needed to survive. Only in 1974, with the passage of the National Mass Transportation Assistance Act, did governmental monies start to flow into public transportation as part of a national public policy. Unfortunately, by 1974, almost all of the trolley, streetcar, and interurban lines in the United States were covered over in asphalt or concrete.

Within the following pages, we will trace the rise and fall of the horsecar, trolley, streetcar, interurban, and trolley bus services within the Commonwealth of Kentucky. (#4)

(#1) The author considers any electric powered car running on one set of wheeled trucks a trolley, and those electric powered cars running on two sets of trucks a streetcar. All non-powered cars having either one or two sets of trucks are a trailer; however, he admits using the words "trolley" and "streetcar" interchangeably within the following pages.

(#2) Some may hold that the Lexington & Ohio's (L&O) use of animals in 1833 to pull its cars from Lexington to Viley (Fayette Co.) or the L&O's use of animals to pull its cars between Portland and Louisville (Jefferson Co.) circa 1834 is the true date of the start of horsecar operations in Kentucky.

(#3) Some dispute the honor of the first electrified overhead electric line in Kentucky being awarded to McCracken County and hold that the honor of being first belongs to Louisville (Jefferson Co.).

(#4) The electrical motors that generated the mechanical power to propel these cars were called Traction Motors, thus this type of public transportation is often referred to in technical journals as Traction Cars.

Rapid Transit in Kentucky.

The Monticello Stage Coach, Burnside, Ky.

MAYSVILLE, KY.   Str. Courier running between Maysville, Ky. and Cincinnati, O.

L. & N. Depot, Bloomfield, Ky.

G. P. BROWN
DRUGS
NT OIL VARNISH WALL PAPER
SCHOOL BOOK
& C.

West Side of Main St., Bloomfield, Ky.

5

Lower Main St., Harrodsburg, Ky.

A SURVEY OF KENTUCKY'S INTERURBAN LINES

At the start of the 20th century, Kentucky had a population of 2.14 million that was largely rural in nature. The few urban areas in the Commonwealth were, with the exception of Lexington, located on the banks of the Ohio River. The principal cities of Kentucky were Ashland, part of the Ironton, Ohio, and Huntington, West Virginia, triangle; Maysville, midway between Huntington and Cincinnati, Ohio; Covington and Newport on the Kentucky side of the Ohio River at Cincinnati, Ohio; Louisville, the largest city of the state; Owensboro and Henderson, located across the river from Evansville, Indiana; and Paducah, at the junction of the Tennessee and Ohio Rivers.

Kentucky's main exports at this time were raw or finished agricultural and mineral products, such as timber and coal and milk and whiskey. To move these goods during the first half of the 19th century, the Commonwealth embraced both the railroad and the steamboat. During the last half of the 19th century, Kentucky sought out the streetcar, trolley, and interurban for local travel. A casual reading of the Louisville newspapers of the period indicates that over 100 different interurban and streetcar lines were proposed for construction within Kentucky during the period 1890 to 1910. A review of the acts of the Kentucky Legislature for the period 1890 to 1920 shows that only 36 companies were actually granted a charter to build a line, and of these, only 12 companies actually laid any track.

Louisville and its suburbs were then, as they are now, the largest centers of urban population in the Commonwealth, and the city was a major rail hub from which steam rail lines radiated out into the Commonwealth. Louisville was an early convert to both the horsecar and the electric streetcar and interurban technology. It opened its first mule car line in 1864, its first electric trolley car line in 1889, and its first interurban line in 1901. The Louisville Chamber of Commerce was soon talking about their city becoming the interurban rail hub of Kentucky. The dreams of those interurban promoters, however, would not ultimately correspond to what was actually built. Only eight interurban lines would lead outward from downtown Louisville.

The city of Louisville would gain some fame as the originating point of a 117-mile interurban line that stretched north to Indianapolis, Indiana, where interurban connecting lines allowed riders to continue their journey to such destinations as Terre Haute, Indiana; Chicago, Illinois; or Columbus, Ohio.

Construction of an interurban line northward into Indiana from Louisville began in 1903 when Louisville & Southern Indiana Traction Company (S&ITC) began to lay track from Louisville into Indiana via the Big Four Railroad Bridge. The interurban cars shared the bridge's two-mile span across the Ohio River with the steam trains of the Big Four Railroad, later New York Central. Prior to S&ITC completing its track from Louisville to Indianapolis, the Indianapolis, Greenwood & Franklin Railroad began laying track southward from Indianapolis toward Louisville in 1895. Both lines battled financial and legal problems that led to work stoppages and reorganizations as they pushed their track forward.

After four years of construction, the two interurban lines finally met each other in 1907 at Sellersburg, Indiana, some 14 miles north of Louisville and 103 miles south of Indianapolis. By this time, the two lines were operating under the names of Louisville & Northern Railway & Light Company and Indianapolis & Louisville Traction Company. In 1912, Samuel Insull gained control of both lines and merged them into Interstate Public Service Company. Insull brought modern management techniques to the line and invested money in its upgrades of the right-of-way and equipment. Freight and passenger services were improved and modernized. While in the short run this led to increased profits, the improved nearby public roads and advances in automobile construction would have a disastrous effect on the Interstate Public Service Company.

The interurban line from Indianapolis to Louisville had been built with little regard to the adjacent roads and their horseless carriages. Thus, the interurban right-of-way hugged the side of the road and crossed it from side to side with little thought to road bound traffic. In the Indiana cities and towns that it served, the interurban car shared the main street of the town with the growing legion of automobiles. Public opinion in the 1920s turned against Interstate Public Service. What in 1907 had been hailed as a boon for the communities along the way was, by 1931, considered a bust.

The effects of the Great Depression drove Insull and his companies into insolvency. In 1931, Interstate Public Service Company was reorganized as Public Service Company of Indiana. Cutbacks in service now became the name of the game in order to save the company. These cutbacks failed to save Public Service, and in 1939, the Louisville to Indianapolis rail line was closed to Louisville traffic at Seymour, Indiana.

Louisville also developed five interurban lines radiating outward from downtown to serve fellow Kentuckians in the outlying districts of Jefferson County and Oldham and Shelby Counties. Two companies, both organized in 1903, built these lines: Louisville and Eastern Railroad (L&E) and Louisville & Interurban Railroad (L&I).

L&E had originally been organized as Louisville, Anchorage & Pewee Valley Electric Railway (LA&PV) in 1899. LA&PV started construction of their line in 1900 but by 1901 had made little progress. At this time, L&E took control of LA&PV and moved to finish the work started by LA&PV. In addition, L&E began to build a line to Shelbyville in Shelby County. Money pledged to L&E for track construction by individuals and governing bodies was slow to arrive. Thus, it was not until 1907 that the L&E Line reached LaGrange, the county seat of Oldham County, located 24 miles east of Louisville. L&E's corporate plans called for this line to be extended 30 miles eastward to Carrollton and then an additional 60 miles to Cincinnati, Ohio; however, financing for this line never materialized.

L&E's line to Shelbyville utilized the first seven miles of the line that ran from downtown Louisville to LaGrange. At Beechwood, the Shelbyville Line branched off and ran due east for 22 miles to Shelbyville that was intended as an intermediate stop. This line was supposed to be extended to Frankfort, 20 miles to the east of Shelbyville. The Frankfort and Shelbyville interurban line was to connect with the Kentucky Traction & Terminal Company (KT&T) line that reached Frankfort from Lexington. Unfortunately, the good citizens of Shelbyville were anti-interurban and for a number of years prevented the L&E from running through their city. L&E's interurban cars were forced to stop on the western outskirts of Shelbyville and transfer their passengers to a local streetcar. By the time the courts ruled that L&E, now operating as Louisville & Interurban, could run its cars through Shelbyville, financing for the line's extension to Frankfort had dried up.

The other Louisville interurban company, L&I, built four lines to the west and south of Louisville: Jeffersontown completed in 1904, Okolona in 1905, Orell in 1907, and Fern Creek in 1908. All of the L&I lines were built to five-foot gauge except the Prospect Line, which was 4 feet 8-1/2 inches. These four lines, while classified as interurban lines and used by both freight motors and interurban cars, were in reality suburban lines. The Jeffersontown Line was thirteen miles long, the Okolona Line ten miles, the Orell Line seventeen miles, the Fern Creek Line ten miles, and the Prospect Line eleven miles.

A charter granted in 1918 to Kentucky Traction Company to extend the Orell Line 15 miles west to Camp Knox (now Ft. Knox) came to naught as material and equipment for track expansion were not available. During World War I, Camp Knox served as the firing range for the Field Artillery Officer Candidate School, then located at Camp Zachary Taylor in Louisville.

The Louisville & Mt. Washington Railway Company was part of a real estate promotion scheme to extend the Okolona Line to Mt. Washington and eventually on to Bardstown. The promoters proclaimed the area to be served as healthy and ready for development as "gentlemen farms." They claimed the proposed line extension had the potential to turn the Okolona Line into a real money earner. Promotional literature for this line pointed out that the existing Louisville & Nashville Railroad (L&N) connection to Bardstown from Louisville was a roundabout route, twice the length of the proposed interurban line. Survey work for laying out the right-of-way of this interurban was undertaken; however, funds to build the line could not be raised.

In 1911, L&E was merged into L&I and lost its corporate identity. The reorganized company provided passenger and freight service on all of its lines. However, all of the lines, except for the Prospect Line, were built to five foot gauge, leaving them with no direct car interchange between L&I and standard-gauge railroads. All goods moving between L&I and the standard gauge railroads had to be transshipped, prompting many shippers located along the L&I to transport their goods an extra mile or so by wagon or truck to avoid the transshipment costs. L&E and L&I developers had not learned from the errors of the early steam railroad promoters who had also failed to see that if the steam railroad system was to grow, all railroads needed to operate on a common gauge, which by 1900 had become 4 feet 8.5 inches. The interurban lines with their mixture of standard gauge, five-foot gauge, and other gauges prevented the development of run-through cars at interurban union terminals.

The effects of the Great Depression and competition from bus lines and jitneys spelled the end of L&I. One-by-one it closed its routes. The Okolona Line was terminated in 1931, and service on the Jeffersontown Line ended in 1932. Traffic on the Fern Creek Line was embargoed in 1933; the last car ran to Shelbyville in 1934. The remaining three lines ceased operations in 1935: Orell on August 17, LaGrange on August 24, and Prospect on October 31. City streetcars, however, would continue to run in Louisville until 1948 when buses took over. Interestingly, the recent Louisville failed light rail line proposal was to have followed the general route of the Okolona Line.

The other major interurban system serving the Commonwealth was centered in Lexington. It consisted of four lines radiating outward from downtown Lexington. In 1902, Georgetown & Lexington Traction Company (G&LT) opened a 12-mile line between Georgetown and Lexington. The following year Blue Grass Traction Company (BGT) began operating an 18-mile route between Paris and Lexington. In 1904, G&LT was merged into BGT, and the company began running through cars from Paris to Georgetown via Lexington. The next year, 1905, Central Kentucky Traction Company (CKT) opened a 14-mile line between Versailles and Lexington. Two years later in 1907, Frankfort & Versailles Traction Company (F&VT) opened a 15-mile line between Frankfort and Versailles. Shortly after the line to Frankfort opened, F&VT was merged into CKT, and through car service was provided between Frankfort and Lexington.

In 1910, Lexington & Interurban Railway Company (Lex&I) built a 12-mile standard gauge line south from Lexington to

Nicholasville. The plan apparently was to exchange freight cars with the Louisville & Atlantic Railroad (L&A) at Nicholasville. This plan all came to naught when the Louisville & Nashville Railroad (L&N) acquired the L&A track in the same year.

Blue Grass Traction Company, Central Kentucky Traction Company, and Lexington & Interurban Railway were all merged into Kentucky Traction & Terminal Company (KT&T) in 1911 and became part of the Samuel Insull Empire. KT&T controlled not only the above interurban lines but also operated streetcar systems in the surrounding cities of Frankfort, Winchester, Paris, Georgetown, and Lexington.

Within the plans of a number of promoters, Lexington was to have become a major interurban hub with lines extending outward into the state. KT&T itself looked at three extensions from Frankfort. The first would have closed the gap between Frankfort and Shelbyville but was shelved due to the Shelbyville City Council's opposition to interurbans running through their city. The second line would have built south from Frankfort to Lawrenceburg. The right-of-way for this line was surveyed but no construction was started. The cost of bridging the Kentucky River at Frankfort is probably what killed the project. The plan to build a line 35 miles north to Monterey and onto Owenton (Owen Co.) was little more than a promoter's dream.

Two interurban extensions were planned south and east from Lexington. The line to the east would have run 25 miles from Lexington to Winchester. This line was surveyed and options taken on land parcels, but no earth was turned, as permission could not be obtained from the Winchester City Council for the interurban cars to operate over their streets. The proposed line south to Richmond is somewhat of a mystery. Three different routes were entertained at different times: a direct route southward from Lexington via Tates Creek, an extension of the proposed Winchester Line, and extension of the track from Nicholasville. All three of these proposed routes would have required bridging the Kentucky River, but the cost of this action was the sticking point that could not be overcome. In addition, three lines were planned to extend beyond Paris. One plan called for an interurban route to run north via Cynthiana, Falmouth, and Newport to Cincinnati, Ohio. This northern extension was to have been accomplished through the chartering of three companies, each of which would have undertaken building a segment of the line between two of the cities listed above. Once the lines were in place, these three companies would have been merged into one operating company. The Newport & Alexandria Electric Traction Company was to have started south from the Kentucky side of the Ohio River at Cincinnati. The Cynthiana & Paris Interurban Railway was to be built north from Paris. As part of this overall plan, the Paris & Mt. Sterling Railway would have tied these two Kentucky towns together. The promoters of this line claimed that it would provide Mt. Sterling with direct rail access to Cincinnati instead of the present rail route that required a change of trains at Winchester, from the Chesapeake & Ohio Railway (C&O) to the L&N. The other proposed line would have run northeast from Paris, and its story is told in the company's name, Maysville, Carlisle, Millersburg & Paris Traction Company. All of these proposed companies remained paper lines due to the inability of their promoters to raise money for construction. Both the Cincinnati and Maysville, Kentucky, lines would have been in direct competition with the L&N.

KT&T was an innovative company during its lifetime. Refrigerated box motor freights were purchased, painted in white, and used to deliver ice from the KT&T ice plant to surrounding communities. In addition, these cars transported milk from the Elmendorf Dairy Farm. In 1922, KT&T became the first company to introduce the Cincinnati Lightweight Curve Side Interurban Cars into revenue service. Both single and double-truck varieties were used by KT&T. Twenty-seven single and twelve double-truck lightweight cars were purchased by KT&T in the 1920s. Weighing less than half of the old wooden streetcars and interurban cars and operated by a one-man crew, these new cars reduced operating costs by two-thirds. With the introduction of these cars, KT&T went from a marginal operation to a profitable company. The company books remained in the black during the 1920s until automobile and truck traffic began to drain away customers. The effects of the Great Depression and a strike by motormen in January 1934 sent the company into bankruptcy. At this time, all KT&T interurban service was ended along with the local Frankfort streetcar service. Lexington streetcar service would continue for a few more years before being displaced by buses on April 21, 1938. The interurban cars were sold to Cleveland, Ohio, but never ran in service there. Conventional wisdom has it that the cars were not used in service in Cleveland due to their inability to climb the local hills, despite having climbed a seven percent grade out of Frankfort while in KT&T service.

The Huntington, West Virginia, Ashland, Kentucky, and Ironton, Ohio, area was the site of an interurban system that provided service in three states. During the last decade of the 19th century, each of these three cities had developed its own local streetcar system. In 1899, these three independent lines were acquired by Zachary T. Vinson and Johnson N. Camden and were merged into Camden Interstate Railway Company (CIRC). Vinson and Camden proposed to join the three lines by bridging the Big Sandy River between West Virginia and Kentucky and operating a car ferry service across the Ohio River from Kentucky to Ohio. In 1903, CIRC bridged the Big Sandy River. CIRC interurban cars could now run over a 25-mile length of track that stretched from Guyandotte, West Virginia, to Ashland. The car ferry across the Ohio River, however, remained a dream. Interurban passengers traveling between Ironton and Huntington had to cross the Ohio River on a foot passenger ferry that ran between Coal Grove, Ohio, and Ashland. In 1907, CIRC changed its name to Ohio Valley Electric Company (OVEC).

OVEC managed two connecting interurban lines, Ashland Street Interurban Railway Company and Huntington & Charleston Railway Company. Ashland Street Interurban Railway built 1.2 miles of track south from Ashland before stopping, while the Huntington & Charleston Railway built two miles of track east of Huntington before stopping. From 1917 to 1929, OVEC connected with Portsmouth Street Railway & Light Company (PSR&LC) at Hanging Rock, Ohio, on the west side of Ironton. Thus, for 12 years, it was possible, if one does not count the ferry, to travel the 70 miles between Huntington and Portsmouth, Ohio, by interurban.

Like many other interurbans, OVEC became a victim of highways and the Great Depression. The Ohio Line was abandoned in 1930 and the Kentucky and West Virginia Line in 1937 after which OVEC continued to operate under the name of Ohio Valley Bus Line. This company would operate until 1971 when a strike by its employees put it into bankruptcy.

In 1924, in an attempt to lower operating costs, OVEC purchased 40 new Kuhlman one-man lightweight cars. These cars would faithfully serve OVEC until the demise of trolley operations. Fourteen of the cars temporarily escaped the scrap heap and found a new home with Lehigh Valley Transit Company (LVT) of Allentown, Pennsylvania. These cars continued to run in revenue service on the LVT until 1952.

At the start of the 20th century, Evansville, Indiana, had begun to build interurban lines radiating outward from its city center. The Southern Indiana Gas & Electric Line ran north to Patoka, Indiana; the Evansville Suburban & Newburgh Railway ran northeast to Newburgh, Indiana, and Boonville, Indiana; and the Evansville & Ohio Valley Railway (E&OV) ran from Mt. Vernon, Indiana, located 22 miles west of Evansville, to Grandview, Indiana, 35 miles east of Evansville. A branch line off the route to Grandview led to McClain, Kentucky, on Green River Island. Due to the silting up of the northern channel of the Ohio River around Green River Island, the island is now attached to the Indiana shore and lies north of the Ohio River but is part of Kentucky. At McClain, E&OV built a dock for its ferry, *Henderson*. This ferry transported the interurban cars across the Ohio River to Henderson. At Henderson, E&OV connected with the local streetcar company, Henderson Traction Company. This ferry service ran from 1912 to 1928.

E&OV also operated two other ferry services across the Ohio River into Kentucky. The Crescent Navigation Company provided passenger ferry service by power launch on the Ohio River between the E&OV terminal at Rockport, Indiana, to Owensboro and from the terminal at Grandview, Indiana, to Lewisport and Hawesville.

Starting in 1903 and for a number of years thereafter, various Owensboro civic leaders promoted a 25-mile extension of the Owensboro City Railroad line westward to Henderson and a connection with E&OV. However, except for a 2.5-mile westward extension of the line in 1905 to reach a coal mine site, nothing came of this proposal. To reach Evansville, the citizens of Owensboro would have to be content with a 30-minute boat ride to Rockport, Indiana, and then a 75-minute interurban ride to Evansville. E&OV quit service to Henderson in 1928 and to Grandview, Indiana, in 1938.

The Nashville & Gallatin Interurban Railway (N&GI) was built in 1913 to tie Nashville, Tennessee, to Gallatin, Tennessee; this 27-mile line paralleled the Louisville & Nashville Railroad (L&N) mainline between the two cities. Promoters of N&GI surveyed a right-of-way north from Gallatin, Tennessee, to Bowling Green, Kentucky. They had plans of extending their line northward from Bowling Green to Louisville and thus emblazoned on the side of one of their cars "The Bluegrass Line." This proposed track would have also run alongside the L&N mainline track. Funds to build this extension were not found, and N&GI proved to not be a moneymaker. N&GI was abandoned in 1932.

The Cincinnati, Newport & Covington Street Railway Company (CN&C) used provisions of the Cincinnati, Covington & Erlanger Railway Company charter to build its Ft. Mitchell Line, as interurban companies had the power, under Kentucky law, to purchase their proposed right-of-way through condemnation.

Twenty-four other interurban companies were chartered by the Kentucky Legislature but failed to build their lines. The reason these companies failed to construct their track was that promoters were generally unable to raise the necessary funds to construct the lines.

Two of the proposed interurban lines were supposed to operate out of Paducah, located at the junction of the Ohio and Tennessee Rivers. The Kentucky & Ohio River Interurban Company was to connect Paducah with Wickliffe on the Mississippi River. There appears to be no rational reason for proposing construction of this line as the Illinois Central Railroad already connected the two towns. The Paducah Southern Electric Railway Company Line was to run from Paducah via Mayfield to Hickman, a port on the Mississippi River. The promoters of this route were hoping to move goods between the Ohio and Tennessee River steamboats and Mississippi River steamboats. They believed this route would save a day in travel time by river, but the promoters apparently failed to consider that it would have resulted in two transshipments of their cargo, from a steamboat to the interurban and from the interurban to a steamboat, thus negating any saving in transportation costs.

The promoters of Ohio Valley Traction (OTV) planned to connect Cincinnati, Ohio, with Madison, Indiana. OVT apparently planned to cross the Ohio River from Cincinnati to Covington via the Suspension Bridge, which was used by the streetcar lines connecting the Covington area with Cincinnati. The line would then have run westward on the Kentucky side of the river through Carrollton to Milton where, via a car ferry, the line would have crossed to the Indiana side of the Ohio River. This car ferry was to be shared with the Shelbyville & Ohio Electric Railroad (S&OE), which was to have tied Shelbyville with Madison, Indiana. S&OE was but a continuation of the dream promoters had been selling since before the Civil War to connect Madison, Indiana, with the Deep South via a railroad through Kentucky. Over the years, various portions of this route had been built by the Cumberland & Ohio Railroad and other companies, but the whole route was never completed. The L&N's Bloomfield and Scottsville branch lines in Kentucky were two disconnected parts of this dream.

A number of interurban lines were chartered to connect a city not served by a steam railroad with a city served by a mainline railroad. Among these was the Eminence & New Castle Electric Railway, which was to connect New Castle with the L&N at Eminence. The Glasgow, Burkesville & Cumberland Traction Company was proposed to connect Burkesville to the L&N at Glasgow at one end of the line and at the other end provide access to steamboats operating on the Cumberland River at Burnside. The Columbia & Lebanon Interurban Railroad was to have connected its two named cities via Campbellsville. This would have provided Columbia with access to the L&N. The Cumberland Valley Interurban Railroad was promoted as a means of providing Monticello with a connection with the Cincinnati, New Orleans & Texas Pacific Railroad (CNO&TP) at Somerset. The Danville Electric Power Railroad would have provided service from downtown Danville to the L&N depot at Junction City. The Mt. Sterling & Sharpsburg Electric Railway Company was to have tied Sharpsburg with the Chesapeake & Ohio Railway (C&O) at Mt. Sterling.

The most interesting of these chartered interurban lines, which failed to lay the first rail, is the Cincinnati, Louisville, Lexington & Maysville Traction Company (CLL&M). Formed by a number of second-string politicians, its charter called for the building of interurban lines between the above named cities via any number of routes. CLL&M appears to have been a preemptive paper company formed in the hopes of being able to sell portions of its charter to companies financially able to build all or parts of the lines. It appears that no portion of the rights conferred by the CLL&M's charter was ever sold to any other company.

One other interurban line needs to be discussed. In the early 1990s, it was proposed that a light rail line would be built from the Greater Cincinnati-Northern Kentucky Airport at Hebron via Covington to Cincinnati, Ohio. In Cincinnati, the line would split with one segment running to Dayton, Ohio, and the other to Kings Island Amusement Park at Mason, Ohio. Branch lines within Kentucky would have served the Florence Mall and the Ohio Riverfront venues in Newport and Bellevue. Voters, however, turned down this concept at the ballot box.

Kentucky thus experienced the interurban phenomena but saw nothing like the construction of lines in its neighboring states of Illinois, Indiana, Ohio, and West Virginia. One thing is obvious from an examination of the interurban lines in Kentucky. In the first half of the 20th century, the citizens of the Commonwealth had public transportation service far superior to that afforded to the citizens of Kentucky in the 21st century. Today there is no public transportation between Ashland and Ironton, Lexington and Paris, Louisville and Shelbyville, or Henderson and Evansville. For Kentuckians living in 2011, the idea that their great grandparents living in the early 20th century could have traveled to neighboring cities using public transportation is the stuff of science fiction. In 2011, there is little public transportation in Kentucky because everyone drives a car. One might switch that around and say, "Everyone drives a car in Kentucky because there is no public transportation!"

In closing, a few words about the cars the interurban lines operated. All the interurban cars had two trucks of two axels each. The cars built in the period before 1920 were built of wood while after 1920, of metal. They were generally 40 to 70 feet long and 8 to 9 feet wide. The cars were powered by direct current electricity gathered from an overhead wire by a trolley pole attached to the roof of the car.

The electricity drawn from the overhead wire powered electrical motors, which turned the wheels. The interurban companies serving Kentucky used four types of passenger cars: closed, combine, open, and convertible. The closed car was fully enclosed with a front and rear door, seats to each side of the aisle, windows along the side, a small baggage area, a separate sitting area for African American riders, and a restroom. Heating was by a small coal stove while air conditioning was provided by opening the windows. A combine car was a closed car in which up to half the interior space was reserved for baggage or packages. The open-air car had only a roof with no sides. Seating was by a series of benches that extended the full width of the car. Protection from rain was provided by a tarp that could be lowered from the roof, however, this hindered entering and exiting the car. A convertible car was a closed car that could have its sides and aisle seating removed in good weather for conversion to an open car.

Some of the interurbans also used trailer cars; these were non powered cars pulled by a powered car. Trailer cars were generally closed cars, but could be convertible or open cars. Also used by the interurban were box motors, which were self-propelled boxcars. Their purpose was to carry freight, generally in the form of numerous small packages. This movement of various small packages destined for different addressees was called Less-Than-Carload (LCL) shipment. Quite often, the box motors were used to pick up and return milk cans that farmers had left at small stations along the right-of-way. Some box motors were insulated for carrying ice and other products that needed to remain cold.

All interurbans operated by the clock. Interurban cars ran over their line on a schedule posted on a company employee timetable. Times on the timetable were departure times from that station, and no car could leave the station until the time posted. In order to ensure that the interurban cars adhered to the timetable, all conductors and motormen had to own a pocket watch that could not be "off" by more than one second in 96 hours. At the start of the day, all watches were compared to the company clock, located at the carbarn, to insure they were in harmony before the conductor and motorman readied their car for the day's operation. Running ahead of schedule was a sure way to have an accident resulting in injury or even death.

It also must be noted that most interurbans ran on single track. Passing was done at a passing siding, which was a short section of double track generally at a station or depot. These passing sidings were entered by a spring switch that would always place cars going in one direction on the main track and those going in the other direction in the passing siding. Spring switches did not require anyone to get on the ground to throw a switch but automatically allowed a car to remain on the mainline or put it in the passing track based on direction of travel. Generally, cars outbound from the main city stayed on the mainline while those returning went into the passing track.

A comment about weather and its effect on interurban systems and the streetcar and trolley lines also needs to be mentioned. Windstorms often shut down the interurban by knocking down the overhead wires or scattering debris on the track. Heavy rains could cause flooding, and any water hitting the electric motors driving the cars' axels would cause the motors to short out and shut down. Ice not only brought down the overhead wires, it caused the trolley pole not to properly engage the overhead wire, thus denying the cars' motors the electricity they needed to operate. Ice and snow allowed the cars' wheels to slip on the rail. Heavy snow would build up to such a height in the track flangeway that it would cause the cars' wheels to derail. Wet leaves on the track could also cause wheel slippage.

In the next four chapters, we will look at the interurban lines that served Ashland, Henderson, Lexington, and Louisville.

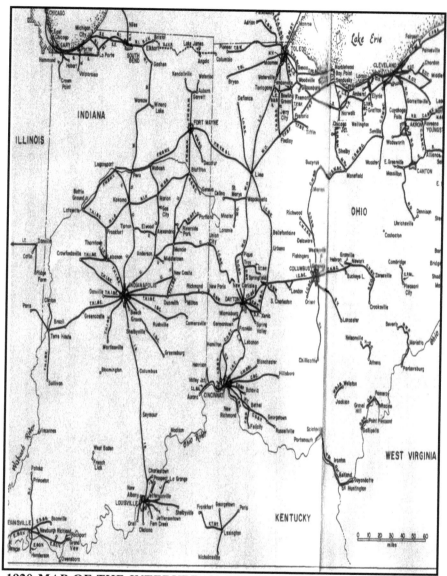

**A 1920 MAP OF THE INTERURBAN SYSTEMS OF OHIO AND INDIANA
AND THEIR SURROUNDING STATES <CM>**

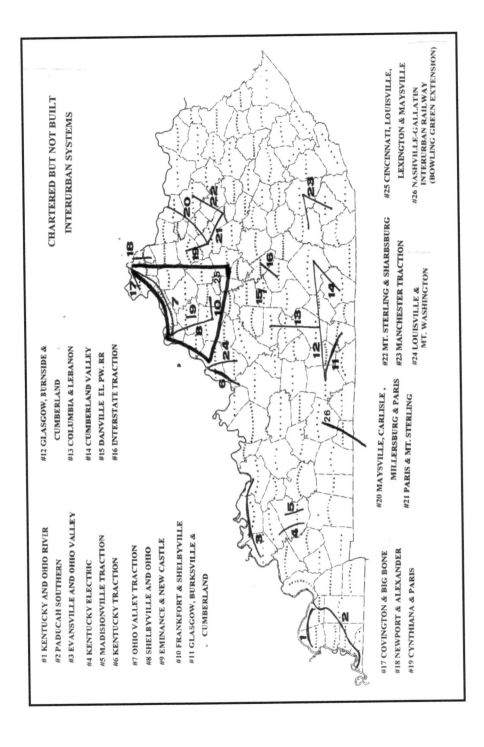

CHARTERED BUT NOT BUILT
INTERURBAN SYSTEMS

#1 KENTUCKY AND OHIO RIVER
#2 PADUCAH SOUTHERN
#3 EVANSVILLE AND OHIO VALLEY
#4 KENTUCKY ELECTRIC
#5 MADISONVILLE TRACTION
#6 KENTUCKY TRACTION
#7 OHIO VALLEY TRACTION
#8 SHELBVILLE AND OHIO
#9 EMINANCE & NEW CASTLE
#10 FRANKFORT & SHELBYVILLE
#11 GLASGOW, BURKSVILLE &
    CUMBERLAND

#12 GLASGOW, BURNSIDE &
    CUMBERLAND
#13 COLUMBIA & LEBANON
#14 CUMBERLAND VALLEY
#15 DANVILLE EL PW. RR
#16 INTERSTATE TRACTION

#17 COVINGTON & BIG BONE
#18 NEWPORT & ALEXANDER
#19 CYNTHIANA & PARIS

#20 MAYSVILLE, CARLISLE ,
    MILLERSBURG & PARIS
#21 PARIS & MT. STERLING

#22 MT. STERLING & SHARBSBURG
#23 MANCHESTER TRACTION
#24 LOUISVILLE &
    MT. WASHINGTON

#25 CINCINNATI, LOUISVILLE,
    LEXINGTON & MAYSVILLE
#26 NASHVILLE-GALLATIN
    INTERURBAN RAILWAY
    (BOWLING GREEN EXTENSION)

22

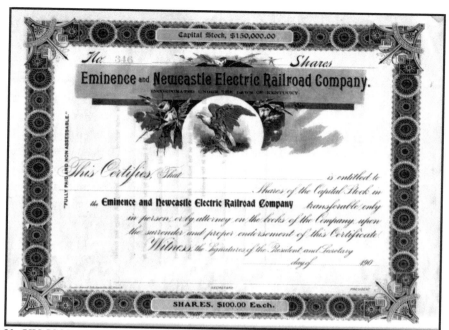

AN UN-ISSUED SHARE OF EMINENCE & NEWCASTLE ELECTRIC RAILROAD COMPANY <CHB>

ASHLAND – IRONTON - HUNTINGTON INTERURBAN

TYING TOGETHER OHIO, KENTUCKY, AND WEST VIRGINIA

With the coming of the Chesapeake & Ohio Railroad, later Chesapeake & Ohio Railway (C&O), to Boyd County in 1875, the economic structure of Ashland and Catlettsburg began to expand. Ashland became the hub of C&O passenger train service, which reached north to Detroit, Michigan; west to Cincinnati, Ohio; southwest to Louisville; south to Elkhorn City; and east to Newport News, Virginia.

Ashland also became a center for iron and steel production and soon replaced Catlettsburg as the major city in Boyd County. Catlettsburg, however, remained the county seat and hosted federal and state offices. Citizens of Ashland involved in legal matters found themselves having to travel to Catlettsburg, the area's judicial seat, to file or adjudicate legal matters. At the same time, Huntington, West Virginia, on the south bank of the Ohio River 22 miles upstream from Ashland, became a major rail and river commercial center while Ironton, on the north bank of the Ohio River 8 miles downstream from Ashland, had become a major iron producer and rail center.

Ashland and Huntington were tied to each other by the C&O. Midway between Ashland and Huntington, the Norfolk & Western Railroad (N&W) came up the Big Sandy Valley and crossed the Ohio River at Kenova, West Virginia, and then ran on to Ironton and Cincinnati, Ohio. Ashland was separated from Huntington by the Big Sandy River, while both Ashland and Huntington were separated from Ironton by the Ohio River. The only bridges were the C&O across the Big Sandy River and the N&W over the Ohio River. Train schedules were inconvenient for the businessperson while horse transportation involved ferries and poor roads. Both the Ohio and Big Sandy Rivers were often dangerous to cross due to debris filling the river while it was in flood or to ice choking the river.

It was not until 1900 that a practical solution, an interurban line, was proposed to correct this problem of traveling between Huntington, Ashland, and Ironton. The proposed interurban line would run from Huntington to Ashland, crossing the Big Sandy by a bridge. At Ashland, the interurban would cross the Ohio, at first by a transfer ferry and later by a bridge. At this time, all three cities had their own electric streetcar system. All that was needed was a means to tie these three systems to each other.

In Kentucky, the Ashland and Catlettsburg Street Railway Company (A&C), 4 feet 8.5 inch gauge, tied these two cities together. The A&C had started in 1890 as a horsecar line within the city of Ashland. In 1893, A&C converted to operating under electric wires and extended its track to Catlettsburg that was located on the west bank of the Big Sandy River. At this time, the Big Sandy was navigated by steamboats for 120 miles upstream to Pikeville.

Huntington was tied to its suburbs by the Huntington Electric Light and Street Railway Company (HEL&SR) built by S. T. Durham. HEL&SR began operating under wires in 1888 and claimed to be the second electric-powered streetcar company in the U.S. In 1890, the HEL&SR was followed by the horse-drawn Huntington Belt Line Railway that provided service between the Baltimore & Ohio Railroad (B&O) Depot and the C&O Depot. These two trolley lines were merged on July 10, 1892, to form Consolidated Light and Railway Company (CL&RC). The CL&RC Line, as constructed, connected the (then) separate town of Guyandotte, West Virginia, with Huntington. The line was later extended westward, circa 1899, to Kenova, located on the east bank of the Big Sandy and was built to 4 foot 8.5 inch gauge.

In 1888, Mr. Dunham had also obtained a franchise from the city of Ironton to build a streetcar line in that city. As built, it was a horse-drawn line and operated as the Ironton and Petersburg Company. The line provided service from the ferry landing at Coal Grove, Ohio, through Ironton to Hanging Rock, Ohio. The ferryboat running between Coal Grove and Ashland provided transportation across the Ohio River. The line was converted to electric operations on November 1, 1896, under the name of Ironton Electric Light and Street Railway Company (IEL&SR) and had four closed and six open cars. IEL&SR was built to a gauge of four feet 8.5 inches. Interestingly, the city of Ironton had a law restricting the speed of the local streetcars to 5 MPH.

By 1895, the only thing that prevented the Ironton, Ashland, and Huntington lines from being operated as one continuous line was the lack of bridges, with the Huntington and Ashland lines being separated by the Big Sandy River at Catlettsburg-Kenova and the Ashland and Ironton lines by the Ohio River at Ashland-Coal Grove. During the 1890s, a number of capitalists had proposed a merger of the three streetcar lines into one company. At the time, the C&O was providing a shuttle service over its railroad from Kenova to Catlettsburg.

In 1899, Zachary T. Vinson and Senator Johnson N. Camden set out to merge the three city lines by forming the Ohio Valley Electric Company (OVE). This company then acquired the stock of Ironton Electric Light and Street Railway Company, Ashland and Catlettsburg Street Railway Company, and Huntington Electric Light and Street Railway Company. On December 13, 1900, OVE, in a reorganization, renamed itself Camden Interstate Railway Company (CIRC).

CIRC's plan for tying its three street railway lines together initially consisted of bridging the Big Sandy and providing car ferry service across the Ohio River. The eventual plan was to bridge the Ohio River. The overall plan seemed to have envisioned an electrical powered interurban line providing service between Cincinnati, Ohio, and Charleston, West Virginia. That envisioned interurban line would have run from Cincinnati via Georgetown, Ohio; Portsmouth, Ohio; Ironton, Ohio; Ashland, Kentucky; Huntington, West Virginia; St. Albans, West Virginia; and ended at Charleston, West Virginia. Unfortunately, only the bridge across the Big Sandy was constructed, being completed in 1903, while the transfer car ferry across the Ohio never progressed beyond a pedestrian ferry. A person traveling between Huntington and Ironton thus had to leave the comfort of their interurban car at Ashland and walk down to the Ohio River. There they boarded the ferry *Winona* for Coal Grove, and upon arrival at the Ohio shore, walked up the riverbank to an Ironton streetcar. This awkward trip was made more difficult if one was carrying packages or luggage. *Winona* was lost in January 1918 and replaced by the ferry *City of Ashland.*

26

The Commonwealth of Kentucky finally bridged the Ohio River in 1924. This bridge between Ironton and Russell, Kentucky, 2 miles below Ashland, while built to carry automobiles, was also envisioned as providing a connecting interurban link between Ironton and Ashland. The bridge, however, had been built too late. By 1924, it had become obvious that the private car was slowly supplementing the streetcar and interurban as America's preferred form of transportation. When Kentucky opened the Ashland to Coal Grove Bridge in 1932, the Ironton streetcar line had already been abandoned.

In 1905, CIRC leased the Huntington and Charleston Railroad (H&C), which had as its goal the tying of these two West Virginia cities together by an interurban line. Construction on this line started on February 24, 1904, but never got much beyond the city limits of Huntington. The line ran from Eighth Street to Ritter Park and then out Charleston Avenue to 20th Street.

In 1906, CIRC reported that it had 30 miles of track and operated 50 cars. Most numerous among these cars were the Niles Car Company's 47-foot cars, which seated 48 passengers (12 rode in the smoking compartment). In regard to the smoking compartment on these cars, I would suspect that their real purpose was to meet the requirements of Kentucky's Jim Crow Law, requiring separate accommodations for African Americans.

By 1912, CIRC had increased its track mileage to 33 miles. Its 50 cars were reported to consist of 41 closed cars and 9 summer open-air cars. CIRC also boasted one box freight motor, three work cars, and three cars listed as "other." The 33 miles of track were divided as follows: 7.6 miles in Ohio, 6.0 miles in Kentucky, and 19.4 miles in West Virginia. The Kentucky and West Virginia lines were served by a powerhouse in Kenova while the Ohio Line received its power from a generating plant in Ironton. The three consolidated lines, operating under one management, were a financial success. In 1912, it was reported that 300 interurban passengers used the ferry each day to cross between Coal Grove and Ashland.

In order to encourage use of the interurban line on Sundays and holidays, CIRC built two amusement parks: Clyffeside Park, east of Ashland, and Camden Park, west of Huntington. Clyffeside Park contained a lake for boating, a casino for dancing and performances of plays and movies, a picnic grove with bandstand, and various rides, including a roller coaster. Clyffeside Park survived until the early 1920s when it was closed and sold off for commercial development. Today Clyffeside's name continues in existence as a block sign on CSX track near where the park once stood .

Camden Park was CIRC's premier park. It started life as a picnic grove but soon developed into an amusement park boasting everything that Clyffeside Park had, but in spades. Clyffeside Park was but a marginal operation; however, Camden Park was a generator of considerable revenue. Both parks also made use of numerous light bulbs and other electrical equipment to encourage residential and commercial use of electricity, but when the interurban's profit margins began to hemorrhage after World War I, it made economic sense to close Clyffeside Park and consolidate all amusement park activities at Camden Park.

In 1913, CIRC picked up considerable passenger service from West Virginia to Kentucky when West Virginia put into effect a statewide ban on the sale of alcoholic beverages within its borders. The sale of alcohol, however, remained legal in Kentucky until 1920 when national prohibition went into effect.

In October 1916, CIRC was reorganized as Ohio Valley Electric Railway Company (OVERC). This reorganization made little difference in day-to-day interurban and city services but did result in the streetcars being repainted. CIRC had operated its cars painted in yellow; OVERC ordered the cars repainted in "Pullman green" with cream trim.

In 1917, an event in Ironton did lead to a change in OVERC service. That year the Portsmouth Street Railroad & Light Company's (PSR&LC) track finally reached Ironton. It was now possible to ride from Coal Grove to Portsmouth, Ohio, by interurban car. This service would last until 1929. Another event that took place sometime circa 1920 was the folding of OVERC into Consolidated Power and Light Company that was controlled by Appalachian Electric Power Company, part of American Electric Power Company, a subsidiary of Middle West Utilities Company. Thus, OVERC became part of

Samuel Insull's traction empire.

At 8:55 A.M. on January 10, 1919, Car 139, with Conductor Mullens and Motorman Frank Farrell on board and carrying 15 passengers, was heading for Ashland from Huntington. Car 139, however, never reached Ashland this day as it was struck by a Norfolk & Western Railroad (N&W) train as it approached the Big Sandy Bridge at Kenova. The N&W had a spur line that served some industries located along the east bank of the Big Sandy River. The N&W spur ran along the fringe of the riverbank some 12 feet before the approach to the OVERC Bridge over the Big Sandy River. The result was that the OVERC crossed this N&W track on grade. OVERC regulations called for their cars to stop upon reaching the N&W crossing. Once stopped, the car's conductor was to walk up to the N&W crossing to visually check that it was clear. After the conductor had ascertained that the N&W crossing was clear, he would waive the OVERC car forward and across the diamond. Mr. Mullens carried out this procedure; unfortunately, however, due to the N&W track curving and some obstructions in the area, sight distance was only 50-feet. It appears from the above description that the crossing was not protected by signal lights nor did the OVERC car have to call a dispatcher to get permission to cross the track.

As Car 139 prepared to cross the bridge, an N&W switching operation was taking place on that railroad's track. An N&W train was shoving twelve cars loaded with stoves, along with ten empty cars, into the Basic Products plant. According to witnesses, there was no flagman at the rear of the N&W train, and the locomotive was not sounding its whistle as it came up onto the crossing. The result was that the boxcar at the rear of the N&W freight clipped the end of Car 139, kicking it off the track and part way down the 40-foot embankment toward the Big Sandy River. Fortunately, before Car 139 had gone too far, it came to rest against a telephone pole and its supporting guide wire. The result of this was that only five passengers were injured from breaking window glass and no lives were lost.

In 1924, with costs rising faster than revenue, OVERC looked into revamping its organization to save money. During the first 30 years of streetcar and interurban service in the United States, no thought had been given to the weight of individual cars, nor to the number of men employed on each car. In a company-wide survey, OVERC found that its 66 cars were of various designs, weighing between 39,000 and 58,000 pounds and required the services of a motorman and conductor. The difference in car weight meant that the heavier cars did more damage to the line than those of less weight. In addition, the heavier cars required more power to attain running speed than those of a lesser weight.

OVERC, therefore, sought to replace its Kentucky and West Virginia cars with lightweight, one-man operator cars. The three Birney cars providing service in Ironton were not replaced. The new cars designed by Kuhlman weighed 34,000 pounds, were 47 feet in length, could seat 48 passengers (12 in the smoking compartment and 36 in general seating), and needed only one man to operate. When the 40 new cars went into service, OVERC's operating costs were reduced 40 percent.

In 1925, OVERC introduced a new concept in public transportation to Ashland. The gasoline bus made its first tentative entrance on the streets of Ashland and Huntington. OVERC acquired buses to extend their services to the new suburbs growing up around Ashland and Catlettsburg. Bus service did not require OVERC to invest in track and its upkeep, rather the government provided the road and kept it in repair for the buses to run on.

Gradually during the 1930s, buses began to replace streetcars on OVERC routes and were also used to extend service into new areas. From an investment point of view, buses enjoyed a number of advantages over interurban cars. The owner of an interurban line had to pay property taxes on his company's right-of-way in addition to maintaining a portion of the street over which his cars ran. The interurban owners thus contributed both directly and indirectly to the maintenance of streets and roads over which their cars ran. A bus company, however, only paid licensing and gasoline taxes, and the government built and repaired the streets on which buses ran.

On December 30, 1927, OVERC was sold to the Central Public Service Commission but continued to operate as OVERC. The start of the Great Depression in 1929 marked the beginning of the end of OVERC streetcar operations. On August 31, 1930, OVERC abandoned its streetcar service in Ironton and sold its interurban franchise to the Blue Ribbon Line, which used this franchise to provide bus service between Ashland and Ironton. Blue Ribbon would build its bus service into a major public service provider between Ashland and Cincinnati during the 1930s and 1940s. It also provided local bus service within the city of Ashland. In 1945, Blue Ribbon transported 11,000,000 passengers. In Ohio, local bus service between Hanging Rock, Ironton, and Coal Grove was provided by the Employees Bus Company.

On July 1, 1933, to raise additional capital, OVERC sold off its remaining bus lines to Fred W. Samworth, who reorganized the bus operations under the name of Ohio Valley Bus Line (OVBL). The infusion of new capital into OVERC only prolonged the slow death of the interurban line from Ashland to Huntington along with their city streetcar lines. Declining ridership, increased maintenance costs, inability to change their fare structure, and failure to meet bond payments resulted in the closing of OVERC interurban service along with its Ashland and Huntington streetcar lines on November 6, 1937. The last OVERC streetcar run, Guyandotte to Huntington, was made by William Jordan who had worked for OVERC and its predecessor companies for 49 years. Only fourteen of the lightweight cars owned by OVERC were not scrapped. These lucky fourteen were sold to Lehigh Valley Transit Company of Allentown, Pennsylvania, where the cars were used until 1952.

Under the leadership of Fred Samworth, OVBL extended its bus lines outward into Kentucky, Ohio, and West Virginia, enjoying prosperity during the 1930s and 1940s. Yearly ridership was often as high as 1.5 million; however, the 1950s saw a steady decline in riders as people switched to private automobiles. In the 1960s, yearly ridership on OVBL decreased to 500,000 patrons, while costs of operating the bus service increased. To save costs, OVBL abandoned some lines and cut service on others; this resulted in fewer riders and less revenue.

In 1971, Ashland and Huntington experienced their first public transportation strike, as the Amalgamated Transit Union #1171 struck OVBL for higher pay. The strike lasted ten long months, and when it finally ended in 1972, the concept of privately owned public transportation in the Ironton-Ashland-Huntington area was but a nostalgic dream. In its place, the publicly funded Tri-State Transit Authority (TTA) was formed to provide bus service between Ironton, Ashland, and Huntington.

TTA started providing bus service on July 17, 1972, and for a short time provided bus service within the Tri-State area. Problems with funding the Ohio match, however, quickly reduced service to just between Ashland and Huntington. Then within a few years, due to further funding difficulties, TTA reduced bus service to only the Huntington and Kenova area. In order to provide public transportation within Boyd County, local government formed the Ashland Bus System. In 2011, this company provides bus service within the Ashland and Catlettsburg area and provides daily connecting bus service with TTA.

In closing, I must note that some rail historians question if CIRC and the resulting OVERC were truly interurban lines or just a glorified city line operation. I will let the readers argue that question.

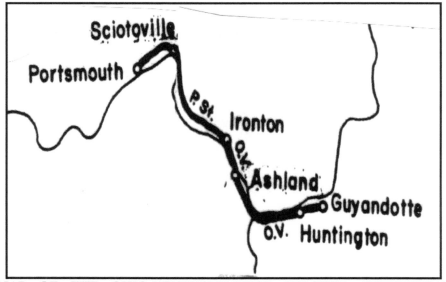

MAP OF THE OHIO-KENTUCKY-WEST VIRGINIA INTERURBAN SYSTEM <CM>

ABOVE AND BELOW IS A CAMDEN INTERSTATE CITY CAR <CHB>

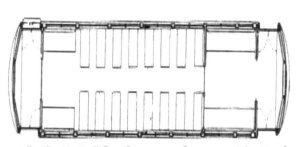

48 Ft. "Double End" Two Compartment Passenger and Smoking Car

Length over buffers................................ 47' 8"	Weight of body, about.............................25,000 lbs.
Length of body.. 37' 0"	Weight complete on track with four 50 H. P.
Length of passenger compartment............ 27' 10¾"	600 V. D. C. motors, about.................26½ tons
Seating capacity.. 48 persons	

A CITY CAR RUNS THROUGH DOWNTOWN ASHLAND. <CHB>.

CLYFFSIDE PARK IS TO THE LEFT WITH ITS INTERURBAN TRACK. ON THE RIGHT IS THE C&O MAINLINE. <CHB>

AN INTERURBAN CAR ON ITS WAY TO HUNTINGTON STOPS AT CLYFFSIDE PARK. <CHB>

THE LAKE AT CLYFFSIDE PARK <CHB>

Clyffeside Park, Catlettsburg, Ky.

CLYFFSIDE PARK AS SEEN FROM THE INTERURBAN TRACK <CHB>

Camden Interstate Street Car Co's Bridge Across Big Sandy River, Catlettsburg, Ky.

INTERURBAN BRIDGE ACROSS THE BIG SANDY RIVER <CHB>

IRONTON, OHIO, SUMMER TIME INTERURBAN CAR <CHB>

AN INTERURBAN CAR ON ITS WAY FROM HUNTINGTON TO ASHLAND ENTERS CATLETTSBURG. <CHB>

AN INTERURBAN CAR PAUSES IN CATLETTSBURG TO PICK UP
PASSENGERS FOR IRONTON, OHIO. THEY WILL NEED TO TAKE THE
FERRY AT ASHLAND TO MAKE THE CONNECTION. <CHB>

CAR #138 PREPARES TO LEAVE ASHLAND FOR HUNTINGTON AFTER
PICKING UP PASSENGERS WHO HAVE CROSSED FROM OHIO TO
KENTUCKY VIA THE FERRY. <CHB>

WEST VIRGINIA HAD VOTED ITSELF DRY BUT PEOPLE STILL WANTED TO DRINK, SO THE CAMDEN INTERURBAN RAN SPECIAL TRAINS TO THE BARS AND SALOONS OF CATLETTSBURG. <CHB>

IT IS A NICE SUMMER SUNDAY AND CAR #21 IS PREPARING TO PICK UP THOSE PLANNING ON A DAY OUT AT CLYFFSIDE PARK. <CHB>

CAMDEN TRAILER CAR #116 <CHB>

CARS AT THE HUNTINGTON CARBARN <CHB>

ABOVE AND BELOW ARE PHOTOS OF THE HUNTINGTON CARBARN.
<CHB

>

ABOVE AND BELOW IS THE HUNTINGTON CARBARN IN 2009. <CHB>

AT CATLETTSBURG THE INTERURBAN LINE CROSSED AT GRADE THE C&O'S MAINLINE BETWEEN HUNTINGTON AND ASHLAND. THE CROSSING WAS GUARDED BY A TOWER THAT CLEARED INTERURBAN CARS TO CROSS. <CHB>

THE DETAILS OF THIS COLLISION HAVE BEEN LOST TO TIME. <CHB>

A TOKEN FOR RIDING THE INTERURBAN CAR <CHB>

THE STREETS OF CATLETTSBURG AND ASHLAND HAVE YET TO BE PAVED. <CHB>

At the start of the 20th century, Evansville, Indiana, saw itself growing to be a competitor with Louisville. Vandenberg County, for which Evansville was the county seat, had a population of 93,000 in 1900. The city was tied by the Louisville & Nashville Railroad (L&N) Bridge over the Ohio River with Henderson, Kentucky, and Nashville, Tennessee. Foreseeing Evansville becoming a regional powerhouse in southwestern Indiana, her boosters began to build interurban lines radiating outward from the city center. These interurban lines were designed to tap the growing rural towns surrounding Evansville and direct their trade towards her.

By 1915, five interurban companies had built electric rail lines based in Evansville: Evansville & Princeton Traction Company, Evansville Suburban & Newburg Railway, Evansville & Eastern Electric Railway, Evansville & Mount Vernon Electric Railway, and Evansville, Henderson & Owensboro Railway Company.

In 1903, the Evansville & Princeton Traction Company opened a line between these two cities. The company planned to build onto Vincennes, Indiana; however, its only extension was 3 miles of track in 1908 onto Patoka, Indiana. ES&N went through a number of receiverships and in 1921 became the Southern Indiana Gas & Electric Company. The line continued to operate under this name until 1933 when it closed, and its four cars were then transferred to Evansville & Ohio Valley Railway.

The Evansville Suburban & Newburgh Railway (ES&N) ran northeast from Evansville to Newburgh, Indiana. It had started as a steam railroad in 1889 but converted to electric operations in 1905. ES&N transported coal from three mines at Newburg to Evansville, provided Less Than Carload (LCL) business, and ran five round trip passenger trains. ES&N was owned by F. W. Cook, owner of F. W. Cook & Sons Brewery, maker of Cook's Goldblume Beer. At Newburg, Cook operated Kuebler's Beer Garden serving Cook's Goldblume Beer. In 1906, ES&N built a branch line to coal mines near Boonville, Indiana. As a side note, in 1912 Cook won a case against the L&N in the U.S. Supreme Court. The L&N had refused to accept beer F. W. Cook was shipping to Dry Counties in Kentucky. The Supreme Court sustained a U.S. Circuit Court finding that as the L&N was an interstate common carrier, it thus had to accept for shipment any cargo presented to it that was not prohibited by the United States Government. With the coal mines playing out, the Boonville Line closed in 1930 and the Newburg Line in 1941. However, as a result of Cook's ownership of F. W. Cook & Son Brewery, a remnant of the line serving the brewery continued in operation until 1956.

In 1907, Evansville & Eastern Electric Railway (E&E) built a 35-mile line from Newburg eastward to Rockport, Indiana. The track of the ES&N was used to reach Evansville from Newburg. In 1908, a dispute with ES&N led E&E to build their own line from Newburg to Evansville. The E&E line to Newburg hauled mostly coal and foundry molding sand. In 1911, the Rockport Line was extended 6 miles east to Grandview, Indiana. A branch line off the E&E at State Line, Indiana, led to McClain, Kentucky, located on Green River Island. Due to the silting up of the northern channel of the Ohio River above Green River Island, the island is now attached to the Indiana shore and thus lies north of the Ohio River but is still part of Kentucky.

In 1906, the Evansville & Mt. Vernon Electric Railway (E&MV) opened its 22-mile line from Evansville to Mt. Vernon, Indiana. The line had plans to build across Illinois onto St. Louis, Missouri, but never got beyond Mt. Vernon. In 1912, however, E&MV established a motorboat passenger ferry service between Mt. Vernon and Shawneetown, Illinois, and Evansville and Spottsville, Kentucky. They used two "new 50-foot, 36 horsepower boats built by Peter Mingst of Evansville." It is thought that this ferry service lasted only for a year. The E&MV Line was closed in 1928 by Evansville & Ohio Valley Railroad (E&OV).

In 1900, Henderson County, Kentucky, had a population of 32,907 with over half living in the city of Henderson, which as befitting a city, had a streetcar system and a desire for an interurban system. Henderson saw itself becoming the premier city in the Green River area. In 1907, Tillman Bethall, A. G. Cruntchfield, and W. W. Cooper proposed to build an interurban line running from Evansville to Henderson and from there west to Uniontown and east to

Owensboro. The interurban line would cross the Ohio River by a bridge and tap the coalfields lying in and around Owensboro and Uniontown. Nothing became of this proposal or a number of other plans that proposed the same routes or added Madisonville or Dixon as additional destinations.

It was only in 1911 that the dream of an interurban line became a reality for Henderson with the formation of the Evansville, Henderson & Owensboro Railway Company (EH&O). EH&O leased 3 miles of former Illinois Central Railroad (IC) track that ran from Henderson to the Ohio River bank at Major. They also leased a little under 3 miles of IC track at McClain. The IC had built the track at McClain in 1889 to reach a car ferry they operated for crossing the Ohio River. In 1904, the IC abandoned the ferry operation for track rights over the L&N Bridge between Henderson and Evansville. EH&O connected the IC track in Henderson to the track of the Henderson City Railway to allow for EH&O cars to run into their depot on North Elm Street in downtown Henderson. The running of EH&O's heavy interurban cars over the track of the city streetcar line necessitated replacing the light rail used by the streetcars with 80-pound rail. Eventually the entire Henderson street rail was replaced with 80-pound rail.

At Major, on the south bank of the Ohio River, and at McClain, on the north bank of the Ohio River, the former IC ferry cradles were re-built to allow the interurban car to be placed on the transfer car ferry *Henderson*. The transfer ferry carried the interurban car back and forth across the Ohio River. *Henderson* had been built at Dubuque, Iowa, in 1912. She had a steel hull and was powered by two gasoline engines producing 120 hp. She was 120 feet long by 25 feet wide and could carry two interurban cars. She drew only 3 feet 6 inches of water. Her captain was R. S. Moats and her engineer was R. L. Duke. Since *Henderson* operated in the days before the Ohio River was canalized, she had to operate in a river of extreme water levels. The river could, depending on rainfall, be overflowing its banks with a fast current or be so shallow that one could walk across the river. The result of these extreme water levels was that the ferry stage on both shores had to be flexible enough to compensate the ferry slip being 50 feet closer or farther from the shore at normal river stage. As a result, each floating cradle was 150 feet long and climbed at a constant 3 percent grade until 48 feet above low water. At times, however, river conditions were such that the interurban car could not be taken onboard *Henderson;* as a result, the interurban passengers became foot passengers for the crossing. It also needs to be remembered that once clear of the ferry cradle, the interurban car had to climb up the river bluff to the flood plain above.

EH&O made its first run on July 28, 1912. The interurban car was described by the *Henderson Gleaner* "as being 50 feet long and nine feet wide, painted an orange color, and has a seating capacity of 59 but will hold nearly twice this number. A compartment of the car is reserved for the colored people and there is also a section which will be used as a smoker and baggage room. The car will be used to check all kinds of baggage. The car is finished in quarter oak and both interior and exterior elegant. The fixtures are the most modern. The car is equipped with comfortable cane seats." Fare was reported to be $.35 one-way and $.65 round trip. EH&O appears to have operated with three American Car Company interurban cars, #126 to #128, all built in 1912. Cars left both Henderson and Evansville at 15 minutes past the hour, every other hour, from 7:15 AM to 11:15 PM. It needs to be noted that while Evansville, Henderson & Owensboro Railway was the official name of the interurban line, it was always called the Evansville Railroad by the locals.

This first run of the interurban car on June 28, 1912, was not a through run, as the incline at McClain was still not completed. Passengers had to walk to the ferry on both sides of the river and travel across the river as foot passengers. The delay was due to problems with the construction of the McClain cradle. Here the bank was of soft mud and required the construction of a concrete pad. Apparently, the first through car between Henderson and Evansville ran on October 14, 1912. That Friday the late night interurban car derailed as it was exiting the boat onto the cradle, causing a scare, but the car stayed upright on the cradle. It was reported that the cradle had not lined up properly with *Henderson* and steps were being taken to correct the problem.

According to an EH&O employee timetable, the 10.9 mile trip between Evansville and Henderson took 44 minutes with the river crossing portion being accomplished in 12 minutes. The 12-minute crossing of the Ohio was under normal river conditions. It was claimed that during the years the *Henderson* operated for EH&O, the Ohio River navigation season consisted of three periods. These periods were three months of the river being frozen, three months of being in flood, and six months of no water. EH&O was to experience all of these river conditions. The winter of 1917-18 was extremely cold and for weeks the Ohio River was frozen over from bank to bank. Once this ice began to melt there was the constant danger of ice flows hitting the *Henderson*. At one point, these ice floats destroyed both ferry cradles requiring them to be rebuilt. Then during periods of high water, all kinds of debris floated down the river ready to puncture the *Henderson's* hull or destroy her propulsion system. Heavy fog also took a toll on *Henderson's* schedule, so during heavy fog, bells were rung at each landing to guide *Henderson* to her landing point.

EH&O would be involved in a number of collisions with automobiles during its life, the worst of which took place on June 6, 1917. On that day an EH&O passenger car struck an automobile carrying six Barret High School students at Watson Lane and Henderson-Evansville Road. The driver thought he could beat the interurban to the crossing but was proven to be Dead Wrong. While the EH&O motorman tried to stop his car, it proved impossible to prevent a collision. The result was four students dead and two seriously injured.

While EH&O provided fast, convenient transportation between Henderson and Evansville, the service was not dependable. As noted, river conditions could cause delays or cancellation of service. The railroad ran less frequently but by using a bridge to cross the Ohio River, its schedule was dependable. During the winter of 1917-18, EH&O passenger service was interrupted for weeks by ice in the Ohio River.

Circa 1920, *Henderson,* while crossing the river with a freight motor and a passenger car carrying some 40 passengers, suffered an engine room casualty. The result was that *Henderson* began to drift down river. After five hours of floating on the river, some of the passengers began to complain of hunger. Captain Moats, to satisfy the hunger of the passengers, authorized commandeering some of the chickens being carried in the freight motor. These chickens had their necks wrung, feathers plucked, and internal organs pulled. The chickens were cooked on the deck of the ferry and eaten by the passengers and crew. Finally, Engineer Duke had the engines repaired and *Henderson* arrived at the far bank. The normal 12-minute trip across the Ohio River had lasted 10 hours.

While *Henderson* was outfitted to carry two interurban cars, she generally only carried one. The exception was the twice-daily round trip of carrying a passenger coach and a freight motor across the river. The other exception was when an extra passenger car was laid on to carry riders to a special event in Evansville.

In 1919, EH&O, E&MV, and E&E were consolidated under the banner of Evansville & Ohio Valley Railway (E&OV). In 1924, E&OV reported that it owned 72.43 miles of track, 9 passenger cars, 3 freight motors, 1 electric locomotive, 1 work car, and 124 freight cars, plus a ferry. A new schedule for EH&O was instituted; now the first train left Henderson at 7:00 AM and the last at 10:25 PM.

Upon starting operations, E&OV added two passenger-only ferries to its operations, which provided services from Indiana across the Ohio River into Kentucky. The Crescent Navigation Company operated the passenger ferry service using gasoline powered river launches. The passenger ferry service was provided between the E&OV terminal at Rockport, Indiana, and Owensboro, and from the E&OV terminal at Grandview, Indiana, to Cannelton, Indiana, and Lewisport and Hawesville, Kentucky. This passenger ferry service lasted until circa 1928. It was also circa 1928 that the car floats at Butler and McClain were modified so that *Henderson* could carry automobiles and trucks. The carrying of autos and trucks soon became the main source of revenue for *Henderson*.

The EH&O Line was never a moneymaker; just the cost of operating the transfer ferry *Henderson* far exceeded any business generated in the city of Henderson. If EH&O had been able to build on to Madisonville, Owensboro, Dixon, and Morganfield it might have generated enough money to cover its costs. There was never enough money for EH&O to undertake this construction and, by 1925, all-weather roads lessened the need for an interurban line to these towns. E&OV had never covered more than the cost of its operations, but by

1925, it was not even doing this.

Interestingly with all this financial gloom, in 1925 E&OV purchased six single ended, lightweight, one-man interurban cars, #300 to 305, from the American Car Company. The new cars weighed 17 tons as opposed to the 37 tons of the cars they were replacing. The new cars were designed to seat 24 in the main compartment, 12 in the smoking or Colored compartment, and 10 in the baggage compartment. E&OV advertised that the general passenger compartment had upholstered seats in green frieze plush, and the Colored compartment had dark green genuine leather upholstery seats. E&OV noted that the seats in the baggage compartment were folding slat seats with rattan covering. A toilet facility was located at the right rear of the general seating compartment

On September 7, 1927, a human error led to a head-on collision of an interurban car and a boxcar at Clay, Indiana, now part of Evansville. Car #117 was returning from Kentucky, having picked up passengers at the Dade Park Race Track, and was running at an estimated 40 MPH when it ran into an open switch that led into a siding. Car #117 went into the siding and crashed into a boxcar parked there. Because of the crash, the motorman and three passengers of Car #117 were killed and fifty passengers injured. The after accident investigation noted that a signal box blocked the motorman's view of the switch stand lamp. The signal box guarding the block that the switch was located in was worked by a dispatcher in Evansville who had set his signal showing the line clear. He was unaware that the switch had been left open after it had been worked. Thus, the signal box indicated that the line was clear for Car #117. The dispatcher just assumed, as he had in the past, once a crew finished working the siding that the switch was relined for the main. This night it was not.

This wreck wrote the end of the Henderson Line. The resulting legal suits forced E&OV into receivership. As a result of the receivership, E&OV temporarily suspended operations over the Henderson Line. Then on April 4, 1928, E&OV ceased all interurban rail service to the city of Henderson and began to use buses for the trip between Henderson and Evansville. This interstate bus service lasted until circa 1965.

With the demise of the EH&O Line, the transfer ferry *Henderson* was sold by E&OV to the Dixie Bee Line Ferry Company who then converted *Henderson* to carrying automobiles and trucks between Henderson and Evansville. In 1931, *Henderson* was bought by the Kentucky Department of Highways who continued to use her as a ferry at Henderson until the new highway bridge (US 41) over the Ohio River opened on July 3, 1932. After this time, *Henderson* is undocumented, and it is thought she was broken up.

In 1927, E&OV was in dire financial trouble, and the next year it was forced into receivership. From this time onward, the death of E&OV would be slow but unremitting. After the Henderson Line was abandoned, the Mt. Vernon Line was closed in early 1928. Passengers wanting to ride the interurban from Mt. Vernon, Indiana, to Evansville had by this time dropped to but a few. The line to Grandview, Indiana, ceased carrying passengers in 1938, but portions of the line would remain in freight service until 1946.

To complete the story of interurban service at Henderson, one must also examine Owensboro. From 1903 through the 1920s, various Owensboro civic leaders promoted a 25-mile extension of Owensboro City Railroad Line westward to Henderson and a connection with E&OV. However, except for a 2.5-mile extension of the line west from Owensboro in 1905 to reach a coal mine, nothing came of these proposals. For the life of E&OV, in order for the citizens of Owensboro to reach Evansville via the interurban, they would have to be content with a 30-minute boat ride to Rockport, Indiana, and then a 75-minute interurban car ride to Evansville. Otherwise, it was a ride onboard one of the Louisville, Henderson & Texas Railroad's (LH&T) passenger trains to Henderson and the transfer to an L&N or an Illinois Central Railroad (IC) train for the final ride into Evansville.

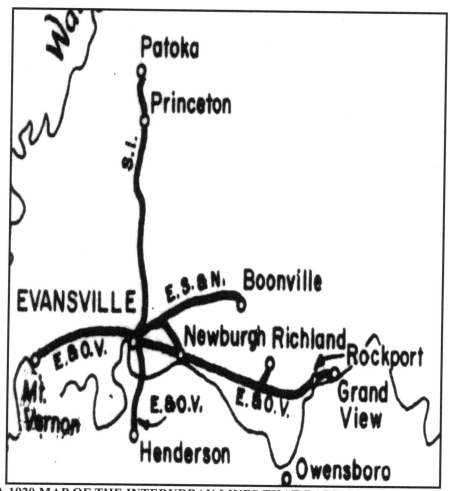

A 1920 MAP OF THE INTERURBAN LINES THAT RADIATED OUT FROM EVANSVILLE, INDIANA <CHB>

1919 EVANSVILLE & OHIO VALLEY RAILWAY COMPANY $5,000 FIVE PERCENT GOLD BOND <CHB>

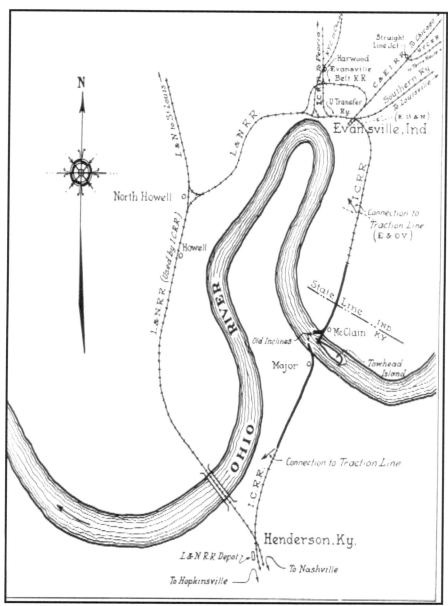

A MAP OF THE FERRY CROSSING BETWEEN INDIANA AND KENTUCKY BY WHICH THE INTERURBAN CARS TRAVELED BETWEEN EVANSVILLE, INDIANA, AND HENDERSON <CHB>

ABOVE AND BELOW, THE CAR FERRY *HENDERSON* <CHB>

A VIEW OF THE DECK OF THE CAR FERRY *HENDERSON* <CHB>

THE INTERURBAN CAR LANDING STAGE ON THE KENTUCKY SHORE <CHB>

THE INTERURBAN CAR COMING ASHORE OVER THE LANDING STAGE <CHB>

CAR #128 AT THE CARBARN IN EVANSVILLE <CHB>

ABOVE AND BELOW: THIS UNIMPOSING BUILDING ON ELM STREET WAS THE HENDERSON INTERURBAN STATION. <CHB>

E&OV CAR #135 WAS USED ON THE EVANSVILLE-HENDERSON RUN. <CHB>

WITH THE DEMISE OF INTERURBAN SERVICE TO HENDERSON FROM EVANSVILLE, BUSES WERE INTRODUCED BY THE E&OV TO COVER THAT SERVICE. <CHB>

Evansville Railways Co.

INTERURBAN STATION

Elm St. Bet. 2 and 3rd.

Phone 363 Cumb.

Cars for Evansville, Mt. Vernon, Newburgh, Yankeetown, Hatfield, Richland, Rockport, Grandview. Cars leave Henderson 7:15, 9:15, 11:15 a. m., 1:15, 3:15, 5:15, 7:15, 9:15, 11:15 p. m. Fare between Evansville and Henderson 35c, single trip; 65c round trip. Tickets good 30 days. I. F. Head, Agt., Henderson, Ky. W. A. Carson, G. M.; D. C. Powell, G. P. A., Evansville, Ind.

INQUIRER, THE FAST MOTOR BOAT, ROCKPORT, IND. TO OWENSBORO, KY.

ENQUIRE PROVIDED A WATER CONNECTION FROM OWENSBORO TO THE EVANSVILLE & OHIO VALLEY INTERURBAN DEPOT AT ROCKPORT, INDIANA. <CHB>

In 1800, Lexington began to propose the canalizing of the Kentucky River and Elkhorn Creek to give it a water connection with the outside world. Before the canal project advanced beyond tentative canalization of the Kentucky River, Lexington turned to the railroad as the answer to its transportation dilemma. In 1832, Lexington began to build the Lexington & Ohio Railroad, which reached the Kentucky River at Frankfort in 1835. During the 1850s, Lexington sought to build railroads north from their city to the Ohio River at Covington and to Maysville. The railroad to Covington was finished just before the Civil War and that to Maysville after the Civil War. After the Civil War, Lexington would also help promote the Cincinnati Southern Railroad, later the Southern Railway (SRy), from Cincinnati, Ohio, to Chattanooga, Tennessee; the Kentucky Union Railroad; and the Elizabethtown & Big Sandy Railroad. The latter two railroads pointed eastward from Lexington for the coalfields of Eastern Kentucky.

Thus, at the beginning of the 20th century when the interurban transportation system concept burst forth over the land, it is no wonder that Lexington embraced this idea and set out to make itself an interurban traction hub. Interurban lines were projected to radiate out from Lexington like spokes from the hub of a wheel. All of the cities surrounding Lexington boasting a county courthouse were to be tied to Lexington via an interurban line. But in the end, only five of these county seats, Frankfort, Georgetown, Paris, Nicholasville, and Versailles, would be connected to Lexington via four interurban rail lines. All of these Lexington based interurban lines were built to standard gauge, 4 feet 8.5 inches.

The first of these spokes to be built was the line to Georgetown, the county seat of Scott County. In 1902, the Georgetown & Lexington Traction Company (G&LT), operator of the city streetcar service in Georgetown, opened a 12-mile line between the two named cities. This line in Georgetown ran west on Main Street and then south on Georgetown Road (US 25) on a private right-of-way alongside the road. The interurban line paralleled the SRy, also called the Queen & Crescent Route, from Georgetown to Lexington. Just north of Lexington it crossed the SRy by a bridge. The G&LT construction had been delayed while it fought to obtain court permission to cross the SRy. The interurban line also crossed on grade the SRy's Versailles to Georgetown route just south of Georgetown. G&LT had two coaches, #10 & #12, and one combine car (Baggage/Coach) #14.

G&LT connected with the SRy in Georgetown and starting in 1905, G&LT hauled coal cars from the SRy to the municipal powerhouse and the local ice plant, both located near Royal Springs. In 1908, SRy refused to interchange coal cars with G&LT, as they had previously been doing, as they had now determined that G&LT was not a railroad as defined under Kentucky state law. G&LT appealed this decision by SRy to the Kentucky Railway Commission who then ruled that G&LT was a legal railroad in that it ran on track and had "locomotives" (freight motors) equipped with couplers and air brakes which were compatible with SRy operating procedures. Thus in February 1909, SRy was ordered by the Kentucky Railway Commission to resume interchange of cars with G&LT.

On October 26, 1903, Blue Grass Traction Company (BGT) began operating an 18-mile interurban line between Paris and Lexington. The line started from a wye behind the Bourbon County Courthouse and ran south on High Street to Main Street. It continued south on Main past the Paris Cemetery, where it crossed at grade the Frankfort & Cincinnati Railroad (F&C) track and passed by the Bourbon County Fair Grounds. The BGT track then ran along the west side of Lexington Road (US 27 or Paris Pike) to Limestone Street in Lexington. Here it ran under the Kentucky Central Railroad (KC) track via an underpass. It then continued into downtown, but only after crossing the Belt Railroad at grade.

During BGT's run from Paris to Lexington, the track of the KC was in constant view to the east of the BGT car. At Elmendorf Farm, a large dairy operation, BGT crossed a KC spur that ran back to the farm's main house. BGT owned six coaches, #20 to #25, and one freight motor, #11. Car #11 was ordered by Elmendorf Farm to haul milk from the farm to Lexington and Paris. This Refrigerated Freight Motor Car was built by American Car Company at St. Louis. It was 50 feet long, built of wood on a semi-steel underframe, and rode on Brill trucks. The interior of the car contained racks for stacking milk cans.

It must be remembered that these were the days before mandatory pasteurization of milk that was sold to the public, and thus Car #11 hauled fresh milk directly from the cow to the local distributor. Elmendorf Farm was an 8,000 acre horse and dairy farm on Paris Pike. During the first two decades of the 20th century, it was owned by James B. Haggin who used the KC spur to his house to park his private rail car on. There was also a BGT spur back to the farm's dairy operation for loading milk into the Refrigerated Freight Motor. This car was equipped with steam railroad compatible couplers and air brake lines. While no documentary evidence exists that this freight motor was used to haul boxcars for inter-exchange with the steam railroads, the possibility exists that such an operation was conducted in the early years.

It needs to be remembered that each and every time an interurban car crossed a steam railroad track on grade, the interurban car had to stop. The conductor then had to get out of the interurban car and go to a telephone on a nearby pole. The conductor would operate a crank next to the phone, which would connect him with the steam railroad's dispatcher for that segment of the line. The interurban conductor would have to ask the steam railroad dispatcher permission to cross the railroad tracks. The steam railroad dispatcher, upon making sure no trains were due at that location within the next five minutes, would clear the interurban to cross the railroad tracks. Once the interurban car had permission to cross the steam railroad, the conductor would unlock and remove the derails placed on the interurban rail on either side of the steam railroad track. A derail is a device placed on a rail so that when a car passes over it the car is lifted from the track and put on the ground. Once the derail was unlocked and opened, the interurban car would proceed past the derails. The conductor would, once the interurban car had passed him, reposition and lock in place the derail.

In 1904, G&LT was merged into the Bluegrass Traction (BGT). As a result after the merger, BGT and G&LT began running through cars from Paris to Georgetown via Lexington, a distance of 30 miles. Interestingly, F&C connected the two towns via 16 miles of track. F&C, however, only ran two round trip passenger trains a day whereas the combined BGT and G&LT ran 12 daily round trips. The F&C, however, operated two freight trains daily between the two towns while BGT only operated a freight motor that carried Less Than Carload (LCL) freight between the two towns twice a day.

In 1905, Central Kentucky Traction Company (CKT) opened a 14-mile line between Versailles and Lexington. CKT built eastward from the Woodford County Court House out along Lexington Street (US 60) to Lexington. The route paralleled the Southern Railway (SRy) line from Louisville via Versailles to Lexington. As CKT left Versailles, it crossed, via a diamond, the track of the Louisville & Atlantic Railroad (L&A) which ran from Versailles to Nicholasville and onto Richmond and Beattyville. CKT ran on private right-of-way alongside the highway until it reached Lexington. It then traveled within the roadway of Angliana Avenue to Broadway and then onto Main Street. At Main, it stopped at the transfer station in front of the Fayette County Courthouse. Within Versailles, CKT built a freight and passenger station on Lexington Street a half a block from Main Street where they had a wye for turning their cars.

In 1908, CKT ordered two Brill semi convertible, bi-directional, heavyweight interurban cars running on high speed trucks. These cars were 54 feet 10 inches long and were purchased for use on the Lexington-Versailles-Frankfort run. The cars were divided into three sections: White, Colored, and Baggage. CKT stated, "In the compartment for White passengers there are 16 walkover seats and four fixed seats, two facing the aisle and two in front of the Color compartment. There are four walkover seats and four fixed seats in the Color compartment. Doors, at either side, at both ends of the car are 40 inches wide to assist in admitting bulk freight." The cars had no restroom facility. They were described as having their "interior finished in cherry with semi-empire ceilings and clear glass in arch top sash windows. There is glass in the partition separating the two compartments at a height above the fixed seats, thus allowing an unobstructed view from the rear platform to the front of the car." These were Cars #111 and #112.

Two years later in 1907, the Frankfort & Versailles Traction Company (F&VT) opened a 15-mile line between these two cities. The track ran north on Main Street in Versailles to Frankfort Road (US 60).

66

It followed Frankfort Road, using private right-of-way, to Main Street in Frankfort. The rails turned west on Main Street in Frankfort and followed Main to the interurban depot at Main and Olive Street. A wye was located at Ann and Main for turning the cars. Then in 1909, the Louisville & Atlantic Railroad (L&A) built a competing steam railroad line between Versailles and Frankfort that ran two miles west of the F&VT track. In reaching Frankfort from Versailles, as it left downtown Versailles, the F&VT crossed at grade the SRy Line from Versailles to Georgetown and crossed by a bridge the L&A track from Frankfort to Nicholasville. It also crossed by a bridge the track of the Louisville & Nashville Railroad (L&N), Lexington to Louisville, a mile outside of Frankfort. Shortly after the interurban line to Frankfort was opened, F&VT was merged into CKT and through car passenger and freight motor service was provided between Frankfort and Lexington. Upon merger with F&VT, CKT had a fleet of nine coaches, #100 to #108, and seven combine cars, #110 to #116.

CKT operations within Frankfort are not well documented, and a number of questions about its operations within the city cannot be answered at the present time. One question is about interurban freight operations within the city of Frankfort. CKT had a rail connection with the L&N in Frankfort. One would assume that if there was a rail connection, there was some inter-exchange of freight cars. One would suspect that it was used to move rail cars between the Old Stagg Distillery (now Buffalo Trace) and possibly the Hermitage Distillery.

It is known that from 1905 to 1910 CKT moved building supplies to the New Capitol Building from the L&N Yard in West Frankfort. CKT built a line along Taylor Avenue and down Second Street to Bridge Street where it connected with the existing city line. The material then moved over Second and up Shelby Street. Then instead of turning at Todd Street as the streetcar line did, CKT's new track ran on up to the building site, with the track making a loop around the New Capitol Building.

In 1910, Lexington & Interurban Railway Company (L&I) built a 12-mile standard gauge line south from Lexington to Nicholasville. Unlike the other three lines, this line was built to steam railroad standards. The line left the Fayette County Courthouse via Limestone Street to Nicholasville Road. Once beyond Lexington, the interurban line ran on private right-of-way next to Nicholasville Road (US27). At Nicholasville, the interurban track then moved to the center of Main Street. The depot was located at Main and Oak Street.

It appears that the reason for building the Nicholasville Line to steam freight standards was a plan to exchange freight cars with the Louisville & Atlantic Railroad (L&A) at Nicholasville. This plan all came to naught when the Louisville & Nashville Railroad (L&N) acquired the L&A track in the same year. The L&N plan was to use the L&A as a route from Louisville via Frankfort, Versailles, Nicholasville, Richmond, and Beattyville to reach the coal fields of Eastern Kentucky. The L&A between Millville, located outside of Frankfort, and Ravenna would be abandoned in 1932.

KT&T and its predecessors had hoped to lay rails from Lexington to Winchester and from Lexington to Richmond. Winchester, located 18 miles east of Lexington, is the county seat of Clark County. The Winchester Line from Lexington to Winchester would have run east following Winchester Road (U.S. 60) out of Lexington to Lexington Road at Winchester. The track between the two cities would have been on roadside private right-of-way. Once at Winchester, it was street running down Lexington Avenue to Main Street where an interurban depot was to have been located. The Winchester Line would have run midway between the L&N and the Chesapeake & Ohio Railway (C&O) track, tying Winchester to Lexington. The Winchester City Council, happy with steam railroad service, refused to grant a franchise to any of the applying interurban companies.

There is some debate about the proposed alignment of the interurban line from Lexington to Richmond. There has been speculation that the connection to Richmond would have been by track rights over the Louisville & Atlantic Railroad (L&A) track between the two cities. This idea has some validity as the L&A had the capability to handle hourly interurban cars. The distance from Nicholasville to Richmond is 15 miles compared to 20 from Lexington to Richmond. By using the Nicholasville to Richmond route, no track would have to be laid and no bridge built over the Kentucky River since the L&A owned such track and bridge. All that would be needed was to string wire over the existing L&A track. The documented route to Richmond, proposed after the L&N gained control of the L&A, was via Tates Creek Road. The interurban line would have run along private right-of-way next to Tates Creek Road from Lexington to the Kentucky River and onto Richmond. The interurban would have crossed the Kentucky River using this route via a steel bridge to be built by the interurban company next to the existing L&A Bridge at Valley View. From the Kentucky River south to Richmond, the interurban would have run within yards of the L&A.

In 1911, to promote efficiency, Bluegrass Traction Company, Central Kentucky Traction Company, and Lexington & Interurban Railway were all merged into Kentucky Traction & Terminal Company (KT&T) and became part of the Samuel Insull Empire. KT&T controlled not only the above interurban lines but also operated streetcar systems in Frankfort, Georgetown, Lexington, Paris, and Winchester. In 1913, KT&T reported that it owned 30.3 miles of city track in Lexington, Paris, Winchester, Frankfort, Versailles, Georgetown, and Nicholasville and 61.43 miles of interurban track. It also owned 15 interurban passenger cars, 4 freight motors, 50 city cars, and 4 line cars. Electrical power to operate the line was obtained from a central station in Lexington, and four sub-stations were located as follows: 1) five miles outside of Paris, 2) in Georgetown, 3) three miles beyond Lexington on the Nicholasville Line, and 4) at the passenger station in Versailles. The sub-stations were built of red brick and housed a 300-kw rotary converter. A portable substation was at times located a mile outside of Frankfort when there was heavy traffic to that city.

Upon taking ownership of all the interurban lines radiating out from Lexington, KT&T started a track upgrade program. While the Nicholasville Line had been built to steam railroad standards, and the line to Versailles and Frankfort with 80-pound rail, the two lines to Paris and Georgetown had not been built to such high standards. Thus during 1912, KT&T completely rehabilitated the track to Georgetown and Paris. New ties and rails riding on heavy cinder ballast were put in place on these two lines.

On February 2, 1913, the *Lexington Herald* ran a two-page article on KT&T. The article noted that Lexington now had a population of 35,000 and was served by the interurban and city cars of the KT&T. It went on to say that KT&T employed 398 men, owned 50 city cars, 15 interurban cars, 4 freight motors, and 4 construction cars. The city cars had transported 4,697,272 passengers and the interurban cars 1,610,093 in 1912. The interurban cars provided 59 trips each day into Lexington; these trips also generated 800,000 visitors to Lexington each year. KT&T announced that due to the increase in interurban ridership, they were going to open a new depot at Broadway & Main Streets (in 2011-De Shay's Restaurant).

The story also noted that KT&T, along with generating electrical power for sale to commercial and residential customers, also managed an ice manufacturing plant that produced 60 tons of ice daily. "During the winter months the excess ice is placed in storage to be ready for increased demand during the summer months. The storage building has a capacity of 2,000 tons." KT&T delivered this ice to residents via wagon routes, the wagons being kept supplied by the ice carrying freight motor, Car #603. The ice carrying freight motor ran a Monday to Saturday set route which allowed the ice wagon operators to meet the ice car at set times and places to replenish their load without having to go to the ice manufacturing plant. Ice could also be delivered out along the interurban line. A $10 deposit was required in advance for delivery of ice to an outlying interurban station.

In 1917, the U.S. entry into WWI would both increase KT&T's business but also raise the cost of conducting business. That year the Kentucky National Guard established the 245-acre Camp Stanley on Versailles Road, just west of Forbs Road, adjacent to the Southern Railway (SRy). The camp had about 100 buildings and served as a mobilization point for the Kentucky National Guard and various volunteer units. Later in 1917, National Guard units would be transferred to Camp Shelby, Mississippi, and new recruits to Camp Zachary Taylor in Louisville.

KT&T also provided Less Than Carload (LCL) package service. Cost of shipping from one terminal city to another terminal city was based on the weight of the package. Packages worth less than $10, and under 10 pounds, cost $.05; 11 to 25 pounds cost $.10; 26 to 50 pounds $.15; and from 51 to 100 pounds $.25. Packages of greater than $10 value had their own shipping rate based on value and weight. Shippers of goods over the KT&T bought pads of $.05 stamps and affixed the proper amount to their package based on weight. The package was then left at the designated station. KT&T promised same day delivery for all packages delivered to one of their depots by noon.

Like most interurbans, KT&T operated over single track outside of the city; however, passing tracks were normally located at a rural depot or station. Within the city, the interurban also ran on single track that made it necessary that all operations over the interurban line be so arranged that no two cars operated on the same track at the same time. This was accomplished by use of timetables that spelled out when a car could leave a station. In addition, before leaving the station, permission had to be received from the stationmaster. When a car did not arrive at a depot when it was supposed to, traffic on the line had to be shut down until it was located. A car could be delayed by slippery track caused by rain, snow or ice, an accident, or mechanical problems. Until the car was located and the problem rectified, interurban operations on that segment of the line were annulled.

Train dispatching on KT&T was by means of the AERA rulebook, timetables, and written orders. The company employed three dispatchers who worked in the company's office in Lexington. Communication between the dispatcher and interurban car was by telephone. Telephones were located at various stations and points along the KT&T right-of-way. The interurban car would stop at one of the phones, and the motorman and conductor would leave the car and go to the phone. The motorman would call the dispatcher and ask for orders. The dispatcher would then read out the order and the motorman would repeat the order. The conductor would write down the order as said by the motorman. The conductor would then read the written order back to the dispatcher for verification. Once the order was verified, they both returned to the car and continued on their way.

Within the dispatcher's office, the dispatcher kept track of where the interurban cars were by a "dispatcher board." This board had the total KT&T track mileage painted on it to include the sidings. At each station and the midway point between each station point, there was located on the dispatcher board a peg hole. Wooden pegs with the train numbers on them were moved along the board by the dispatcher as trains acknowledged and completed train orders. Thus, the dispatcher had a visual picture in front of him of the location of each passenger, freight, and work car on the line.

The interurban routes radiating out from Lexington were a blessing for those wanting to attend college in Lexington. The interurban allowed one to live at home while attending class at State College (University of Kentucky) or Transylvania College. Those living in the cities served by the interurban quickly learned to use it to attend the theater in Lexington or watch a semi pro baseball game in a neighboring community.

As previously stated, many interurban promoters saw Lexington becoming a major interurban hub. Besides the Winchester and Richmond extensions, a number of other lines were proposed. KT&T looked at three extensions from Frankfort. The first would have closed the gap between Frankfort and Shelbyville but was shelved due to the Shelbyville City Council's opposition to interurbans running through their city. The second would have built a 20-mile line south from Frankfort to Lawrenceburg, the county seat of Anderson County. The right-of-way for this line was surveyed but no construction was started. The cost of bridging the Kentucky River at Frankfort is probably what killed this project. The plan to build a line 35 miles north from Frankfort to Monterey and onto Owenton, the county seat of Owen County, was little more than a promoter's dream.

Extensions of interurban lines were also planned for running north and east from Lexington. The interurban line east to Winchester would have run onto Mt. Sterling, the county seat of Bath County, with a branch line running north to North Middletown In addition, a line was planned to extend north beyond Paris. The proposal was for an interurban route to run north to Cincinnati, Ohio, via Cynthiana, Falmouth, and Newport.

The Paris to Cincinnati Line was to have been accomplished through the chartering of four construction companies each of whom would have undertaken the building of a segment of the line. Once all three segments were in place, the individual lines would have been merged into one operating company. The Newport & Alexandria Electric Traction Company was to have started south from Newport, Kentucky, across the Ohio River from Cincinnati, to Alexandria. The Cynthiana & Paris Interurban Railway was to build north from Paris to

Cynthiana. Two other un-named companies would have closed the Alexandria to Falmouth and the Falmouth to Cynthiana gaps. As a part of this overall plan, the Paris & Mt. Sterling Railway would have tied these two towns together, providing Mt. Sterling with direct access to Cincinnati instead of requiring a change of trains at Winchester from the C&O to the L&N. The other proposed interurban line would have run northeast from Paris, and its story is told in the company's name, Maysville, Carlisle, Millersburg & Paris Traction Company. All of these proposed companies remained paper lines due to the inability of their promoter to raise money for construction. Both the Cincinnati and Maysville Lines would have been in direct competition with the L&N.

During its lifetime, KT&T was an innovative company. The freight and passenger cars it inherited from its predecessor companies were all heavy, wooden, two-man cars operated by a conductor and motorman. One of KT&T's first steps was to purchase a refrigerated freight box motor, paint it white, and use it to deliver ice manufactured at the KT&T ice plant to surrounding communities. In addition, the refrigerated car was used to transport milk from the Elmendorf Dairy Farm to Lexington. Then in 1922, KT&T became the first interurban to introduce the Cincinnati Car Company Curved Side Lightweight Interurban Car into revenue service.

KT&T purchased ten of these interurban curved sidecars, #300 to #310. The cars were 40 feet 3 inches long and seated forty-four persons in three compartments: twenty-three in the White compartment, twelve in the Colored section, and nine in the Smoking/Baggage section. A restroom was also located in the baggage section. These cars rode on double trucks. KT&T also purchased 27 single truck Cincinnati Curved Side Cars for city service in Frankfort and Lexington. The Cincinnati Curve Side Interurban Cars weighed less than half of the old wooden interurban cars and were operated by a one-man crew. When placed in service by KT&T, these lightweight cars were credited with reducing the company's operating costs by two-thirds. With the introduction of these cars, KT&T went from a marginal operation to a profitable company. The company books remained in the black for the next five years until automobile traffic, using the newly paved government built roads radiating out from Lexington, began to drain away customers.

The Cincinnati Curved Side Cars were so named as the sheet metal forming their sides had a horizontal bow to it. This bow added strength to sheet metal while at the same time allowed a reduction in the weight of the metal. Cars #300 to #309 were delivered in 1922 and Cars #310 to #311 in 1923. Car #305 was lost in a fire in 1926 and was replaced with an identical car numbered #305. Car #311 was wrecked in 1928 and was replaced with an identical car marked #311. The Lexington *Herald Leader* reported that all of these cars had "interiors of cherry stained mahogany woodwork, white ceilings, and roomy seats upholstered in Pullman green plush. The cars are painted in yellow with black lettering and striping edged with silver. Aluminum window posts appear prominent in the color scheme." It was the yellow paint that earned them the name "The Yellow Perils."

The toilet facilities on all interurban cars dumped directly to the ground so they were only supposed to be used outside the city limits. Philip Ardery reported that "The design of the toilets on the Cincinnati Curved Side Cars was such that one could feed toilet paper down it so it would go out the bottom while remaining attached to the roll of toilet paper by the toilet seat. Then as the car went down its route, it would trail a floating, flapping festoon of toilet paper."

The 1922 order with Cincinnati Car Company also included two one-man freight motors, #350 and #351, for LCL service. In 1925, KT&T owned five LCL freight motors: #350, #351, #600, #602, and #603. The LCL freight motors in KT&T service had straw colored roofs, a body painted a deep red, a Saxon red-letter board, and lemon yellow striping. Also on KT&T"s roster were #200, a snow sweeper, "A," a portable substation, and #11, an insulated freight motor used to carry milk and ice. In 1931, Car #11 was scrapped and Freight Motor #603 was rebuilt to carry ice from the icehouse in Lexington that was now owned by a subsidiary of Kentucky Utilities. Portable substation Car "A" was often assigned to Frankfort to provide additional power during periods of peak usage for cars climbing up Main Street Hill.

In 1925, shortly after the purchase of the Cincinnati Curved Side Cars, KT&T rationalized its interurban service. Before 1924, KT&T operated its cars over two divisions, Paris to Frankfort via Lexington, a distance of 46 miles, and Georgetown to Nicholasville via Lexington, a distance of 24 miles. In 1925, management decided to equalize the length of the two divisions, and they were changed to Frankfort to Nicholasville, 40 miles, and Paris to Georgetown, 30 miles. This change in division structure reduced by one the number of cars in daily service that were needed to meet the schedule.

As did most interurbans, KT&T used electricity that was converted from Alternating Current (AC) to Direct Current (DC) to power their cars. Generally, this conversion was done at a permanent substation. However, at times a portable substation needed to be used when a permanent substation was down for maintenance, had encountered some mechanical problem, or there was a need to boost current on a segment of a line experiencing heavy use. Portable substations were thus built to be shifted around the line where a temporary increase in traffic was overloading power lines. A county fair, inauguration of the Governor, Fourth of July Parade, or a major sporting event all could call for a portable substation to be put on the line to meet increased power demands.

With the introduction of the Cincinnati Curved Side Cars, KT&T issued a new schedule. Speed of the cars over the line was now faster, averaging 23 MPH. The 40.1 mile run from Frankfort to Nicholasville now took 1 hour 44 minutes, and the 29.9 mile Paris to Georgetown run was accomplished in 1 hour 12 minutes. These new cars were outfitted with a general seating compartment, a smoking section, and Colored seating area. The Colored seating area was a result of Kentucky's 1892 Separate Coach Law that prohibited African Americans and Whites from riding in the same section of a public transportation vehicle.

To increase revenue on the weekend, KT&T operated two amusement parks: Joyland Park was on Paris Pike just north of present day I-75 near Mary Todd Park, and Blue Grass Park was located at Versailles and Rosalie Road at Fort Spring. Blue Grass Park was opened by Central Kentucky Traction in 1909 and closed in 1925. It offered amusement rides, dancing, swimming, a penny arcade, and a vaudeville stage. Joyland Park opened in 1925 replacing Blue Grass Park. Joyland offered amusement rides including a roller coaster, dance pavilion, shows, and a midway. Joyland began to decline in the years after World War II. The 1950s saw Joyland with operating facilities that deteriorated a little bit more each year as revenue declined. In 1963, Joyland closed part way through the summer season, and Central Kentucky was left without an amusement park offering rides and a midway.

The effects of the Great Depression, a strike by motormen in January 1934, a bond issue due for payment in February 1934, and a treasury empty of money sent KT&T into bankruptcy. On 15 January 1934, all KT&T interurban service, along with the local Frankfort streetcar service, ended. Replacing the interurbans were the buses of Southeast Greyhound Lines, a sister corporation of KT&T. (#1) The Southeast Greyhound buses not only served the cities of Versailles, Frankfort, Nicholasville, Georgetown, and Paris but reached out to cities KT&T had only dreamed about serving: Richmond, Winchester, Mt. Sterling, Lawrenceburg, and Shelbyville. The Frankfort to Shelbyville gap was closed by providing bus service between Lexington and Louisville via Frankfort and Shelbyville. By the 1950s, Southeast Greyhound buses tied Lexington to all of Kentucky's major and not so major cities. In 2011, Greyhound from Lexington only services Cincinnati, Ohio; Louisville; and Ashland. Lexington streetcar service would continue for a few more years before being replaced by buses on April 21, 1938.

Ten of the surviving KT&T Cincinnati interurban cars, #300 to #304 and #306 to #310, were sold to Cleveland, Ohio, but never ran in service there. Conventional wisdom has it that the cars were not used in service in Cleveland due to their inability to climb the local hills. Since the cars handled with ease the six percent grade up Main Street Hill to get out of Frankfort, this reason for non-use is suspect. Interurban car #311 was converted into an automobile service station at Broadway and Russell Cave Road in Lexington but burned circa 1954. Car #305 was used to provide service from downtown Lexington to Joyland Park until streetcar service ended in 1938 and was then burned for scrap metal circa 1943. One of the freight motors became a café on the Kentucky River. A number of city cars were sold for summer use on the banks of various streams in Central Kentucky, but as far as it is known, none of these cars exist today. All have become victims of rot and fire.

It needs to be noted that all of the railroad passenger train service KT&T competed against is also a thing of the past. Passenger service from Lexington to Frankfort ended in 1971, to Paris in 1951, to Versailles in 1937, to Georgetown in 1971, and to Nicholasville in 1971

(#1) The fascinating story of Southeast Greyhound and its relationship to KT&T can be found in the book *Pick of the Litter* by Kenneth R. Hixson.

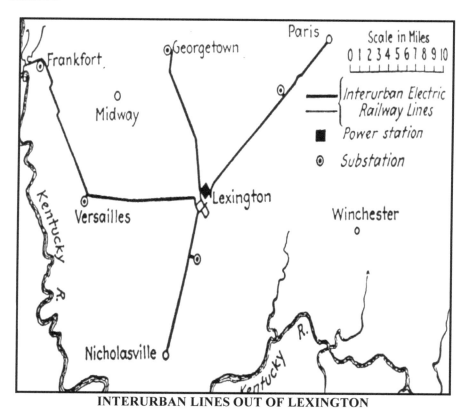

INTERURBAN LINES OUT OF LEXINGTON

1904 BLUE GRASS TRACTION COMPANY $100 FIRST MORTGAGE, FIVE PERCENT, GOLD BOND <CHB>

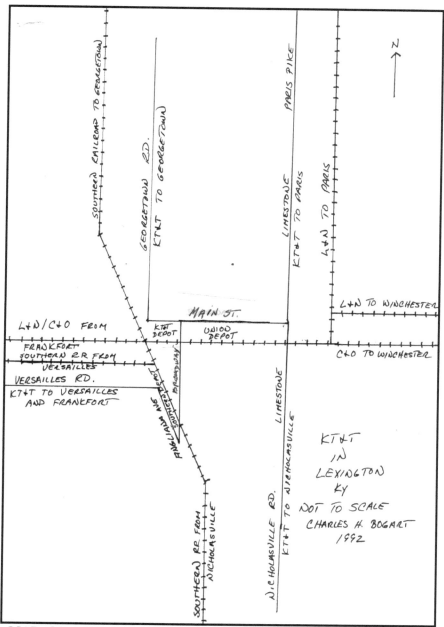

A MAP OF THE VARIOUS RAILWAY TRACKAGE IN LEXINGTON
<CHB>

ABOVE AND BELOW, THE KT&T CARBARN ON LOUDON AVENUE. BUSES WILL SOON DISPLACE THE STREETCAR AND INTERURBAN AS THE MEANS OF MOVING THE GENERAL PUBLIC AROUND THE BLUEGRASS. <CHB>

Milk Stables, Elmendorf Farm, Lexington, Ky.
The finest Dairy in the world.

ELMENDORF FARM WAS A MAJOR MILK PRODUCER, AND THE FARM USED THE INTERURBAN TO TRANSPORT ITS PRODUCT TO THE CITY. <CHB>

Main Entrance to Elmendorf, Lexington, Ky., J. B. Hagins Stock Farm.

NOTE THE INTERURBAN PASSENGER WAITING STATION AT THE ENTRANCE TO THE FARM. <WA>

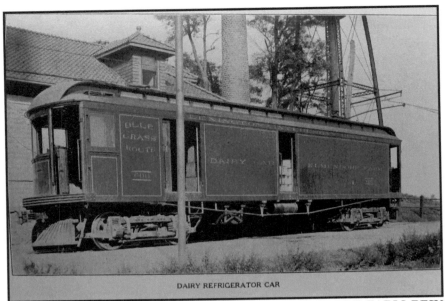

DAIRY REFRIGERATOR CAR

THE INTERURBAN FREIGHT MOTOR AT ELMENDORF FARM BEING LOADED WITH MILK FOR DELIVERY TO THE CITY. <WA>

Milk Stables, Elmendorf Farm,
Lexington, Ky. The Finest Dairy in the World.

THE INTERURBAN TRACK IS IN THE FOREGROUND AND A SPUR LEADS INTO THE ELMENDORF FARM. <WA>

One of Kentucky's Worlds famous oiled Roads. August Belmont's stock farm on the right.

One of Kentucky's World Famous Oiled Roads.

NOTE THAT IN THE ABOVE TWO PHOTOS AND THE PHOTO AT THE TOP OF THE NEXT PAGE, THE INTERURBAN TRACK IS IMMEDIATELY ADJACENT TO THE PUBLIC ROAD. THUS, WHEN THE HIGHWAY DEPARTMENT WANTED TO WIDEN THE ROAD, THE TRACK BECAME AN IMPEDIMENT. NOTE THE HANGERS ON THE POLES USED TO SUPPORT OVERHEAD ELECTRIC POWER LINES. <WA>

Kentucky's Oiled Roadway along the Interurban, near Lexington, Ky.

2513

RESIDENCE VIEW ON NORTH MAIN STREET,
NICHOLASVILLE, KY.

THE INTERURBAN TRACK RUNS DOWN THROUGH THE CENTER OF THE ROAD. WHEN THERE WERE FEW AUTOMOBILES, THIS CAUSED NO PROBLEM; HOWEVER, BY 1930, WITH INCREASED CAR OWNERSHIP, CENTER STREET RUNNING LED TO INTERURBAN – CAR COLLISIONS. <BF>

Main Street, Looking West, Georgetown, Ky.

ABOVE AND BELOW IS THE SHARED INTERURBAN AND CITY TROLLEY TRACK RUNNING IN THE CENTER OF THE STREET IN GEORGETOWN. <CHB>

BROADWAY, Georgetown, Ky.

Kane Run Bridge
Lexington Pike, Georgetown Ky.

A CITY CAR HAS VENTURED OUT ONTO THE INTERURBAN TRACK BETWEEN GEORGETOWN AND LEXINGTON. PERHAPS IT IS CARRYING A GROUP OUT FOR A DAY IN THE COUNTRY. <CHB>

KT&T CAR #311 IN FRONT OF THE FRANKFORT INTERURBAN DEPOT AT MAIN AND OLIVE STREET <EC>

Business Men's Club, Frankfort, Ky., Assembling for a "Boosting" Trip

THIS VIEW IS OF ANN AND MAIN STREET IN FRANKFORT WHERE A WYE TURNED THE INTERURBAN CAR. THE INTERURBAN PASSENGER FREIGHT DEPOT IS BEHIND THE CAR. <CHB>

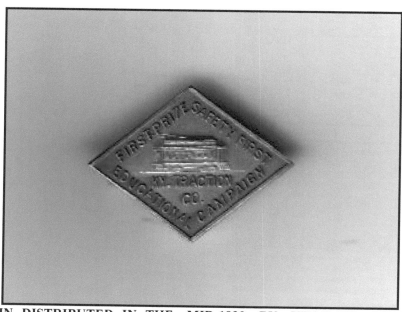

A PIN DISTRIBUTED IN THE MID-1920s BY KT&T TO SCHOOL CHILDREN WHO PARTICIPATED IN A SAFETY AWARENESS POSTER CAMPAIGN. <CHB>

Kentucky Traction & Terminal Company

EFFECTIVE MAR. 22, 1925

FROM FRANKFORT TO VERSAILLES, LEXINGTON AND NICHOLASVILLE

STATIONS	A.M.	A.M.	A.M.	A.M.	A.M.	A.M.	A.M.	P.M.	P.M.	P.M.	P.M.	P.M.	P.M.	P.M.	P.M.	P.M.	P.M.
Miles																	
3.0 Lv Frankfort		6.23	7.23	8.23	9.23	10.23	11.23	12.23	1.23	2.23	3.23	4.23	5.23	6.23	8.09	9.43	10.46
3.8 Sta. 66, Hoge		6.32	7.32	8.32	9.32	10.32	11.32	12.32	1.32	2.32	3.32	4.32	5.32	6.32	8.09	9.52	10.54
4.6 Sta. 63 Jett		6.35	7.35	8.35	9.35	10.35	11.35	12.35	1.35	2.35	3.35	4.35	5.35	6.35	8.12	9.55	10.57
9.1 McKee		6.45	7.45	8.45	9.45	10.45	11.45	12.45	1.45	2.45	3.45	4.45	5.45	6.45	8.22	10.05	11.07
14.5 Versailles Ar.		6.58	7.58	8.58	9.58	10.58	11.58	12.58	1.58	2.58	3.58	4.58	5.58	6.58	8.35	10.20	11.20
Lv. Versailles		6.58	7.58	8.58	9.58	10.58	11.58	12.58	1.58	2.58	3.58	4.58	5.58	6.58	8.35	10.20	11.20
0.0 For Lexington		7.07	8.07	9.07	10.07	11.07	12.07	1.07	2.07	3.07	4.07	5.07	6.07	7.07	8.44	10.29	11.30
5.8 Sta. 29, Jesse	6.18	7.13	8.13	9.13	10.13	11.13	12.13	1.13	2.13	3.13	4.13	5.13	6.13	7.13	8.50	10.35	11.37
5.9 B. G. Park	6.25	7.25	8.25	9.25	10.25	11.25	12.25	1.25	2.25	3.25	4.25	5.25	6.25	7.29	9.02	10.47	11.49
10.6 Sta. 9, Stanley	6.29	7.29	8.29	9.29	10.29	11.29	12.29	1.29	2.29	3.29	4.29	5.29	6.29	7.40	9.06	10.51	11.53
11.9 Sta. 3, Gentry	6.40	7.40	8.40	9.40	10.40	11.40	12.40	1.40	2.40	3.40	4.40	5.40	6.40	7.40	9.15	11.00	12.00
13.5 Lexington Ar.																	
Lv. Lexington	Day																
0.0 For Nicholasville	5.40	6.40	7.40	8.40	9.40	10.40	11.40	12.40	1.40	2.40	3.40	4.40	5.40	6.40	7.40	9.15	11.12
1.3 Rose St.	5.52	6.52	7.52	8.52	9.52	10.52	11.52	12.52	1.52	2.52	3.52	4.52	5.52	6.52	7.52	9.27	11.15
3.4 Sta. 6, Berry	5.58	6.58	7.58	8.58	9.58	10.58	11.58	12.58	1.58	2.58	3.58	4.58	5.58	6.58	7.58	9.33	11.18
6.1 Sta. 12, Hulett	6.03	7.03	8.03	9.03	10.03	11.03	12.03	1.03	2.03	3.03	4.03	5.03	6.03	7.03	8.03	9.38	11.30
9.7 Sta. 19, Lyne	6.10	7.10	8.10	9.10	10.10	11.10	12.10	1.10	2.10	3.10	4.10	5.10	6.10	7.10	8.10	9.45	11.30
12.1 Nicholasville Ar.	6.17	7.17	8.17	9.17	10.17	11.17	12.17	1.17	2.17	3.17	4.17	5.17	6.17	7.17	8.17	9.52	11.37

FROM NICHOLASVILLE TO LEXINGTON, VERSAILLES AND FRANKFORT

STATIONS	A.M.	A.M.	A.M.	A.M.	A.M.	A.M.	A.M.	A.M.	P.M.	P.M.	P.M.	P.M.	P.M.	P.M.	P.M.	P.M.	P.M.	P.M.	P.M.
Miles																			
0.0 Lv. Nicholasville		6.23	7.23	8.23	9.23	10.23	11.23	12.23	1.23	2.23	3.23	4.23	5.23	6.23	7.23	8.38	10.23	11.40
2.4 Sta. 19, Lyne		6.30	7.30	8.30	9.30	10.30	11.30	12.30	1.30	2.30	3.30	4.30	5.30	6.30	7.30	8.45	10.37	11.47
6.0 Sta. 12, Hulett		6.37	7.37	8.37	9.37	10.37	11.37	12.37	1.37	2.37	3.37	4.37	5.37	6.37	7.37	8.52	10.37	11.54
8.7 Sta. 6, Berry		6.42	7.42	8.42	9.42	10.42	11.42	12.42	1.42	2.42	3.42	4.42	5.42	6.42	7.42	9.08	10.42	11.59
10.8 Rose Street		6.48	7.48	8.48	9.48	10.48	11.48	12.48	1.48	2.48	3.48	4.48	5.48	6.00	7.00	7.48	9.15	10.48	12.03
12.1 Lexington Ar.		7.00	8.00	9.00	10.00	11.00	12.00	1.00	2.00	3.00	4.00	5.00	6.00	7.00	8.00	9.15	11.00	12.12
0.0 Lv. Lexington For & Frank't	5.45	6.00	7.00	8.00	9.00	10.00	11.00	12.00	1.00	2.00	3.00	4.00	5.00	6.00		8.00	9.15	11.00
1.6 Sta. 3, Gentry	5.53	6.08	7.08	8.08	9.08	10.08	11.08	12.08	1.08	2.08	3.08	4.08	5.08	6.08		8.10	9.23	11.13
2.9 Sta. 9, Stanley	5.57	6.13	7.13	8.13	9.13	10.13	11.13	12.13	1.13	2.13	3.13	4.13	5.13	6.13		8.16	9.28	11.13
7.6 B. G. Park	6.08	6.24	7.24	8.24	9.24	10.24	11.24	12.24	1.24	2.24	3.24	4.24	5.24	6.24		8.26	9.39	11.24
10.0 Sta. 29, Jesse		6.31	7.31	8.31	9.31	10.31	11.31	12.31	1.31	2.31	3.31	4.31	5.31	6.31		8.33	9.46	11.31
13.5 Versailles Ar.		6.40	7.40	8.40	9.40	10.40	11.40	12.40	1.40	2.40	3.40	4.40	5.40	6.40		8.45	9.55	11.40
0.0 Lv. Versailles For Frankfort		6.40	7.40	8.40	9.40	10.40	11.40	12.40	1.40	2.40	3.40	4.40	5.40	6.40		8.45	9.55	11.40
5.4 McKee		6.53	7.53	8.53	9.53	10.53	11.53	12.53	1.53	2.53	3.53	4.53	5.53	6.53		8.58	10.07	11.57
9.9 Sta. 63 Jett		7.02	8.02	9.02	10.02	11.02	12.02	1.02	2.02	3.02	4.02	5.02	6.02	7.02		9.11	10.21	12.05
11.2 Sta. 66, Hoge		7.06	8.06	9.06	10.06	11.06	12.06	1.06	2.06	3.06	4.06	5.06	6.06	7.06		9.14		
14.5 Frankfort Ar.		7.15	8.15	9.15	10.15	11.15	12.15	1.15	2.15	3.15	4.15	5.15	6.15	7.15		9.20	10.30	12.15

FROM GEORGETOWN TO LEXINGTON AND PARIS

STATIONS	A.M.	A.M.	A.M.	A.M.	A.M.	A.M.	A.M.	A.M.	P.M.	P.M.	P.M.	P.M.	P.M.	P.M.	P.M.	P.M.	P.M.
Miles																	
0.0 Lv. Georgetown		6.20	7.20	8.23	9.23	10.23	11.23	12.23	1.23	2.23	3.23	4.23	5.23	6.23	7.23	8.53	10.23
3.2 Sta. 26 Coleman Ave		6.28	7.28	8.31	9.31	10.31	11.31	12.31	1.34	2.31	3.31	4.31	5.31	6.31	7.31	8.46	10.31
4.3 Donerail		6.31	7.31	8.34	9.34	10.34	11.34	12.34	1.37	2.37	3.34	4.37	5.37	6.37	7.37	8.52	10.37
5.6 Tanner		6.35	7.35	8.37	9.37	10.37	11.37	12.37	1.41	2.41	3.41	4.41	5.41	6.41	7.41	8.56	10.41
8.1 Greendale		6.40	7.40	8.41	9.41	10.41	11.41	12.41	1.46	2.46	3.46	4.46	5.46	6.46	7.46	9.01	10.46
9.4 Sta. 7, Hill		6.45	7.45	8.46	9.46	10.46	11.46	12.46	1.51	2.51	3.51	4.51	5.51	6.51	7.51	9.06	10.51
11.3 Hickory Street		6.50	7.50	8.51	9.51	10.51	11.51	12.51	1.55	2.55	3.55	4.55	5.55	6.55	8.00	9.15	11.00
12.8 Lexington Ar.		7.00	8.00	9.00	10.00	11.00	12.00	1.00	2.00	3.00	4.00	5.00	6.00	7.00			
0.0 Lv. Lexington For Paris	5.50	7.00	8.00	9.00	10.00	11.00	12.00	1.00	2.00	3.00	4.00	5.00	6.00	7.00		9.15	11.00
3.9 Country Club	6.07	7.17	8.17	9.17	10.17	11.17	12.17	1.17	2.17	3.17	4.17	5.17	6.17	7.17		9.32	11.17
6.4 Elmendorf	6.17	7.24	8.24	9.24	10.24	11.24	12.24	1.24	2.24	3.24	4.24	5.24	6.24	7.24		9.39	11.24
10.0 Sta. 36 Piper	6.32	7.32	8.32	9.32	10.32	11.32	12.32	1.42	2.42	3.42	4.42	5.42	6.42	7.42		9.47	11.32
15.8 Sta. 54	6.35	7.42	8.42	9.42	10.42	11.42	12.42	1.49	2.49	3.49	4.49	5.49	6.49	7.49		9.57	11.42
17.6 Paris Ar.	6.42	7.49	8.49	9.49	10.49	11.49	12.49									10.04	11.49

FROM PARIS TO LEXINGTON AND GEORGETOWN

STATIONS	A.M.	A.M.	A.M.	A.M.	A.M.	A.M.	A.M.	P.M.	P.M.	P.M.	P.M.	P.M.	P.M.	P.M.	P.M.	P.M.	P.M.
Miles																	
0.0 Lv. Paris		6.50	7.53	8.53	9.53	10.53	11.53	12.53	1.53	2.53	3.53	4.53	5.53	6.53	8.26	10.11	11.53
1.8 Sta. 54		6.57	7.59	8.59	9.59	10.59	11.59	12.59	1.59	2.59	3.59	4.59	5.59	6.59	8.32	10.17	11.59
7.6 Sta. 36 Piper		7.10	8.10	9.10	10.10	11.10	12.10	1.10	2.10	3.10	4.10	5.10	6.10	7.10	8.43	10.28	12.10
11.2 Elmendorf		7.18	8.18	9.18	10.18	11.18	12.18	1.18	2.18	3.18	4.18	5.18	6.18	7.18	8.51	10.36	12.18
13.7 Country Club		7.23	8.23	9.23	10.23	11.23	12.23	1.23	2.23	3.23	4.23	5.23	6.23	7.23	8.56	10.41	12.23
17.6 Lexington Ar.		7.42	8.42	9.42	10.42	11.42	12.42	1.42	2.42	3.42	4.42	5.42	6.42	7.42	9.15	11.00	12.40
0.0 Lv. Lexington For Georgetown	6.40	7.42	8.42	9.42	10.42	11.42	12.42	1.42	2.42	3.42	4.42	5.42	6.42	7.42	9.15	11.00	
1.0 Hickory Street	6.49	7.51	8.51	9.51	10.51	11.51	12.51	1.51	2.51	3.51	4.51	5.51	6.51	7.51	9.29	11.14	
2.9 Sta. 7, Hill	6.54	7.56	8.56	9.56	10.56	11.56	12.56	1.56	2.56	3.56	4.56	5.56	6.56	8.00	9.33	11.18	
4.2 Greendale	6.58	8.00	9.00	10.00	11.00	12.00	1.00	2.00	3.00	4.00	5.00	6.00	7.00	8.05	9.38	11.23	
6.7 Tanner	7.03	8.05	9.05	10.05	11.05	12.05	1.05	2.06	3.06	4.05	5.05	6.05	7.05	8.07	9.43	11.28	
8.0 Donerail	7.05	8.07	9.07	10.07	11.07	12.07	1.10	2.10	3.10	4.07	5.07	6.07	7.10	8.10	9.46	11.30	
9.1 Sta. 26 Coleman Ave	7.08	8.10	9.10	10.10	11.10	12.10	1.12	2.13	3.13	4.10	5.10	6.10	7.19	8.19	9.52	11.37	
12.8 Georgetown Ar.	7.17	8.19	9.19	10.19	11.19	12.19	1.19	2.19	3.19	4.19	5.19	6.19	7.19	8.19			

Note—Car leaves Sta. 23 Paris Division for Lexington at 6:17 a. m. Daily except Sunday.

*Indicate that cars run daily except Sunday.

'The arrival and departure of trains upon time scheduled is not guaranteed.

These time tables are subject to change without notice to the public.

HENRY BUSH, Superintendent of Transportation

Kentucky Traction & Terminal Company

INTERURBAN TIME TABLE, EFFECTIVE JULY 1, 1930

FROM FRANKFORT TO VERSAILLES, LEXINGTON AND NICHOLASVILLE

Miles	STATIONS	A.M.	A.M.	Da'y A.M.	Da'y A.M.	Da'y A.M.	Da'y A.M.	Da'y A.M.	Da'y A.M.	Da'y P.M.	Da'y P.M.	Da'y P.M.	Da'y P.M.	Da'y P.M.	Da'y P.M.	Da'y P.M.	Da'y P.M.	Da'y P.M.
0.0	Lv Frankfort		6.25	7.25	8.25	9.35	10.55	11.55	12.55	1.55	2.55	3.55	4.55	5.55		6.55	8.45	10.00
3.3	Sta. 66, Hoge		6.32	7.32	8.32	10.02	11.02	12.02	1.02	2.02	3.02	4.02	5.02	6.02		6.52	8.52	10.07
4.6	Sta. 63 Jett		6.35	7.35	8.35	10.05	11.05	12.05	1.05	2.05	3.05	4.05	5.05	6.05		6.55	8.55	10.10
9.1	McKee		6.45	7.45	8.45	10.15	11.15	12.15	1.15	2.15	3.15	4.15	5.15	6.15		7.05	9.05	10.20
14.5	Versailles Ar.		6.59	7.59	8.59	10.29	11.29	12.29	1.29	2.29	3.29	4.29	5.29	6.29		7.19	9.20	10.35
0.0	Lv. Versailles	5.59	6.59	7.59	8.59	10.29	11.29	12.29	1.29	2.29	3.29	4.29	5.29	6.29	6.45	7.19	9.20	10.40
3.5	Sta. 29, Jesse	6.07	7.07	8.07	9.07	10.36	11.36	12.36	1.36	2.36	3.36	4.36	5.36	6.36	6.53	7.26	9.28	10.48
6.0	Fort Spring	6.13	7.13	8.13	9.13	10.44	11.44	12.44	1.44	2.44	3.44	4.44	5.44	6.44	6.57	7.34	9.34	10.54
11.0	Sta. 9, Stanley	6.26	7.26	8.26	9.26	10.56	11.56	12.56	1.56	2.56	3.56	4.56	5.56	6.56	7.09	7.46	9.46	11.06
11.9	Sta. 3, Gentry	6.30	7.30	8.30	9.30	11.00	12.00	1.00	2.00	3.00	4.00	5.00	6.00	7.00	7.12	7.50	9.50	11.10
13.5	Lexington Ar.	6.40	7.40	8.40	9.40	11.10	12.10	1.10	2.10	3.10	4.10	5.10	6.10	7.10	7.20	8.00	10.00	11.20
0.0	Lv. Lexington For Nicholasville	5.40	6.40	7.40	8.40	9.40	11.10	12.10	1.10	2.10	3.10	4.10	5.10	6.10		8.00	10.00	
1.3	Rose St.	5.52	6.52	7.52	8.52	9.52	11.22	12.22	1.22	2.22	3.22	4.22	5.22	6.22		8.12	10.12	
5.4	Sta. 6, Berry	5.58	6.58	7.58	8.58	9.59	11.28	12.28	1.28	2.28	3.28	4.28	5.28	6.28		8.18	10.18	
6.1	Sta. 12, Hulett	6.03	7.03	8.03	9.03	10.07	11.33	12.33	1.33	2.33	3.33	4.33	5.33	6.33		8.23	10.23	
9.7	Sta. 19, Lyne	6.10	7.10	8.10	9.10	10.13	11.40	12.40	1.40	2.40	3.40	4.40	5.40	6.40		8.30	10.30	
12.1	Nicholasville Ar.	6.17	7.17	8.17	9.17	10.20	11.47	12.47	1.47	2.47	3.47	4.47	5.47	6.47		8.37	10.37	

FROM NICHOLASVILLE TO LEXINGTON, VERSAILLES AND FRANKFORT

Miles	STATIONS	A.M.	A.M.	Da'y A.M.	* A.M.	Da'y A.M.	Da'y A.M.	Da'y A.M.	Da'y A.M.	Da'y P.M.	Da'y P.M.	Da'y P.M.	Da'y P.M.	Da'y P.M.	Da'y P.M.	Da'y P.M.	Da'y P.M.	Da'y P.M.
0.0	Lv. Nicholasville		6.25	7.25	8.25	9.55	11.55	12.55	1.53	2.55	3.55	4.55				5.55	7.25	9.23	10.45
2.4	Sta. 19, Lyne		6.30	7.30	8.30	10.00	11.00	12.05	1.00	2.00	3.00	4.00	5.00			6.00	7.30	9.30	10.47
6.5	Sta. 12, Hulett		6.37	7.37	8.37	10.07	11.07	12.07	1.07	2.07	3.07	4.07	5.07			6.07	7.37	9.37	10.54
8.7	Sta. 6, Berry		6.42	7.42	8.42	10.12	11.12	12.12	1.12	2.12	3.12	4.12	5.12			6.12	7.42	9.42	10.59
10.3	Rose Street		6.48	7.48	8.48	10.18	11.18	12.18	1.18	2.18	3.18	4.18	5.18			6.18	7.48	9.48	11.05
12.1	Lexington Ar.		7.00	8.00	9.00	10.30	11.30	12.30	1.30	2.30	3.30	4.30	5.30			6.30	8.00	10.00	11.12
0.0	Lv. Lexington For Versailles & Frank't	5.20	6.00	7.00	8.00	9.00	10.30	11.30	12.30	1.30	2.30	3.30	4.30	5.30	6.00	6.30	8.00	10.00
1.6	Sta. 3, Gentry	5.26	6.06	7.06	8.08	9.08	10.58	11.38	12.38	1.38	2.38	3.38	4.38	5.38	6.08	6.38	8.08	10.08
2.5	Sta. 9, Stanley	5.30	6.13	7.13	8.13	9.13	10.43	11.43	12.43	1.43	2.43	3.43	4.43	5.43	6.13	6.43	8.13	10.13
7.6	Fort Spring	5.41	6.24	7.24	8.24	9.24	10.54	11.54	12.54	1.54	2.54	3.54	4.54	5.54	6.24	6.54	8.24	10.24
10.0	Sta. 29, Jesse	5.47	6.31	7.31	8.31	9.31	11.01	12.01	1.01	2.01	3.01	4.01	5.01	6.01	6.31	7.01	8.31	10.31
13.5	Versailles Ar.	5.56	6.40	7.40	8.40	9.40	11.10	12.10	1.10	2.10	3.10	4.10	5.10	6.10	6.40	7.10	8.40	10.40
0.0	Lv. Versailles For Frankfort		6.45	7.46	8.46	9.46	11.16	12.16	1.16	2.16	3.16	4.16	5.16	6.16		7.16	8.46	10.46
5.4	McKee		6.55	7.53	8.53	9.55	11.25	12.25	1.25	2.25	3.25	4.25	5.25	6.25		7.25	8.53	10.53
9.9	Sta. 63 Jett		7.02	8.02	9.02	10.07	11.32	12.32	1.32	2.32	3.32	4.32	5.32	6.32		7.32	9.02	11.02
11.2	Sta. 66, Hoge		7.06	8.06	9.06	10.11	11.36	12.36	1.36	2.36	3.36	4.36	5.36	6.36		7.36	9.06	11.06
14.5	Frankfort Ar.		7.15	8.15	9.15	10.20	11.45	12.45	1.45	2.45	3.45	4.45	5.45	6.45		7.45	9.15	11.15

FROM GEORGETOWN TO LEXINGTON AND PARIS

Miles	STATIONS	Da'y A.M.	A.M.	Da'y A.M.	Da'y A.M.	Da'y A.M.	Da'y A.M.	Da'y A.M.	Da'y A.M.	Da'y P.M.	Da'y P.M.	Da'y P.M.	Da'y P.M.	Da'y P.M.	* P.M.	Da'y P.M.	Da'y P.M.	Da'y P.M.
0.0	Lv. Georgetown	6.20	7.25	8.25	9.25	10.25	11.25	12.25	1.25	2.25	3.25	4.25		5.25	6.25	7.25	9.25	10.43
2.9	Coleman Ave.	6.28	7.29	8.31	9.31	10.31	11.31	12.31	1.31	2.31	3.31	4.31		5.29	6.31	7.31	9.31	10.49
4.0	Donerail	6.31	7.32	8.34	9.34	10.34	11.34	12.34	1.34	2.31	3.34	4.32		5.32	6.34	7.34	9.34	10.52
5.3	Tanner	6.35	7.55	8.37	9.37	10.37	11.37	12.37	1.37	2.37	3.35	4.35		5.35	6.37	7.37	9.37	10.55
7.8	Greendale	6.40	7.40	8.41	9.41	10.41	11.41	12.41	1.41	2.41	3.49	4.40		5.40	6.41	7.41	9.41	10.58
9.3	Sta. 7 Hill	6.45	7.45	8.46	9.46	10.46	11.46	12.46	1.46	2.46	3.45	4.45		5.45	6.46	7.46	9.46	11.03
11.0	Hickory Street	6.50	7.51	8.51	9.51	10.51	11.51	12.51	1.51	2.51	3.51	4.51		5.51	6.51	7.51	9.51	11.08
12.0	Lexington Ar.	7.00	8.00	9.00	10.00	11.00	12.00	1.00	2.00	3.00	3.06	5.00		6.00	7.00	8.00	10.00	11.15
0.0	Lv. Lexington For Paris	5.50	6.50	7.00	8.00	9.00	10.00	11.00	12.00	1.00	2.00	3.00	4.00	5.00	5.30	6.00	8.00	10.00
3.9	Country Club	6.07	6.47	7.17	8.17	9.17	10.17	11.17	12.17	1.17	2.17	3.17	4.17	5.17	5.47	6.17	8.17	10.17
6.4	Elmendorf	6.17	6.54	7.24	8.24	9.24	10.24	11.24	12.24	1.24	2.24	3.24	4.24	5.24	5.54	6.24	8.24	10.24
10.0	Sta. 36 Piper	6.25	7.02	7.32	8.32	9.32	10.32	11.32	12.32	1.32	2.32	3.32	4.32	5.32	6.02	6.32	8.32	10.32
10.3	Sta. 64	6.30	7.12	7.42	8.42	9.42	10.42	11.42	12.42	1.42	2.42	3.42	4.42	5.42	6.12	6.42	8.42	10.42
17.6	Paris Ar.	6.42	7.19	7.49	8.49	9.49	10.49	11.49	12.49	1.49	2.49	3.49	4.49	6.49	6.19	6.49	8.49	10.49

FROM PARIS TO LEXINGTON AND GEORGETOWN

Miles	STATIONS	A.M.	Da'y A.M.	Da'y A.M.	* A.M.	Da'y A.M.	Da'y A.M.	Da'y A.M.	Da'y A.M.	Da'y P.M.	Da'y P.M.	Da'y P.M.	Da'y P.M.	Da'y P.M.	Da'y P.M.	* P.M.	Da'y P.M.	Da'y P.M.
0.0	Lv. Paris		6.50	7.23	7.53	8.53	9.58	10.53	11.53	12.53	1.53	2.53	3.53	4.53	5.53	6.23	7.10	9.10	10.53
1.8	Sta. 64		6.57	7.29	7.59	8.59	9.59	10.59	11.59	12.59	1.59	2.59	3.59	5.29	5.59	6.29	7.16	9.16	10.59
7.6	Sta. 36 Piper		7.10	7.40	8.10	9.10	10.10	11.10	12.10	1.10	2.10	3.10	4.10	5.10	6.10	6.40	7.27	9.27	11.10
11.2	Elmendorf		7.18	7.48	8.18	9.18	10.18	11.18	12.18	1.18	2.18	3.18	4.18	5.18	6.18	6.48	7.35	9.35	11.18
13.7	Country Club		7.23	7.53	8.23	9.23	10.23	11.23	12.23	1.23	2.23	3.23	4.23	5.23	6.23	6.53	7.41	9.41	11.23
17.6	Lexington Ar.		7.42	8.12	8.42	9.42	10.42	11.42	12.42	1.42	2.42	3.42	4.42	5.42	6.42	7.12	8.00	10.00	11.40
0.0	Lv. Lexington For Georgetown	5.40	6.42	7.42		8.42	9.42	10.42	11.42	12.42	1.42	2.42	3.42	4.42	5.42	6.42	8.00	10.00
1.0	Hickory Street	5.49	6.51	7.51		8.51	9.51	10.51	11.41	12.51	1.51	2.51	3.51	4.51	5.51	6.51	8.09	10.09
2.9	Sta. 7 Hill	5.54	6.56	7.56		8.56	9.56	10.56	11.56	12.56	1.56	2.56	3.56	4.56	5.56	6.56	8.14	10.14
4.2	Greendale	5.68	7.00	8.00		9.00	10.00	11.00	12.00	1.00	2.00	3.00	4.00	5.00	6.00	7.00	8.18	10.18
6.7	Tanner	6.03	7.05	8.05		9.05	10.05	11.05	12.05	1.05	2.05	3.05	4.05	5.05	6.05	7.05	8.23	10.23
8.0	Donerail	6.05	7.07	8.07		9.07	10.07	11.07	12.07	1.07	2.07	3.07	4.07	5.07	6.07	7.07	8.25	10.25
9.1	Coleman Ave.	6.08	7.10	8.10		9.10	10.10	11.10	12.10	1.10	2.10	3.10	4.10	5.10	6.10	7.10	8.28	10.28
12.0	Georgetown	6.17	7.19	8.19		9.19	10.19	11.19	12.19	1.19	2.19	3.19	4.19	5.19	6.19	7.19	8.37	10.37

NOTE:—The * indicates that cars run daily except Sunday.

These time tables are subject to change without notice.

HENRY BUSH, Superintendent of Transportation.

89

CENTRAL TRACTION INTERURBAN CAR #113 HAS TURNED VIA THE WYE AT ANN AND MAIN STREET AND IS HEADED FOR THE INTERURBAN DEPOT AT OLIVE AND MAIN. <WF>

ONE OF THE BIG, HEAVY CENTRAL KENTUCKY TRACTION WOODEN INTERURBAN CARS IS INBOUND TO FRANKFORT NEAR JETT. <CCM>

MR. RICHARD CHEEK, A CENTRAL KENTUCKY TRACTION CONDUCTOR, SHOWS OFF HIS NEW UNIFORM. <CCM>

CENTRAL KENTUCKY TRACTION TRACKS ADJACENT TO VERSAILLES ROAD NEAR THE JUNCTION OF I-64, LOOKING SOUTH TOWARD VERSAILLES <CCM>

KT&T FREIGHT MOTOR #351 IS SEEN IN DOWNTOWN LEXINGTON STARTING OUT FOR HER MORNING RUN OF DELIVERING PACKAGES AND MILK CANS TO STATIONS ALONG HER ROUTE. <CHB>

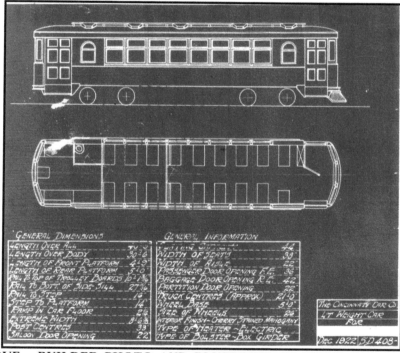

GENERAL DIMENSIONS		GENERAL INFORMATION	
LENGTH OVER ALL		SEATING CAPACITY	44
LENGTH OVER BODY	30'6"	WIDTH OF SEATS	39"
LENGTH OF FRONT PLATFORM	4'9"	WIDTH OF AISLE	22"
LENGTH OF REAR PLATFORM	5'0"	PASSENGER DOOR OPENING F.E.	36"
RAIL TO TOP OF TROLLEY BOARDS	10'7⅛"	BAGGAGE DOOR OPENING R.E.	42"
RAIL TO BOTT. OF SIDE SILL	27⅝"	PARTITION DOOR OPENING	22"
RAIL TO STEP	16"	TRUCK CENTRES (APPROX.)	21'0"
STEP TO PLATFORM	14"	WHEEL BASE	5'0"
RAMP IN CAR FLOOR	2½"	SIZE OF WHEELS	26"
EXTREME WIDTH	8'0⅞"	INTERIOR FINISH - CHERRY STAINED MAHOGANY	
POST CENTRES	33"	TYPE OF HEATER - ELECTRIC	
SALOON DOOR OPENING	22"	TYPE OF BOLSTER - BOX GIRDER	

THE CINCINNATI CAR CO
LT WEIGHT CAR
FOR
DEC. 1922 S.D. 408

ABOVE - BUILDER PHOTO AND BLUEPRINT OF KT&T CAR #310, A CINCINNATI CAR COMPANY LIGHTWEIGHT CURVE SIDE CAR. THE CAR IS DIVIDED INTO THREE SECTIONS. FROM RIGHT TO LEFT: WHITE, COLORED, BAGGAGE/WHITE SMOKING. <CS>

INTERIOR VIEW OF KT&T CAR #310 LOOKING FORWARD. NOTE THE FARE REGISTER IN THE CENTER AISLE. <CS>

INTERIOR VIEW OF KT&T CAR #310 LOOKING TOWARD THE REAR OF THE MAIN SEATING AREA. NOTE THE WORD "WHITE" ABOVE THE DOOR LEADING INTO THE "COLORED" SEATING AREA. <CS>

INTERIOR OF KT&T CAR #310 LOOKING INTO BAGGAGE/SMOKING AREA. NOTE THE WORD "COLORED" ABOVE DOOR. SUCH SIGNS WERE PLACED AT EITHER END OF A COMPARTMENT TO DESIGNATE ITS ALLOWED OCCUPANCY. <CS>

MR. JACK GORDON, A BLUEGRASS TRACTION CONDUCTOR, IS SEEN IN HIS UNIFORM. <CCM>

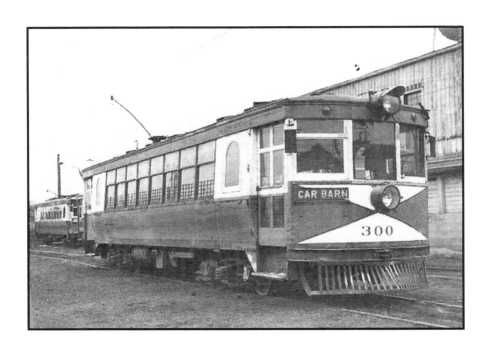

A CENTRAL KENTUCKY TRACTION CAR ON VERSAILLES PIKE NEAR MILLVILLE ROAD <WA>

VERSAILLES & FRANKFORT TRACTION COMPANY WORKERS LAYING RAIL ALONGSIDE VERSAILLES ROAD NEAR JETT <CCM>

THIS PHOTO AND THE NEXT ARE OF THE INTERURBAN FREIGHT STATION AT MAIN AND OLIVE STREET.<CHB>

Pay as You Enter Cars

Save delays by handing conductor your ticket or correct fare as you enter car.

Tickets cheaper than cash fare between all points.

Ticket Rates

Between	One Way	Round Trip
Lexington & Frankfort	80c	$1.35
Lexington & Paris	50c	.75
Lexington & Versailles	40c	.70
Lexington & Georgetown	35c	.60
Lexington & Nicholasville	35c	.60
Versailles & Frankfort	45c	.80

COMMUTATION AND SCHOOL BOOKS AT REDUCED RATES

Special Interurban Cars and Motor Coaches

TIME TABLE

KENTUCKY TRACTION & TERMINAL COMPANY

CONNECTING

Lexington—Versailles

Frankfort—Georgetown

Paris

TRACTION LINES

Connect with

CONSOLIDATED

COACH

CORPORATION

For points throughout the United States at low rates of fare

General Offices

MAIN & BROADWAY

Lexington, Ky.

Phone Ash. 19

Effective July 1, 1930

PACKAGE EXPRESS SERVICE

Packages ranging in weight according to the schedule set forth below may be shipped from any point between Terminal Cities or regular stop at the following rates:

Stamp Rates and Insurance

	Rate	Liability
Less than 1 lb.	10c	$10.00
1 lb. to 5 lbs.	15c	10.00
6 lbs. to 12 lbs.	20c	10.00
13 lbs. to 25 lbs.	25c	10.00
26 lbs. to 50 lbs.	30c	10.00
51 lbs. to 100 lbs	40c	10.00
101 lbs. to 200 lbs.	40c per cwt.	10.00
Each 100 lbs. thereafter 30c additional 10.00		

Liability Insurance

	Rate
$10.00, less than $25.00	10c
$25.00, less than $50.00	15c
$50.00, less than $100.00	25c
Each $100.00 thereafter	20c

Liability not to exceed $600.00. All parcels valued at $100.00 and over must be sealed. Jewelery not accepted except at shipper's risk. All goods shipped to non-agency points are shipped at shippers risk without insurance.

C. O. D. Packages handled on passenger cars between agency points—non-perishable and not to exceed $100.00 in value.

Package stamps can be purchased at Agencies of the Company for the shipment of individual packages or in quantities, stamps being pasted on the package in accordance with the above schedule.

Package properly stamped and delivered to agencies of the company will be shipped on all regular cars arriving at destination not later than 6.00 p. m.

TIME TABLE

Table shows time cars are scheduled to arrive and depart from stations named.

The company does not guarantee the time shown herein nor hold itself responsible for any errors and reserves the right to deviate therefrom without published notice.

SERVICE

Passengers are requested to report any misconduct, discourtesy or neglect of duty shown by any employee.

HENRY BUSH,
Supt. of Transportation

Interurban Freight Service

Connecting
—Lexington
—Versailles
—Frankfort
—Georgetown
—Nicholasville
—Paris
—Louisville

Free Telephone Service for placing orders to be shipped over Interurban lines—Telephone your order to our tation Agent.

Baggage

There will be a charge made for all baggage except grips or parcels personally carried.

The minimum charge for each piece carried on one division is 25 cents.

The maximum charge for each piece carried on more than one division is 50 cents.

DOOR DELIVERY

on all freight shipments made to Frankfort, Versailles, Georgetown, Nicholasville and Paris at request of shipper and when so indicated on bill of lading. For information regarding rates apply to local agent.

LOUISVILLE

JOINING KENTUCKY & INDIANA TOGETHER

Kentucky's main exports during the 19th century were agricultural products such as tobacco, hemp, lumber, and corn; however, the Commonwealth had also developed a large manufacturing and commercial center based around Louisville. To move these raw and finished goods into and out of the city, the Commonwealth of Kentucky embraced both the railroad and the steamboat during the first half of the 19th century.

During the last half of the 19th century, Kentucky continued to develop rail and water transportation. As part of the infatuation with rail travel, Louisville embraced the electric-powered streetcar and interurban. A casual reading of the Louisville newspapers of the day indicates that over 100 different interurban and streetcar lines were proposed for construction in Kentucky during the period 1890 to 1920, with many including Louisville within their proposed route. A review of the acts of the Kentucky Legislature for the period 1890 to 1920 shows that only 36 of these proposed interurban companies were granted a charter to build a line, and of these, only 12 companies actually started to construct their line.

Louisville and its suburbs were then, as they are now, the largest center of urban population in Kentucky. Louisville was a major hub from which steam rail services radiated out into the Commonwealth and north into Indiana. Three railroad bridges crossed the Ohio River at Louisville: Kentucky & Indiana Terminal Railroad below the Falls of the Ohio, The Pennsylvania Railroad at the Falls, and the Big Four Railroad (Cleveland, Cincinnati, Chicago & St. Louis Railroad) above the Falls.

Louisville was an early convert to streetcar and interurban technology, with its first mule car running in 1864, its first electric trolley line opening in 1889, and its first interurban line which began providing service in 1901. The Louisville Chamber of Commerce was soon talking about Louisville becoming the interurban rail hub of Kentucky. The dreams of those promoters, however, would not correspond to what was actually built. Only eight interurban lines would lead outward from downtown Louisville, five into Kentucky and three into Indiana.

Louisville developed eight inter-connected interurban lines radiating outward from downtown to serve fellow Kentuckians in the outlying districts of Jefferson County and the surrounding counties of Oldham and Shelby. These Kentucky interurban lines were built by two companies, both organized in 1903: Louisville and Eastern Railroad (L&E) and Louisville & Interurban Railroad (L&I).

L&E had originally been organized as Louisville, Anchorage & Pewee Valley Electric Railway (LA&PV) in 1899. The purpose of the line was to tie Anchorage and Pewee Valley to Louisville; both of these communities were being promoted by the owners of the LA&PV as an upscale place for the successful businessman to live on a gentleman's farm. In 1900, LA&PV started construction of their line from their Louisville depot, located in the 500 block on Green Street, but by 1901, had made little progress. In 1903, LA&PV was reorganized as the L&E and at once set out to finish the work started and extend the line onto La Grange, the county seat of Oldham County. In addition, L&E announced that it would also build a line to Shelbyville, the county seat of Shelby County. Money pledged toward construction of the line, however, was not paid to L&E in a timely manner. Thus, it was not until 1907 that the line reached LaGrange, 24 miles east of Louisville. Plans called for this line to be extended 30 miles eastward to Carrollton, the county seat of Carroll County, and then an additional 60 miles to Cincinnati, Ohio, but financing for this construction never materialized.

The L&E Line to Shelbyville utilized the first seven miles of the line from downtown Louisville to LaGrange. At Beechwood, it branched off and ran due east about 35 miles to Shelbyville. The L&E put in five miles of double track leading into Beechwood to facilitate the diverging of these two rail lines. Shelbyville was not intended to be the end of the track but instead an intermediate stop, as the line was supposed to be extended onto Frankfort, 20 miles to the east. The Frankfort & Shelbyville Interurban was to connect at Frankfort with Kentucky Traction & Terminal Company that ran between Frankfort and Lexington. Unfortunately, the good citizens of Shelbyville were anti-interurban and for a number of years prevented L&E from running through their city. L&E interurban cars were forced to stop on the western outskirts of Shelbyville and transfer their passengers to a local streetcar. By the time the courts ruled that L&E interurban cars could run through Shelbyville, financing for the extension to Frankfort had dried up. One-way fares from Louisville to LaGrange, a distance of 27 miles, was $.55, while the 31 mile trip to Shelbyville was $.60. Upon opening, the Line saw hourly passenger cars plus four freight motors making round trips each day.

L&E definitely overbuilt its rail line considering the amount of traffic it generated during its lifetime. The Shelbyville/LaGrange Line was built to light steam railroad standards, with crushed rock ballast and 70-pound rails, but it did have a few sharp curves and grades of over 3 percent. The worst grade was on the Shelbyville Line when, while running east, the motorman faced a 4.3 percent descending grade to the 1,250 foot bridge over Floyds Fork Creek, located east of Eastwood, and then a 3.9 percent climb out of the valley. The approach to the crossing of the L&N track outside of Anchorage, on the line to LaGrange, was via 3 percent reverse curves from either direction. However, like the steam railroads, L&E ran on a private right-of-way near, but not adjacent, to any public road; at times, it veered away from the highway it paralleled to take a more direct route. Interurban cars could reach speeds of 45 MPH on some stretches of track. One has to suspect that the sections of the line that were built by L&E were built in the belief that L&E track would eventually reach Cincinnati, and that once the L&E Line connected Cincinnati with Louisville, L&E would become a hauler of freight needing expediting service. Since the line never got beyond LaGrange, it never saw the heavy daily freight usage for which it was built.

At Marcia, some 9.26 miles east of their Louisville Station, the L&E built their shop, carbarn, powerhouse, offices, and a boarding house for crews. Portions of this facility would remain in use until the end of the Shelbyville and LaGrange service; however, with the merger into the L&I, much of the Marcia functions were transferred to the L&I car facility at Brook and Green Streets in Louisville. The principle cars used on the L&E Lines were motor cars #111 to #120 and trailer cars #121 to #125. The line was also served by box motors pulling as many as two freight trailers.

The L&E powered its cars with Direct Current (DC) electricity. To push the DC current over the route run by the interurban, substations were necessary to maintain even loads over the line. At times, operating factors or other conditions would cause the current to drop which would result in the cars on the line losing speed or even stalling out. To prevent this, substations were spaced along the L&E lines. The substations acted as transformers and accomplished this using large rotary equipment. The substation received high voltage Alternating Current (AC) from overhead high-tension lines. The substation took the high AC voltage, converted it to DC, and fed it into the interurban overhead wires. Two substations from the Shelbyville Line still stand, one at Eastwood and the other at Scotts Station. These two facilities served both as substations and as freight/passenger stations.

The other Louisville interurban company, the L&I, advertising itself as the Beargrass Line, was a subsidiary of the Louisville Railway Company. While L&E built their lines to steam railroad standards, L&I built their lines to light interurban standards with virtually no fills and cuts, crossing and re-crossing of roads, and using 60-pound rail. L&I built four lines to the west and south of Louisville. These were the 12.3 mile Jeffersontown Line finished on May 2, 1904; the 9.2 mile Okolona Line opened on June 1, 1905; the 14.8 mile Orell Line completed on April 13, 1907; and the 12.3 mile Fern Creek Line put into operation on June 6, 1908. The Orell Line was often listed as the Salt River Line on early timetables. These four L&I lines operated out of a common passenger station at 318 Jefferson Street in Louisville. One-way fares for these lines were Prospect, Jeffersontown, Okolona, and Fern Creek, $.15 and Orell, $.20.

All of the L&I Lines were built to five-foot gauge, which prevented them from hauling steam railroad cars. These four lines, while classified as interurban lines as they hosted both freight motors and interurban cars, were in reality suburban city lines. In 1904, the Louisville Railway Company ordered city cars, while L&I ordered interurban cars, from the St. Louis Car Company. The city cars and the interurban cars were almost identical in design and appearance. The LRC city and the L&I interurban cars were described in *Street Railway Journal* as "The interurban car is slightly longer than the city car and of heavier construction. The city car is 39 feet 4 inches long by 8 feet 3 inches wide with a seating capacity of 40 passengers. The L&I car is 43 feet long by 8 feet 3 inches wide with a seating capacity of 44." Both cars had the same internal layout, but the city car had 10 windows to a side and the interurban car 11 windows.

The Okolona Line was always a money losing line for L&I except during WWI when it served Camp Zachary Taylor. Upon completion, the line terminated at a settlement of less than 50 people. Thus for most of its life, the line saw every other hour service.

The Fern Creek Line was the second biggest loser of money. While it provided hourly service and additional cars at rush hour plus freight motor service, the revenue generated barely covered operating expenses. Until 1923, there was no turning loop at the end of the line, and dual end operating cars had to be used until 1923 when a loop was installed. Duel end operating cars had a motorman's operating station at each end of the car.

L&E's charter allowed its track to be extended to Cincinnati, Ohio, and Lexington. This provision of the charter was not executed. Also, the L&I charter allowed extension of its lines into the neighboring Kentucky counties of Spencer, Nelson, and Hardin, but these proposed extensions never got beyond the talking stage.

L&I also operated the Prospect Line, a steam railroad line that ran from Louisville to Prospect. In 1877, the 3-foot narrow gauge Louisville, Harrods Creek & Westport Railroad (LHC&W), a steam railroad, began to build eastward from Louisville. The line ran out of funds after it reached Prospect some 11 miles from Louisville. The LHC&W was in financial trouble from the laying of its first tie in 1877 and was soon acquired by the Louisville, Cincinnati & Lexington Railroad (LC&L). In 1881, the Louisville & Nashville Railroad (L&N) acquired the LC&L and its Prospect Line. The Prospect Line became a commuter line serving the estates of the rich and influential who ran Louisville and Jefferson County. In 1888, the Prospect Line was rebuilt to 4 feet 9 inch gauge. (#1) Then in 1904, the Prospect Line was sold to L&I, but with L&N retaining track rights. L&I immediately electrified the line. The Prospect Line, due to its 4 feet 9 inch gauge, could not be served by the cars used on L&I's 5 foot gauge lines. The line was a favorite for weekend pleasure seekers to the scenic beauty of the line and the major bridges over Big Goose Creek and Harrods Creek.

The Prospect Line experienced the worst accident in L&I history on May 6, 1926. On that morning on the Goose Creek Bridge, while running in fog, two cars hit head on. G. H. Pate, conductor of Car #917 west bound, over ran his meet at the Harrods Creek Siding and met Car #915 in the center of the bridge. Car #915 caught fire and set on fire both Car #917 and the bridge. The two cars were destroyed and the trestlework of the bridge damaged. W. P. Edwards, motorman of Car #915, was killed and five passengers injured. Pate was discharged from L&I due to his violation of work orders.

In seeking men to operate its cars, L&I stated that they sought men who were at least 5 feet tall, weighed less than 190 pounds, and were at least 21 years old but no older than 35. Potential employees had to be able to read and pass a physical examination that covered both seeing and hearing and had to be of good character and of a non-excitable nature that was courteous to all. They had to be able to pass a rulebook test and a field operation test. Once hired, employees would be placed on the extra board until promoted by seniority to a full time job on one of the routes.

All of the interurban lines offered Less Than Carload (LCL) freight service using freight motors and trailers. On March 4, 1911, L&I opened a LCL freight terminal in Louisville at Brook and Liberty Streets. Some of the main products moved by L&I were milk, vegetables, and fruits from nearby farms. The freight terminal also housed the L&I dispatchers. The interurbans provided stock cars for the transportation of livestock to the Bourbon Stockyard via a connecting track that L&I installed in 1917. Before 1917, livestock had been unloaded at the freight house and carried by wagon to the stockyard. Livestock also posed a problem for L&I as it ran through farm country. L&I recorded numerous incidents of hitting livestock on its track. To combat this, L&I fenced its right-of-way and put up cattle guards at every on-grade road crossing.

In 1910, L&E was placed in receivership. Among the companies and individuals it owed money to was L&I, $1,717,500. L&E's inability to pay its debt resulted in an adverse court judgment, and as a result, it was merged into the L&I on January 3, 1911. It should be stated that none of the L&E or L&I lines were ever truly profitable passenger carrying lines. Yes, the fares collected by L&E and L&I covered operating costs, but there was little left over to pay off bond issues and stock dividends. The lines to Orell, Okolona, and Fern Creek terminated in what was still farm country, and the other lines all ran through farm country. In 1915, L&E stated that they served a population base of 12,000 who lived beyond the Louisville city limits. Amazingly, L&I reported that it carried 3.6 million passengers that year. It is obvious that most of these passengers lived within the city of Louisville and were using the L&I as an express streetcar service.

With the merger of L&E into L&I, the L&E's passenger depot on Green Street was closed, and L&E cars began to use the L&I passenger depot at Brook and Liberty Streets. Since L&E operated 4-feet 9-inch gauge cars and L&I broad gauge cars, this necessitated the laying of two different gauge tracks within the L&I passenger depot.

L&I purchased its electricity from the Louisville Railway Company that owned two steam power plants, one producing 15,800 kw and the other 27,800 kw. The power was transported via 13,250-volt transmission lines to the substations. The current fed into the overhead power lines varied from 500 to 600 volts. However, L&I reported that on the Jeffersontown Line, due to occasional heavy usage such as during the county fair when cars ran in two sections of two cars, power at times dropped to as low as 200 volts.

During the county fair and other weekend special events, the Jeffersontown Line not only ran two car section trains but increased service from on the hour by adding half hour service. Service from one end of the line to the other took 50 minutes. In approaching Jeffersontown, the line ran under the Southern Railway (SRy) and threaded through a cut with curves at both ends. To protect this block of track, L&I built passing tracks at both ends of the block and installed automatic block signaling at each entrance to this block. The signal system allowed two section trains to run through while protecting the block and indicated to the following section that there was a section in front of him. Upon arrival at the block signal, the car operator noted if the signal gave an approach, clear or occupied. If he saw an approach signal or stop signal, he stopped his car. The car that was listed as superior by timetable then would enter and clear the block. If the signal was clear, the car entered the block and ran through.

None of L&I's interurban lines ever generated the residential and commercial development along their routes that the promoters had hoped for. As testimony to the rural character of these lines, they all were served by box motors pulling freight trailers that daily hauled milk, cream, livestock, and vegetables into Louisville.

In order to increase patronage of the interurban lines, L&E and L&I provided charter service to Louisville Colonel's baseball games plus other sporting events, political and fraternal gatherings, and social outings. World War I, with the establishment of Camp Zachary Taylor on Preston Highway, provided an influx of business for the L&I. The L&I had also investigated extending the Orell Line to Camp Knox but wartime shortages prevented this endeavor. In 1920, Camp Taylor was closed and Camp Knox reduced to caretaker status, thus negating any reason to build beyond Orell.

1919 was the year of the Great Strike against the Louisville Railroad Company and its subsidiary, L&I. The strike was called by the Amalgamated Association of Street & Electrical Railway Employees of America. It started at midnight on August 18, 1919, over higher wages. Management refused to meet the strikers' demands and soon violence reared its ugly head. On September 14, a Fern Creek car being run by "scabs" was blown up at Blake Station by unknown perpetrators using dynamite. The same fate befell a Prospect car on September 15, and on September 19, the Market Street Carhouse was dynamited. Management, however, did not budge and slowly most of the men returned to work. Those men who were most vocal against the Louisville Railroad Company and L&I were, however, not rehired.

In 1924, L&I reported that it owned 102.5 miles of track, 42 passenger cars, 7 trailers, 12 motor freight, 5 freight trailers, and 8 service cars. It needs to be reported that all the passenger cars were cooled in the summer by opening the windows and heated in the winter by a coal stove. A blower was mounted on the coal stove. It blew hot air through a return duct that ran the perimeter of the car's floor. This air rapidly cooled as it traveled on its journey. The result was that one side of the car was hot while the other cold. In addition, during the day the interurban cars did not run with their arch headlights mounted. These were placed on the front of the car by the motorman only when running at night. The arch light sent out a powerful but flickering white light that had to be dimmed in the city by placing a cover over it that only allowed light to escape through a small slit. Placed on the rear of the car were two kerosene rear end marker lights.

Fare on L&I was $.03 a mile. Kentucky Traction & Terminal Company of Lexington was at this time charging $.036 per mile and Evansville & Ohio Valley $.03 per mile. The L&I freight depot in Louisville was located at Brook and Liberty Streets. It had opened on March 4, 1911. The L&I passenger station was located on Liberty Street between Third and Fourth. Repairs of L&I cars, except for the Prospect Line cars, was conducted at 29th and Garland, a Louisville Railroad Company facility. Since the Prospect cars ran on 4 foot 9 inch gauge, they were repaired at Brook and Green. The citizens of Louisville, when speaking of an L&I car, referred to it as a country car since it ran beyond the city limits, unlike the Louisville Railway Company whose cars never ventured beyond Louisville's city limits.

During the 1920s, the Commonwealth of Kentucky began to build all-weather roads that radiated out from Louisville; many of these roads paced the interurban lines. L&I was, at this time, only collecting enough money to cover operating costs. The development of all-weather roads alongside the interurban soon saw most of the L&I freight business being lost to trucks. Revenue from passenger traffic just did not cover operating costs plus pay debt interest and stock dividends. Thus, there was no money available to modernize the L&I's rolling stock during the 1920s. Therefore, while other interurban companies were getting rid of their old two-man heavyweight cars in favor of one-man lightweight cars, L&I did not have the funds to reequip their fleet of wooden interurban cars. L&I, however, did slowly convert its cars from two-man cars, conductor and motorman, to one-man cars, motorman only. The Fern Creek and Jeffersontown Lines were converted to one-man operation in 1922; Okolona, Orell and Prospect Lines in 1923; and Shelbyville and LaGrange Lines in 1931. It needs to be noted that throughout L&I and its predecessor lines' lives, they had to operate in accordance with Kentucky's Jim Crow segregation laws. African Americans had to ride at the back of the interurban cars.

The Great Depression of the 1930s only added to L&I's loss of freight and passenger business. To keep its lines open, L&I cut both service and maintenance. With no government funds to subsidize the cost of operating L&I lines, the company slid into insolvency. The 1930s would see the slow closure of all the L&I Lines. First to close was the Okolona Line on May 5, 1931. This was followed by the Jeffersontown Line on November 29, 1932; Fern Creek Line on December 28, 1933; Shelbyville Line on April 11, 1934; La Grange Line on August 10, 1935; Orell Line on August 17, 1935; and Prospect Line on October 31, 1935. When the Prospect Line closed, only the track beyond the Louisville Water Plant was abandoned as the L&N serviced the Water Plant with carloads of coal. In 2011, this line is operated by R J Corman Central Kentucky Lines.

Interestingly, the city of Shelbyville, which had so bitterly fought to prevent L&E from running its cars over the streets of Shelbyville after L&I folded, complained bitterly about the loss of $500 in yearly franchise tax fees generated by L&I.

When L&I interurban service ended, various bus companies stepped forward to transport former L&I passengers. Virgil Price (Bus Company) serviced the Okolona Line; Blue Motor Coach Company, the Jeffersontown and Fern Creek Lines; Louisville Railway Company extended one of its bus routes out to Orell; Southeast Greyhound provided service from Lexington via Frankfort and Shelbyville to Louisville; and Paxton Bus Line ran from LaGrange into Louisville. The 31 remaining interurban cars, all heavy wooden cars, could not find a buyer and were burned to recover any scrap metal. The L&I freight house was converted for use by trucks while the passenger depot remained in service until the New Albany & Louisville Electric Railroad ceased rail operations between its two namesake cities on December 31, 1945.

During its lifetime, L&I operated 48 passenger cars, all built between 1901 and 1912, 17 freight motors built between 1902 and 1916, and three service cars built between 1898 and 1916. Six passenger cars and two freight motors were equipped with standard gauge trucks for running on the Prospect Line. When new, the cars were painted Pullman Green. Beginning in 1918, they were slowly painted Murphy Red. When converted to one-man cars, they were repainted Chrome Yellow. All freight motors were painted Murphy Red.

No discussion of interurban service within Louisville would be complete without mention of the shuttle trolley service from L&I to the Central Kentucky Asylum for the Insane. This facility was located at 10510 La Grange Road, beyond Louisville's city limits, and had opened in 1873. Its location away from the city meant that it was almost impossible for family members to visit without riding out to the hospital site on an L&N passenger train. To facilitate visitors in reaching the institution from the railroad stop, a .75-mile horsecar rail line was established in 1885. With the coming of L&E's LaGrange Line, the horsecar line was converted to electricity. A single truck wooden trolley was purchased from the Louisville Railroad Company. In 1908, a new double-ended car was purchased from American Car Foundry of Jeffersonville, Indiana. The Central Kentucky Asylum Line closed at the same time L&I closed the LaGrange Line, in 1935; visitors were now responsible for their own transportation to the Asylum.

Louisville is mainly remembered for being the originating point of a 117-mile interurban line that stretched north to Indianapolis, Indiana. At Indianapolis, other connecting interurban lines allowed riders, with a change of car, to continue their journey to such destinations as Terre Haute, Indiana; Chicago, Illinois; Detroit, Michigan; or Columbus, Ohio.

Electric streetcar service in Southern Indiana commenced in 1892 with the opening of the New Albany Highland Railway Company (NAHRy). This company operated a 1.5-mile line from New Albany, Indiana, to its Silver Hills Subdivision. The opening of the NAHRy Line led to a desire by many to tie New Albany to Jeffersonville and Charlestown, Indiana. Once this was accomplished, the plan was to extend the line to Louisville. From its first year of operation, NAHRy lost money and in 1895 was sold and reorganized as the Highland Railroad Company (HRC). In 1904, HRC was merged into the Louisville & Southern Indiana Traction Company (L&SIT) which in 1925 was merged into Interstate Public Service Company.

In 1885, the Kentucky & Indiana (K&I) Bridge Company opened their bridge between New Albany, Indiana, and the Portland section of Louisville. Upon the opening of the bridge, K&I began to provide steam powered commuter train service between New Albany and Portland. The public's response to this service was so overwhelming that in 1893 the New Albany Street Railway Company (NASRy), controlled by K&I, was chartered and began electrification of the track over the bridge. On August 25, 1893, electric passenger service commenced between New Albany and Louisville via the K&I Bridge. This is claimed to have been the first electrification of a mainline steam railroad in the United States. The electrified line was 4.11 miles long with ten stops, and the cars ran with fifteen-minute headways. The line originated at Vincennes Street in New Albany and ended at First Street in Louisville. In 1902, NASRy had 14 passenger cars and 4 work cars. NASRy ran only from the Indiana shore to the Kentucky shore. Upon crossing the Ohio River, passengers had to transfer to a local streetcar at each end of the bridge. In 1906, NASRy reported that it had transported 1,250,000 riders across the bridge. Within a short time, NRC also began to run its broad gauge streetcars across the K&I Bridge to Kentucky. In 1910, K&I reported that 96 streetcars a day were using the bridge.

In 1901, NASRy was reorganized as the New Albany Street Railroad Company (NASRR). Then in 1903, NASRR was sold to Louisville & Southern Indiana Traction Company and in 1925 became part of Interstate Public Service Company. NASRy and its successors were referred to locally as the Daisy Line.

The year 1901 saw the existing Jeffersonville, Indiana, horsecar lines being reorganized as the Jeffersonville City & Suburban Railway Company (JC&SR). The new company set out to electrify its property and completed this task in 1904. Then in 1903, JC&SR was sold to Louisville & Southern Indiana Traction Company (L&SIT). Under the control of L&SIT, JC&SR and NASRR built a line tying New Albany to Jeffersonville. The completion of the New Albany to the Jeffersonville streetcar line allowed a person in New Albany to make a circle ride from his town to Louisville, all under overhead electric wires. The trip started by boarding a car in New Albany and traveling to Louisville via the K&I Bridge. In Louisville, the rider would board a car for Jeffersonville via the Big Four Bridge. In Jeffersonville, the rider would switch to a car to New Albany. This was a trip of 12.5 miles. In 1925, L&SIT became part of Interstate Public Service Company.

In 1903, L&SIT began construction of an interurban line running north from Louisville via Jeffersonville, Indiana, for Indianapolis, Indiana. That year L&SIT reached Jeffersonville via the Big Four Railroad Bridge. In 1906, the line was extended north to Charlestown, Indiana, and in 1907, to Sellersburg, Indiana. As they crossed the Ohio River, the interurban cars shared the Big Four Bridge's two-mile span with the railroad's steam trains.

Prior to L&SIT starting construction of its track from Louisville to Indianapolis, Indiana, the Indianapolis, Greenwood & Franklin Railroad (IG&F) had begun in 1895 to lay track southward from Indianapolis toward Louisville. Both L&SIT and IG&F battled financial and legal problems during their construction that resulted in work stoppages and reorganizations. These financial and legal problems led to numerous delays in completion of the track.

After four years of construction, L&SIT and IG&F finally met each other on October 2, 1907, at Sellersburg, Indiana, some 14 miles north of Louisville and 103 miles south of Indianapolis. By this time, the two lines were operating under the names of Louisville & Northern Railway & Light Company and Indianapolis & Louisville Traction Company. In 1912, Samuel Insull gained control of both lines and merged them into the Interstate Public Service Company (IPSC). The interurban cars of IPSC that ran into Louisville carried letter boards reading "Indiana Railroad." As a result, the line between Louisville and Indianapolis is often listed as Indiana Railroad. Insull brought modern management techniques to the line and invested money in upgrading the IPSC right-of-way and equipment. The ISPC freight and passenger service were improved and modernized. Its passenger trains running from Indianapolis to Louisville wore a sign on the front of their cab proclaiming that they were the "Dixie Flyer" while cars running from Louisville to Indianapolis carried a sign proclaiming they were the "Hoosier Flyer." The run on these "Flyer" trains between the two cities took 3 hours and 45 minutes.

IPSC saw its Less Than Carload (LCL) as the money-making segment of its business. Next in profitability for IPSC was the movement of carload freight. Passenger traffic in and of itself was never a profitable operation. To please its LCL customers, IPSC had freight stations located in every major town it served and a combination freight/passenger station in smaller towns. One of the main LCL cargos carried was milk. The line also moved sealed mail pouches, express agency shipments, and various small finished goods. Its freight cars hauled logs, lumber, livestock, gravel and sand, and finished and unfinished manufactured goods.

To handle its LCL shipment, in 1929, the IPSC built a freight house complex in Louisville between First and Brook just north of Prospect Alley. The freight house, often referred to as the Indiana Railroad facility, was 210 feet by 38 feet and had three home and two team tracks. The freight depot opened its doors just as the U.S. economy went into a downward tailspin leading into the Great Depression. Thus, the new freight house never got used to its true potential.

In 1906, passengers in Louisville bound for Indiana were accommodated at the IPSC Passenger Station at 3rd Street and Prospect Alley. The station, as built, was a one story building, 191 feet by 100 feet, housing three tracks for Louisville–Jeffersonville service, a passenger waiting room, and an express and package freight room. In 1909, the building was reconfigured to hold six tracks, three standard gauge and three wide gauge. Both the New Albany and Jeffersonville lines were then able to use the station. A new passenger station was to have been built after World War I, but declining passenger service made the existing station more than adequate. It needs to be noted that during WWI the U.S. Railroad Administration obtained five IPSC 1910 Niles passenger car trailers and assigned them to the Piedmont & Northern Railway (P&N) where these became #3000 to #3004 in P&N service.

While in the short run these Insull improvements to IPSC's equipment and services led to increased profits for the company, in the long run these innovations were unable to save IPSC. Concurrently with IPSC improvements that Insull was financing, both state and federal governments were putting taxpayer money into improved roads that competed directly with IPSC. At the same time, improvements were being made to trucks and automobiles that turned them into all-weather vehicles. Shippers and travelers now had a convenient alternative form of travel from that of using IPSC.

During its first years of operation, the interurban line between Indianapolis and Louisville saw little use beyond daily passenger service with freight motors carrying LCL lots. However, IPSC soon developed a formidable passenger and freight service. Travelers on its passenger train could enjoy a full course meal and obtain a sleeper for a good night's rest. Cars were modernized from heavy wooden two-man cars into high-speed lightweight steel cars. New steel freight motors were acquired to pull boxcars, hoppers, flatcars, and gondolas loaded with various raw and manufactured goods to customers along the way or for inter-exchange with other interurban or steam railroad lines. The lightweight passenger cars purchased by IPSC during the early 1920s were designed and built by American Car & Foundry. These new cars were 62 feet long and divided into passenger, smoking, and baggage sections. The baggage compartment contained fold-down seats, and African Americans, in observance of Kentucky's Jim Crow Laws, had to move to these seats when the car started across the Ohio River to Kentucky or before it left from Kentucky.

The promoters of the interurban line from Indianapolis to Louisville had built their line with little thought of the potential development of the horseless carriage. Both L&SIT and IG&F had built immediately adjacent to existing roads and down the center of streets as they passed through towns. Therefore, in the country, the interurban right-of-way hugged the side of the road and crossed from one side of the road to the other side with little thought to road bound traffic or further widening of the road. While within the cities and towns it served, the interurban car shared the street with the growing legion of automobiles. Public opinion in Indiana during the 1930s turned against IPSC. What in 1907 had been hailed as a boom for the communities along the way was, by 1931, considered a bust.

The effects of the Great Depression drove Insull and his companies into insolvency. In 1931, IPSC was reorganized as Public

Service Company of Indiana (PSCI). Surprisingly, that year PSCI opted to buy new passenger equipment. These cars purchased from American Car & Foundry of Jeffersonville, Indiana, were operated by one man. They weighed 26-tons and were powered by four 100 hp motors. These cars could reach a top speed of 83 MPH. As a result of the purchase of these new lightweight cars, PSCI moved to 7th position among interurban companies for the best speed over a rail line. PSCI was credited with averaging 39 MPH during its run from Louisville to Indianapolis. This included dwell time for stops. The fastest interurban line in the United States was the Chicago, North Shore & Milwaukee Railroad that moved over its track at 51 MPH.

Cutbacks in service after 1932 became the name of the game as management tried to preserve PSCI's core interurban track. In 1934, local streetcar service in Southern Indiana was discontinued by PSCI. The New Albany–Jeffersonville Line was abandoned while the New Albany–Louisville Line was sold to New Albany & Louisville Railway (NA&L) and the New Albany city service to Home Transit. Other IPSC lines in Indiana were also abandoned or had service reduced, but all these cutbacks would not be enough to save PSCI.

NA&L would continue to provide service between New Albany and Louisville until December 31, 1945. NA&L access to downtown Louisville was via the K&I Bridge, and once in Louisville, NA&L ran over the rails of the Louisville Railway Company (LRC) into downtown Louisville. Since LRC's track was broad gauge, gauntlet tracks were laid in the K&I Bridge to accommodate the standard gauge steam railroad and NA&L. On January 1, 1946, LRC converted the line over which NA&L ran into downtown Louisville to buses. With this, LRC took down the overhead wire from the K&I Bridge to downtown Louisville. This act denied NA&L the electricity it needed to operate their streetcars within Louisville. NA&L, in response to this loss of overhead electric wires, switched to buses. In 1976, NA&L was sold to Free Enterprise System that in turn was purchased by Transit Authority of River City (TARC) in 1983.

The cutbacks management made in service failed to save PSCI. The company was faced with a continual decline in passengers and freight. In addition, the industries it served were changing, and the interexchange of freight with the steam railroads was disappearing.

118

On October 31, 1939, as a result of deferred track maintenance, PSCI was forced to close that portion of its line between Louisville and Seymour, Indiana. The Seymour to Indianapolis segment of the line would remain open until September 18, 1941, when it was also abandoned. A portion of the PSCI Line at Speed, Indiana, would, however, survive as a connecting track between a concrete plant and the Baltimore & Ohio Railroad, now Louisville & Indiana Railroad track. This line was converted from electric locomotive operations to diesel power in 1947.

A complete listing of the Louisville interurban cars can be found in *Trolley Sparks B-90* published by the Central Electric Railfans Association.

(#1) The L&N had been built to 5-foot gauge. In 1881, the L&N was supposed to be converted to standard gauge, 4 feet 8.5 inches. Due to locomotive frame mechanical constraints, the gauge of L&N locomotives could only be narrowed from 5 feet to 4 feet 9 inches, thus the necessity of a 4 feet 9 inch gauge instead of 4 feet 8.5 inches. Some claim that L&N did not change its entire line of track to 4 feet 8.5 inches until the 1920s. As long as L&N kept their track to a constant 4 feet 9 inch gauge, they could pull standard gauge cars, but any wider deviation from 4 feet 9 inches would put a standard gauge car on the ground.

All of the interurban routes that served Kentucky originated and terminated their service from the interurban station at Third and Jefferson Street. Charles Murphy developed the following driving directions for each of these routes.

PROSPECT LINE

Upon leaving the terminal turn south on Third Street to Prospect Court. Turn east on Prospect to Brook Street. North on Brook Street to Madison Street. East on Madison to Wentzell Street. North on Wentzell to Main Street. East on Main to Mellwood Avenue. East on Mellwood to River Road and then follow River Road to Prospect. The interurban cars were double-ended so the overhead poles were swapped at the end of the line.

LAGRANGE LINE

Upon leaving the terminal turn south on Third Street to Liberty Street. Turn east on Liberty to Preston Street. Then turn south on Preston to Fehr Avenue. Take Fehr east to Baxter Avenue. At Baxter go east to Lexington Road and then north on Lexington to Payne Street. Head north on Payne to Frankfort Avenue. At Frankfort Avenue take Frankfort until it becomes Shelbyville Road and then continue east to Lyndon where the road turns north on KY 146 for LaGrange. At LaGrange the cars turned on a balloon track for the return run.

SHELBYVILLE LINE

Upon leaving the terminal turn south on Third Street to Liberty Street. Turn east on Liberty to Preston Street. Then turn south on Preston to Fehr Avenue. Take Fehr east to Baxter Avenue. At Baxter go east to Lexington Road and then north on Lexington to Payne Street. Head north on Payne to Frankfort Avenue. At Frankfort Avenue take Frankfort until it becomes Shelbyville Road. Continue east on Shelbyville Road to Eastwood where the interurban line crosses over the Louisville & Nashville Railroad (L&N) track hidden

120

below in a tunnel. (The Eastwood interurban depot/substation still stands.) At Simpsonville the interurban line and the L&N duck under the road. Continue east following US 62 through Shelbyville. Note at Scott Station the depot/substation still exists. The interurban car turned on a wye at the east side of Shelbyville for its return journey.

FERN CREEK LINE

Upon leaving the terminal turn south on Third Street to Liberty Street. Turn east on Liberty to Preston Street. Then turn south on Preston to Fehr Avenue. Take Fehr east to Baxter Avenue. Turn south on Baxter to Bardstown Road. Continue east on Bardstown Road to Fern Creek. The cars were double-ended so the overhead poles were swapped at the end of the line.

JEFFERSONTOWN LINE

Upon leaving the terminal turn south on Third Street to Liberty Street. Turn east on Liberty to Preston Street. Then turn south on Preston to Fehr Avenue. Take Fehr east to Baxter Avenue. Turn south on Baxter to Bardstown Road. Continue east on Bardstown Road to Taylorsville Road and then follow Taylorsville Road to Jeffersontown. The cars were double-ended so the overhead poles were swapped at the end of the line.

OKOLONA LINE

Upon leaving the terminal, turn south on Third Street to Liberty Street. Turn east on Liberty to Preston Street. Then turn south on Preston and run out to Okolona. The cars were double-ended so the overhead poles were swapped at the end of the line.

ORELL LINE

Upon leaving the terminal turn south on Third Street to Liberty Street and then west on Liberty to Seventh Street. North on Seventh to Jefferson Street and then west on Jefferson to Eighteenth Street. At Eighteenth turn onto Broadway and follow US 60 to Orell. The cars were double-ended so the overhead poles were swapped at the end of the line.

121

LOUISVILLE'S ELEVATED RAILWAY TRACK

At the end of the 19th century, Louisville was one of the largest cities in the United States, twelfth in population, and faced with all the normal problems such a large city encountered in providing public transportation in an urban hub. The main problem Louisville faced was conflict between competing traffic flows crossing perpendicular to each other at on grade crossings. Louisville's solution to this problem was the building of elevated track that ran above street level. Roughly three miles of elevated track was built within the downtown area. These elevated tracks were used by both electric and steam railroads and served both long distance and commuter service.

In 1889 when the Kentucky & Indiana Bridge Company (K&I) built their bridge across the Ohio River, they added an elevated connecting track that ran along the Louisville River Front. This elevated track not only served the Central Depot but connected with the Big Four Bridge. Both steam railroad trains and electric powered streetcars and interurbans used this track. The elevated track from the K&I Bridge along the waterfront had three elevated trackside commuter stations. The electric powered cars, when first used on this line in 1893, were multi unit cars; later the company used streetcars pulling trailers. This 1893 electric powered car operation marked the first time within the United States that electric powered commuter rail cars ran over elevated track that also had adjacent stations trackside.

This electrified elevated rail operation between Louisville and New Albany, Indiana, over the K&I Bridge lasted until 1908 when the streetcars were re-routed into downtown Louisville using local streets. The theory was that this re-routing would allow the company to serve more passengers. Instead, it caused a slow loss in ridership as the time to complete the trip was lengthened due to extra stops and street congestion.

The other electric elevated railway operation was over the Big Four Bridge. This commuter and long distance rail service ran from 1905 until 1939. At Jeffersonville, Indiana, there was located an elevated station that was 60-feet above ground level.

The K&I Bridge still carries Norfolk Southern Railway and CSX Transportation trains. The Big Four Bridge has lost both its Indiana and Kentucky approaches and is being converted to a pedestrian bridge. The elevated track along Louisville's riverfront was lost during 1980 highway construction. There is a long-term plan within the Greater Louisville area to construct a walking trail that would duplicate the lost streetcar/interurban rail loop.

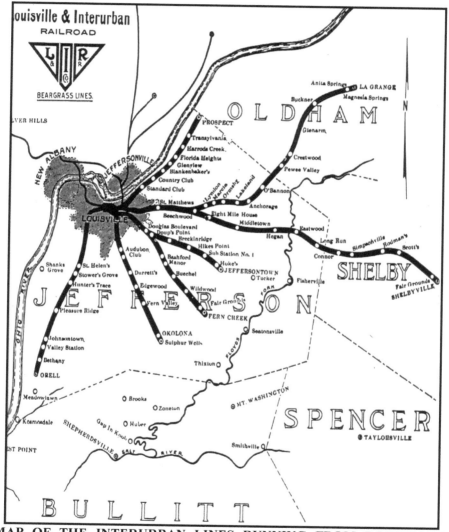

MAP OF THE INTERURBAN LINES RUNNING FROM DOWNTOWN LOUISVILLE OUT INTO THE RURAL AREAS <CM>

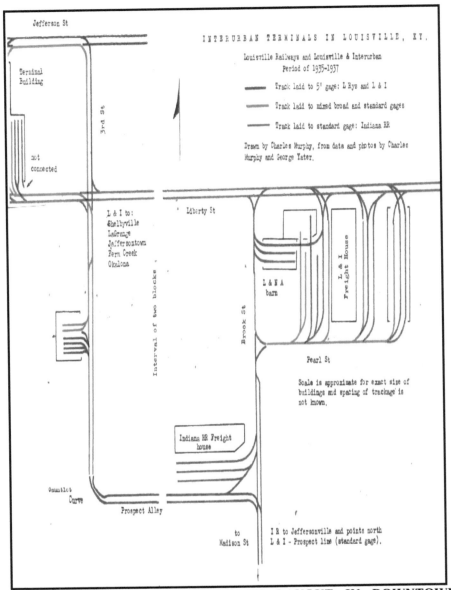

MAP OF THE INTERURBAN TRACK LAYOUT IN DOWNTOWN LOUISVILLE <CM>

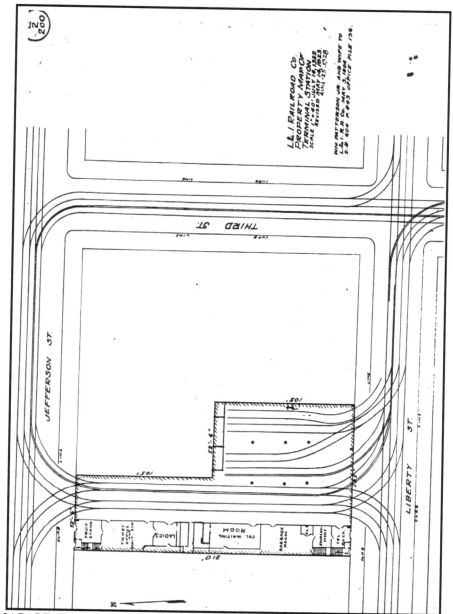

MAP OF THE TRACK LAYOUT AT THE LOUISVILLE INTERURBAN STATION <CM>

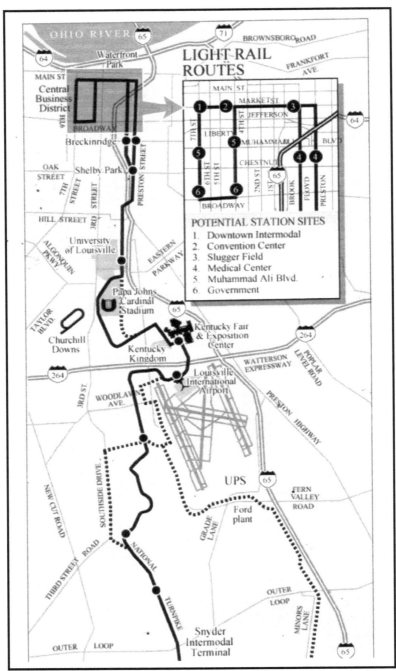

PROPOSED 2005 LOUISVILLE LIGHT RAIL LINE <CHB>

Louisville's northside elevated in Jeffersonville, In. circa mid 1930's

THIS PAGE AND THE NEXT FOUR PAGES CONTAIN PHOTOS OF THE ELEVATED TRACK WITHIN THE LOUISVILLE AREA USED BY STEAM AND ELECTRIC POWERED RAILROADS. <CHB>

Fig. 2. Electric Train and Freight Train Passing on Double-Track Trestle.

BIG FOUR R.R. BRIDGE BETWEEN LOUISVILLE, KY. AND JEFFERSONVILLE, IND.   76697

Viaduct used by Dixie Hoosier Flyers, Louisville. Ky.

Bridge used by Dixie Hoosier Flyers, Indianapolis, Columbus & Southern Traction Co., Louisville, Ky

Hoosier Flyer Crossing Ohio River, Louisville, Ky.

LOUISVILLE MUNICIPAL BRIDGE BETWEEN JEFFERSONVILLE, IND. AND LOUISVILLE, KY.

Interurban Trail car No. 124   1/24/28

ABOVE AND BELOW ARE PHOTOS OF INTERURBAN CARS USED WITHIN JEFFERSON COUNTY. <CHB>

43 FT INTERURBAN CAR-1917

Lou. Ry. Co.
Mech. Dept.

Hoosier Flyer, Interurban Station, Indianapolis, Columbus & Southern Traction Co., Louisville, Ky.

THE LOUISVILLE & EASTERN INTERURBAN STATION IN LOUISVILLE <CHB>

THE LOUISVILLE INTERURBAN FREIGHT DEPOT <CS>

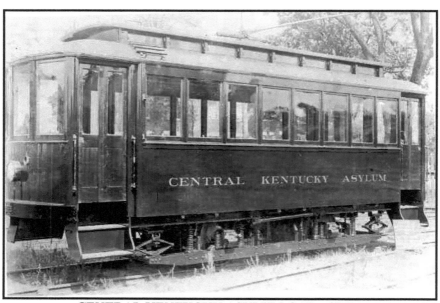

CENTRAL KENTUCKY ASYLUM CAR <CHB>

L. & E. Electric R. R. Station, La Grange, Ky.   1234   HAND COLORED   MC DOWELL & SON PUB

ABOVE AND BELOW, THE LAGRANGE INTERURBAN STATION. TRACK. IN THE FOREGROUND IS THE LOUISVILLE & NASHVILLE RAILROAD TRACK. <CHB>

ABOVE AND BELOW ARE VIEWS OF THE LOUISVILLE INTERURBAN FREIGHT STATION. <CS>

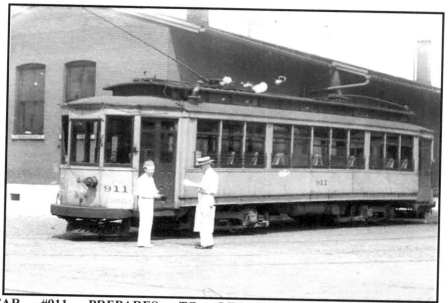

CAR #911 PREPARES TO LEAVE THE CARBARN FOR JEFFERSONTOWN. <CS>

A 900 SERIES CAR IN THE PROSPECT LOOP <CS>

CAR #916, ON THE LEFT, RAN TO PROSPECT AND CAR #166, ON THE RIGHT, TO LAGRANGE AND SHELBYVILLE. <CS>

BOX TRAILER #209 AT THE FREIGHT HOUSE. IT LOOKS LIKE IT WAS USED TO MOVE LIVESTOCK. <CS>

FREIGHT MOTOR #202 WAS BUILT BY CUMMINGS IN 1907. <CS>

LOUISVILLE & EASTERN FREIGHT MOTOR #1 WAS BUILT BY THE ST. LOUIS CAR COMPANY IN 1904. <CM>

CAR #111 AS SHE ARRIVED ON THE PROPERTY IN 1910. SHE COST $18,000. <CS>

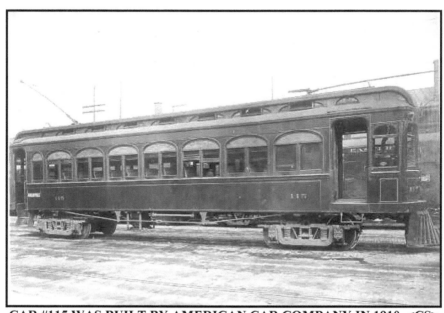

CAR #115 WAS BUILT BY AMERICAN CAR COMPANY IN 1910. <CS>

LOOKING WEST DURING THE CONSTRUCTION OF THE TRESTLE AT LONG RUN ON THE SHELBYVILLE LINE <CHB>

LOOKING EAST AT THE REMAINS OF THE LONG RUN TRESTLE IN 2011 <CHB>

AT BEECHWOOD JCT., THE L&E LINE SPLIT FOR LAGRANGE AND SHELBYVILLE. THE CAR IS HEADED FOR SHELBYVILLE. <CS>

THE INTERURBAN DEPOT AT LONG RUN STILL STANDS IN 2011. THE ROAD USES THE INTERURBAN RIGHT-OF-WAY. THE VIEW IS TOWARD SIMPSONVILLE. <CHB>

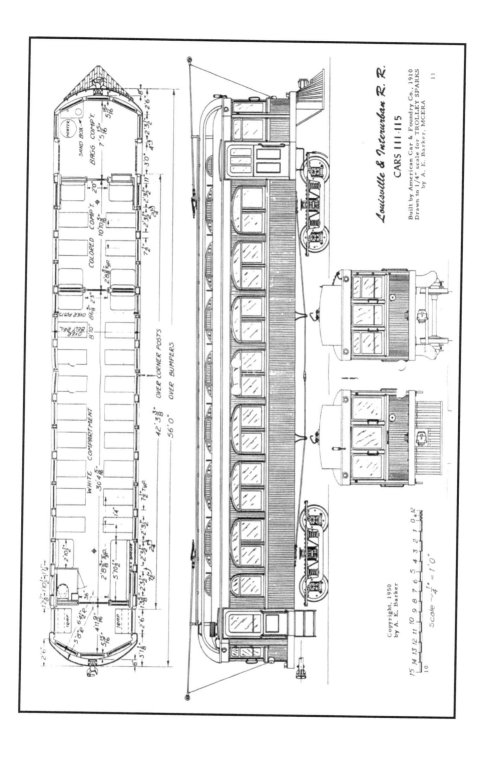

Louisville & Interurban R. R.

CARS 111-115

Built by American Car & Foundry Co., 1910
Drawn to 1/4" scale for TROLLEY SPARKS
by A. E. Barker, MCERA

11

Copyright, 1950
by A. E. Barker

Scale $\frac{1}{4}" = 1'0"$

CAR #111 WAS ONE OF FIVE IDENTICAL CARS, #111 TO #115, ORDERED IN 1910 FROM AMERICAN CAR & FOUNDRY. <CM>

LOOKING REARWARD IN CAR #111 TOWARD THE COLORED COMPARTMENT. THE SEATS ARE, FOR SOME REASON, FACING REARWARD. <CM>

CAR #111 LOOKING REARWARD FROM THE COLORED COMPARTMENT TO THE BAGGAGE COMPARTMENT. <CM>

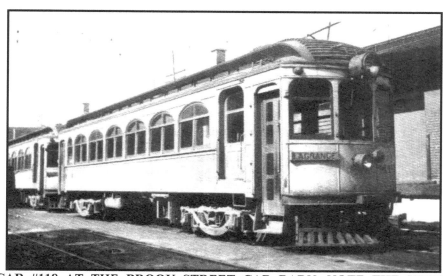

CAR #118 AT THE BROOK STREET CAR BARN. NOTE THE UPPER HEADLIGHT WAS FOR USE OUTSIDE THE CITY; THE LOWER WHILE RUNNING ON CITY STREETS. <CS>

NOTE THE WIGWAG SIGNAL GUARDING THE INTERURBAN RAILROAD CROSSING. <CS>

L&E BALLAST CAR BEING FILLED DURING CONSTRUCTION OF THE LINE TO LAGRANGE. <CS>

THE L&E DEPOT AT ANCHORAGE. IT LATER WAS USED AS A RESTAURANT. <CS>

THE DEPOT AT MIDDLETOWN <CS>

HIGH SPEED TRACK ON THE INTERURBAN LINE TO SHELBYVILLE <CS>

ABOVE AND BELOW, THE INTERURBAN SHOPS AT MARCIA, 9.26 MILES EAST OF LOUISVILLE <CS>

TWO VIEWS ALONG THE SHELBYVILLE LINE. THE CONDUCTOR IS CALLING THE DISPATCHER FOR PERMISSION TO PROCEED ON DOWN THE TRACK. <EC>

LEXINGTON & EASTERN FREIGHT MOTOR #204 <GY>

ABOVE AND BELOW, FLAG STOP STATIONS ALONG THE LINE TO LAGRANGE. CARS ONLY STOPPED WHEN SIGNALED BY A WAITING PASSENGER. <CHB>

A CITY STREETCAR IS PASSING IN FRONT OF THE LIBERTY STREET INTERURBAN STATION. <CS>

EXPRESS SERVICE AT FREIGHT RATES

Express Cars Leave Louisville,
Daily Except Sunday

11:35 am.   2:40 pm.   5:30 pm.

10:00 am. Sunday only.
ASK FOR A COPY EXPRESS CAR SCHEDULE.

Low Rates on Express Matter and Less than Car Load consignments of all classes of Freight.

PROMPT AND CAREFUL HANDLING.

Ask for rates on Car Load Lots of Building Material and other Bulk Freight.

Louisville Station open for receipt and delivery of Express and Freight 7.00 A. M. to 5.30 P. M. Sundays and Holidays 7.30 A.M. to 10.00 A.M. Other Stations 7.00 A. M. to 6.00 P. M. Daily.

"Take the Pewee Valley Limited"

Fastest, Safest and Most Luxurious Trolley Service in the World.

Lv. Crestwood (Beard) 7.15 am	Lv. Louisville........5.15 pm
" Pewee Valley....7.17 "	" Anchorage ......5.50 "
" Anchorage ......7.26 "	" Pewee Valley....5.57 "
Ar. Louisville........7.57 "	Ar. Crestwood (Beard) 6.00 "

LIMITED CARS have Smoking Compartment and stop to receive and discharge passengers only at Stations noted.

TICKET OFFICES.

LOUISVILLE,	TERMINAL STATION
"	BUSHEMEYER'S DRUG STORE, 4th & Green Sts.
CRESCENT HILL,	NONWEILER'S DRUG STORE
LYNDON,	STATION
LAKELAND,	STATION
ANCHORAGE,	STATION
O'BANNONS,	A. H. COLLINS
PEWEE VALLEY,	STATION
CRESTWOOD (BEARD),	STATION
GLENARM,	STATION
BUCKNER,	STATION
LAGRANGE,	STATION
"	McDOWELL'S DRUG STORE

Lower Rates can be secured by purchasing Round-trip, Business and other Forms Commutation Tickets.

Special cars can be chartered to run direct to Parks and other places of amusement in Louisville; also for Fraternal Society Visitations and "Trolley Parties."

ALL TICKET OFFICES OPEN 7.00 A. M. TO 6.00 P. M.

Direct connection at Lakeland with cars to and from Asylum.

RICHARD MERIWETHER, Gen'l Supt.
W. B. MEEK, General Agent

GENERAL OFFICES, - - - MARCIA, KY.
P. O. 511 W. GREEN STREET, - - LOUISVILLE, KY.
HOME TELEPHONE No. 20.

INDIANA RAILROAD SYSTEM

TABLE

Public Service Company Of Indiana

2 INDIANAPOLIS TO FRANKLIN - COLUMBUS - SEYMOUR - LOUISVILLE

SOUTH BOUND

STATIONS	Mi	2 A AM	4 A AM	6 A AM	8 A AM	10 A AM	12 A AM	14 A AM	16 A PM	18 A PM	20 A PM	22 A PM	24 A PM	26 A PM	28 A PM	30 A PM	32 A PM	34 A PM	36 Y PM
Lv INDIANAPOLIS, Ind.	0		5 30	6 30	7 30	9 30	10 30	11 30	12 30	1 30	2 30	3 30	4 30	5 30	6 10	7 30	9 30	11 30	
Southport	8		5 54	6 55	7 55	9 55	10 55	11 55	12 55	1 55	2 55	3 55	4 55	5 55	6 36	7 55	9 55	11 56	
Greenwood	12		6 00	7 01	8 01	10 01	11 01	12 01	1 01	2 01	3 01	4 01	5 01	6 01	6 42	8 01	10 01	12 02	
Whiteland	16		6 08	7 08	8 08	10 08	11 08	12 08	1 08	2 08	3 08	4 08	5 08	6 08	6 48	8 08	10 08	[illegible]	
FRANKLIN	22		6 16	7 16	8 16	10 16	11 16	12 16	1 16	2 16	3 16	4 16	5 16	6 16	6 56	8 16	10 16	[illegible]	
Edinburg	32		6 32	7 32	8 32	10 32	11 32	12 32	1 32	2 32	3 32	4 32	5 32	6 32	7 12	8 32	10 32	12 16	
Taylorsville	38		6 38	7 38	8 38	10 38	11 38	12 38	1 38	2 38	3 38	4 38	5 38	6 38	7 18	8 38	10 38	12 32	
COLUMBUS	43		6 50	7 50	8 50	10 50	11 50	12 50	1 50	2 50	3 50	4 50	5 50	6 50	7 30	8 50	10 50	12 50	
Azalia	52		7 00		9 00	11 00		1 00		3 00		5 00		7 00		8 59	10 59		
Reddington	57		7 07		9 07	11 07		1 07		3 07		5 07		7 07		9 04	11 04		
SEYMOUR	62	5 30	7 17		9 17	11 17		1 17		3 17		5 17		7 17		9 13	11 15		11 17
Crothersville	75	5 47	7 34		9 34	11 34		1 34		3 34		5 34		7 34		9 30			11 34
Austin	78	5 52	7 38		9 38	11 38		1 38		3 38		5 38		7 38		9 35			11 38
SCOTTSBURG	83	6 00	7 46		9 46	11 46		1 46		3 46		5 46		7 46		9 43			11 46
Underwood	89	6 08	7 55		9 55	11 55		1 55		3 55		5 55		7 55		9 50			11 55
Henryville	93	6 16	8 00		10 00	12 00		2 00		4 00		6 00		8 00		9 54			[illegible]
Memphis	97	6 22	8 05		10 05	12 05		2 05		4 05		6 05		8 05		9 58			[illegible]
Speeds	102	6 27	8 11		10 11	12 11		2 11		4 11		6 11		8 11		10 03			[illegible]
Sellersburg	103	6 30	8 13		10 13	12 13		2 13		4 13		6 13		8 13		10 06			[illegible]
Watson Junction	107	6 40	8 20		10 20	12 20		2 20		4 20		6 20		8 20		10 13			12 20
Jeffersonville	114	6 56	8 30		10 30	12 30		2 30		4 30		6 30		8 28		10 25			12 30
Ar LOUISVILLE, KY	117	7 10	8 45		10 45	12 45		2 45		4 45		6 45		8 45		10 40			12 45
		AM	AM	AM	AM	PM	AM	PM	PM	PM	PM	PM	PM	PM	PM	PM	PM	AM	AM

LOUISVILLE TO SEYMOUR - COLUMBUS - FRANKLIN - INDIANAPOLIS

NORTH BOUND

STATIONS	Mi	1 A AM	3 A AM	5 A AM	7 A AM	9 A AM	11 A AM	13 A AM	15 A PM	17 A AM	19 A PM	21 A PM	23 A PM	25 A PM	27 A PM	29 A PM	31 A PM	33 A PM	35 Y AM
Lv LOUISVILLE, KY	0			5 30		7 30		9 30		11 30		1 30		3 30		5 30	8 20	11 15	
Jeffersonville, Ind	3			5 45		7 45		9 45		11 45		1 45		3 45		5 45	8 35	11 30	
Watson Junction	10			5 54		7 54		9 54		11 54		1 54		3 54		5 54	8 44	11 41	
Sellersburg	14			6 02		8 02		10 02		12 02		2 02		4 02		6 02	8 50	11 48	
Speeds	15			6 05		8 05		10 05		12 05		2 05		4 05		6 05	8 53	11 51	
Memphis	20			6 11		8 11		10 11		12 11		2 11		4 11		6 11	8 57	11 56	
Henryville	24			6 15		8 15		10 15		12 15		2 15		4 15		6 15	9 01	12 00	
Underwood	28			6 20		8 20		10 20		12 20		2 20		4 20		6 20	9 05	12 04	
SCOTTSBURG	34			6 28		8 28		10 28		12 28		2 28		4 28		6 28	9 15	12 12	
Austin	[illegible]			6 34		8 34		10 34		12 34		2 34		4 34		6 34	9 21	[illegible]	
Crothersville	43			6 39		8 39		10 39		12 39		2 39		4 39		6 39	9 26	12 22	
SEYMOUR	55		5 56	6 59		8 59		10 59		12 59		2 59		4 59		6 59	9 44	[illegible]	[illegible]
Reddington	60		6 02	7 07		9 07		11 07		1 07		3 07		5 07		7 07	9 52		12 44
Azalia	66		6 07	7 13		9 13		11 13		1 13		3 13		5 13		7 13	9 56		[illegible]
COLUMBUS	74	5 25	6 20	7 25	8 20	9 25	10 20	11 25	12 20	1 25	2 20	3 25	4 20	5 25	6 10	7 25	10 10		1 02
Taylorsville	81	5 34	6 29	7 34	8 29	9 34	10 29	11 34	12 29	1 34	2 29	3 34	4 29	5 34	6 19	7 34	10 20		1 12
Edinburg	85	5 42	6 39	7 42	8 39	9 42	10 39	11 42	12 39	1 42	2 39	3 42	4 39	5 42	6 26	7 42	10 26		1 18
FRANKLIN	96	6 00	7 00	8 00	8 55	10 00	11 00	12 00	1 00	2 00	3 00	4 00	5 00	6 00	6 47	8 00	10 42		1 36
Whiteland	101	6 02	7 02	8 02	9 02	10 02	11 02	12 02	1 02	2 02	3 02	4 02	5 02	6 02	6 50	8 02	10 49		[illegible]
Greenwood	105	6 14	7 14	8 14	9 10	10 14	11 14	12 14	1 14	2 14	3 14	4 14	5 14	6 14	7 03	8 14	10 55		[illegible]
Southport	109	6 19	7 19	8 19	9 15	10 19	11 19	12 19	1 19	2 19	3 19	4 19	5 19	6 19	7 08	8 19	11 00		1 54
Ar INDIANAPOLIS, Ind.	117	6 45	7 50	8 45	9 45	10 45	11 45	12 45	1 45	2 45	3 45	4 45	5 45	6 45	7 35	8 45	11 25		[illegible]
		AM	AM	AM	AM	AM	AM	PM	PM	PM	PM	PM	PM	PM	PM	PM	PM	AM	AM

A—Daily train Y—Sundays and Holidays only

Regular Riders

Now you can buy 500-Penny Coupon Books at $3.75--good one whole year for bearer and party.

Also 10-Ride Commutations at 1.35c a mile good 30 days

C. D. HARDIN
SALES MANAGER
310 Traction Terminal Building
Riley 8461
INDIANAPOLIS, INDIANA

Travel by Interurban *...the fast, dependable low cost transportation*

1½c a mile Round Trip — *Cheaper than Driving* — 2c a mile one way

C. D. HARDIN, Sales Manager .. 310 Traction Terminal Bldg. .. Phone Riley 8461 .. Indianapolis

IN 1930, EIGHT TRAINS PER DAY RAN BETWEEN LOUISVILLE AND INDIANAPOLIS. <CHB>

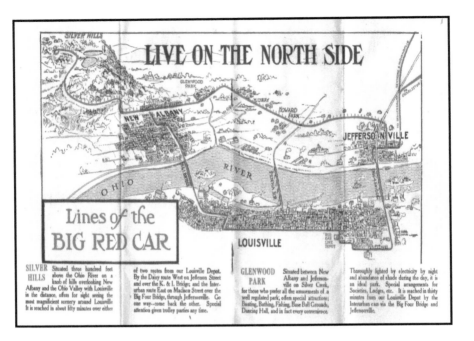

LIVE ON THE NORTH SIDE

Lines of the BIG RED CAR

LOUISVILLE

SILVER HILLS Situated three hundred feet above the Ohio River on a knob of hills overlooking New Albany and the Ohio Valley with Louisville in the distance, offers for sight seeing the most magnificent scenery around Louisville It is reached in about fifty minutes over either of two routes from our Louisville Depot. By the Daisy route West on Jefferson Street and over the K. & I. Bridge; and the Interurban route East on Madison Street over the Big Four Bridge, through Jeffersonville. Go one way—come back the other. Special attention given trolley parties any time.

GLENWOOD PARK Situated between New Albany and Jeffersonville on Silver Creek, for those who prefer all the amusements of a well regulated park; offers special attraction; Boating, Bathing, Fishing, Base Ball Grounds, Dancing Hall, and in fact every convenience. Thoroughly lighted by electricity by night and abundance of shade during the day, it is an ideal park. Special arrangements for Societies, Lodges, etc. It is reached in thirty minutes from our Louisville Depot by the Interurban cars via the Big Four Bridge and Jeffersonville.

GET A HOME

ON THE

.. PEWEE VALLEY LINE ..

Superbly Equipped and running through

THE GARDEN SPOT OF THE STATE

To an elevation of 350 feet above Louisville, to the beautiful suburban towns of Anchorage, Pewee Valley, Crestwood (Beard), Magnesia Springs, Anita Springs, and La Grange.

Here are unsurpassed sites for residences. Genial society for all. Convenient distances from business and shopping. Children carried into center of Louisville within easy reach of schools.

Monthly School, Business, and Family Tickets between all Stations and Louisville at Low Rates.

POPULARITY.

Our first-class service and our desire to supply the every want of our patrons has gained for us a wide-spread reputation, which we can maintain only by courteous treatment to our patrons by every officer and employe; therefore, any reliable report to the contrary will be gratefully received by the management.

The Company respectfully solicits the co-operation of its patrons in keeping the aisles of its passenger cars free from packages and baggage and in being ready to promptly board and leave cars.

When a large number of persons contemplate movement in a body on a regular car the Company would appreciate advance information.

Lost articles found by employes are left at office of Trainmaster at Marcia.

2571   GIBBS-INMAN CO., LOUISVILLE

HENRY GLOVER Receiver

LOUISVILLE AND EASTERN RAILROAD

THE YELLOW FLYER

LOUISVILLE
ST. MATTHEWS
LYNDON
LAKELAND
ANCHORAGE
PEWEE VALLEY
BEARD
GLENARM
BUCKNER
LAGRANGE

No. 8.

IN EFFECT JAN. 3, 1910.

SUBJECT TO CHANGE WITHOUT NOTICE.

NEW ALBANY & LOUISVILLE CAR #770 HAS JUST COME OFF THE K&I BRIDGE INTO NEW ALBANY <CS>

NEW ALBANY & LOUISVILLE INTERURBAN CAR #772 IS IN THE BALLOON TRACK IN NEW ALBANY PREPARING TO RETURN TO LOUISVILLE. <CS>

SHELBYVILLE

THE CITY OBJECTS TO HAVING A STREETCAR LINE

In February 1901, the Shelby County Electric Power and Railway Company was chartered. The company's charter stated that it could build a line that was "12 miles in length, unless a larger distance was determined upon." The proposed line was to run from the Shelby County Courthouse in Shelbyville, to the fairgrounds of the A&M Association, and then north to Eminence. Tentative plans called for extension of the line beyond Eminence to New Castle and then to Pewee Valley to connect with the interurban line running from there to Louisville. This line was never built, as the company was unable to raise the necessary funds to start the work.

April 1901 saw the Louisville, Anchorage, and Pewee Valley Electric Railway Company (LA&PV) announce its intention to build a line to Shelbyville via Simpsonville. The company proposed to start the line from a point on the Louisville to LaGrange Line near Middletown. Upon completion of the line to Shelbyville, the LA&PV would commence construction of a line onto Frankfort. Then on June 13, 1902, the company announced that the line to Shelbyville would begin at Lakeland. The proposed interurban line would follow the south side of State Pike (U.S. 60) to Long Run Creek. From there the line would parallel the south side of the Louisville and Nashville Railroad (L&N) to Simpsonville. Here it would cross along the north side of State Pike to the Shelbyville A&M Fairgrounds and then follow Washington Street to the Shelby County Courthouse.

By 1903, a number of reorganizations of the various interurban companies that had stated they were going to build a line to Shelbyville had taken place. LA&PV was now under the control of the Louisville & Eastern Railway Company (L&E). On May 18, 1902, L&E announced that construction of the rail extension from the Louisville to LaGrange Line to Shelbyville would begin from Lakeland on June 1, 1903. After the track reached Shelbyville, the line would be extended to Frankfort. Once the line to Frankfort was completed, a branch line from Shelbyville to New Castle and on to Bedford and Milton would be built. Ferry service from Milton, across the Ohio River to Madison, Indiana, would be provided. Upon completion of the Versailles-Milton Line, a sub-branch line would be built from Milton to Carrollton. L&E stated that the line to Milton, after it was built, would within a few years be upgraded to be part of a main line that would extend from Madison, Indiana, to Nashville, Tennessee.

L&E, the promoter of this new interurban line to Shelbyville, however, was unable to raise the necessary money to build this line. Over the next few years, every six months or so, a new press release would come out stating that L&E would begin work on the line within the next few months. A few weeks later, it would be noted in the newspaper that L&E engineers and contractors were looking over the proposed road, and contracts were being signed for the purchase of the route's right-of-way, but beyond a ceremonial shovel of dirt, little actual work was done.

In 1906, it was proclaimed that Eastern Capitalists were begging to invest money into the Shelbyville Line. How much money Eastern Capitalists invested is unknown, but in February 1907, ground was broken by L&E at Beechwood for construction of the Shelbyville Line. At the same time, L&E also started to extend the Louisville-Pewee Valley Line to LaGrange.

By the end of February 1907, a total of 22 miles of grading contracts were issued for the line to Shelbyville. L&E proclaimed that interurban service, between Louisville and Shelbyville and between Louisville and LaGrange, would start in October 1907. LaGrange would see L&E reaching its city by that date, but Shelbyville would not.

While the raising of capital was one reason for the delay in building the Shelbyville Line, another reason was the attacks by a set of NIMBYs (Not in My Back Yard). These persons objected to the interurban cars traveling down Shelbyville's Main Street to the courthouse. Those favoring the operation of interurban cars on Main Street contended that there would only be one track on Main Street, unlike Fourth Street in Louisville or Main Street in Lexington. Those favoring the interurban also pointed out that Shelbyville's Main Street was wider than these other two streets. They also stated that the most prosperous streets in Lexington and Louisville were the streets with the most streetcar and interurban traffic, and that Frankfort, Versailles, Georgetown, and Paris all had interurban rail lines running on single tracks down the main streets of their cities.

Those opposed to the interurban running within Shelbyville replied that Main Street had only three blocks of businesses but ten blocks of residential homes, and that interurban cars would have to pass these ten blocks of residential housing before reaching the business district. The result would be that the now-quiet residential area would be assailed with the clanging of streetcar bells, the blowing of horns, and the flashing of headlights. In addition, the interurban line would result in the erecting of more poles and wires along the street. The street would be torn up for a considerable period of time while the tracks were being laid. Interurban cars would operate at unreasonable speeds within town, and that despite what L&E's charter said, the company would, in the near future, begin to haul freight cars down the street, just like it was a steam railroad. The end result of this would be that one of the most desirable residential neighborhoods in Shelbyville would suffer irredeemable blight and therefore would no longer be a desirable place to live.

L&E, in response, said it had no plans to haul freight cars down Main Street. Furthermore, the interurban line would be built to a five-foot rail gauge and, thus, not be able to pull steam railroad cars on its track, as steam rail cars were built to run on a four-foot 8.5-inch gauge track. The interurban cars would only use bells in town at street crossings and would stop at all street crossings in the city before crossing them. In addition, the interurban cars would not speed through the city endangering lives but would observe the speed limit established by the city while the cars were within Shelbyville.

These statements did nothing to lessen the attacks by the NIMBYs. The NIMBYs organized to gain control of the Shelbyville City Council and hired lawyers to file lawsuits against L&E. The NIMBY coalition stormed the city council and fought to have the sitting council declare the existing L&E franchise to operate in Shelbyville null and void due to the company's failure to meet certain deadlines. In a closing argument at the city council meeting, the group proclaimed, "This is both the age of civil improvement and the age of civic suicide. City fathers do not rob us of the best we have given to others. Save our city (from the interurban) and immortalize yourselves." The result was that the city council requested a meeting with L&E to renegotiate the franchise. At the same time, L&E began to face challenges by some individuals concerning who actually owned the right-of-way the company had acquired in Shelby County.

Construction of the line from Beechwood to Shelbyville, which began in February 1907, was not completed to Shelbyville by October 1907. January 1908 found the grading and bridge work on the line still incomplete. The two miles of grading, immediately to the west of Shelbyville, had not yet been started. The first drill hole had not been sunk into the rock for the cut at Middletown. The bridge over Floyd's Fork was lacking a deck. These failures to finish work on schedule were due to bad weather and a national financial crisis.

At the same time, a new controversy concerning the Interurban broke out in Shelbyville. For operating in Shelbyville, L&E's franchise required it to pave half of Main Street with brick when the city paved its half. The trouble was that the existing city council preferred the dirt street due to the cost of laying brick, the main problem being the city would have to borrow the money to pay for its half of the paving. This would mean the city would have to pay interest on the money borrowed instead of living off its tax income. The result would be less money to do other work that was needed. The city, thus, would have to raise taxes or go deeper into debt.

Many, however, felt that a bricked Main Street, for which the city had to pay only 50 percent of the cost, was a golden opportunity for the city to improve its image. Bricked streets were, to these people, a sign of a city with civic pride. The *Shelby Record* editorialized on the subject as follows:

"If a thousand dollars in interest means a good brick street, from one end of the town to the other, would it not be better to pay this, than to pay two-thousand dollars a year for alleged repairs of the street, that result in nothing but mud holes and miserable crossings in the winter, and blinding and stifling dust in the summer?"

July 1907 saw Main Street in Shelbyville being torn up by L&E for the laying of track. Completion of the work was subject to stop-and-go construction. The NIMBY group filed a number of lawsuits against the company claiming property damages and seeking monetary rewards. In addition, a number of injunctions were requested, and some were obtained to stop work until one or another issue of a lawsuit or claim had been settled.

While L&E was bending every effort to complete its road, weather, financial difficulties, lawsuits, and injunctions were delaying completion of the line. It soon became apparent to L&E that the line's track, within the city of Shelbyville, would not be in place by August 1, 1907, as called for by its franchise.

Appealing to the city for an extension of the completion date of the line in Shelbyville, the council informed L&E that there would be no extension granted. The city did agree, however, to negotiate a new franchise with L&E, which would allow a delay in completing the line. But this new franchise would require L&E to completely pave five blocks of Main Street with brick. L&E's response to this was to transfer all its contract workers to Shelbyville to complete the track and overhead line work in the city by the deadline. Even with this extra work force, L&E was unable to complete the track work on time.

Shelbyville filed a lawsuit against L&E demanding that it remove all the track and poles it had placed in and along Main Street and that the street be returned to the condition it had enjoyed before track work had begun. This action helped throw L&E into bankruptcy. The city of Shelbyville, with L&E in bankruptcy and a receiver appointed to run it, threw another obstacle into the path of the company. The city annexed property for another half-mile beyond its present western city boundary. Upon completion of this action, the city informed the receiver that he would have to take up all the track that had been laid in this area and return the street to its former glory. Also, any future building by the interurban company within this area would be in compliance with a new franchise to be negotiated with the city. The city of Shelbyville also ordered the interurban company to cease using the depot it had opened outside the city, but which was now within the city limits because of the annexation.

This attempt by the city of Shelbyville to impose new rules on L&E, after it had finished its track work in compliance with the franchise it had obtained from the Shelby County Fiscal Court, was to be fought in federal and state courts until 1913. L&E's position was that it was legally in possession of its track, wire, and depot in the newly annexed area, being upheld in every state and federal court rendering a decision on this issue.

L&E, in 1913, to end future court action against it by the city of Shelbyville, agreed to maintain a brick pavement between its tracks, plus three feet on each side of the track, from the old city limits to the new city limits. This financial drain within L&E, from contesting the lawsuits filed by the city of Shelbyville, had gutted its financial sheet.

It was only late in 1909 that L&E began final construction of its line to Shelbyville; however, once again, money was short and work proceeded slowly. It was not until August 1910 that the Shelbyville Line was completed and ready for operation. Opening day was set for August 20, 1910. L&E would operate its cars from the station at the A&E Fair Grounds, on the far west side of Shelbyville, to Louisville. Running time between the two depots was to be 80 minutes. Fare was set at 60 cents one way and one dollar for the round trip. Express passenger cars would run in the mornings and evenings, which would make the trip in 66 minutes. Motor freight cars that would carry milk and small packages would operate over the line in the mornings and afternoons.

The L&E Depot, being located over a mile west of the courthouse, soon gained the local name of "Council Bluff" because it was so far west. In August 1910, L&E finished its track from the "Council Bluff" Depot to the Shelby County Courthouse, but difficulties with the city of Shelbyville prevented L&E from operating over this portion of the line. L&E proposed, as an interim measure, to operate a streetcar from the depot to the courthouse. In addition, L&E proposed to relocate the end of its city track from a loop around the courthouse to a depot located three blocks east of the courthouse at First Street. There L&E would build a wye to turn the cars and erect a passenger and freight depot. Once this was in place, the streetcar operation would be discontinued and the interurban cars would run through town to First Street. Until this was allowed, the streetcar would be used to carry passengers through the city.

On August 20, 1910, at 5:40 AM, the first L&E interurban car carrying fare-paying passengers from Louisville reached Shelbyville's "Council Bluff" Station with little fanfare. This first car was named the "City of Shelbyville." The last car for that day left Shelbyville for Louisville at 12:40 PM. During the day, there was a steady stream of interurban cars running back and forth between Louisville and Shelbyville. In addition to numerous flag stops made by L&E's interurban car on its way to Louisville, regular stopping points were Scott Station, Record, Simpsonville, Connor, Eastwood, Middletown, and Beechwood. There was, however, no connecting streetcar to carry people from the "Council Bluff" Station to downtown Shelbyville. The city had vetoed its operation.

While L&E had reached the west side of Shelbyville, the battle with the city raged on. The newspaper was full of rumors that L&E would build a branch line from Scott Station, three miles west of the Shelby County Courthouse, northward to Eminence in 1911. The paper also reported that a branch line would be built south from Scott Station to Mt. Eden. In another edition, the paper stated that once Shelbyville allowed the interurban cars access to the east side of Shelbyville, L&E would start work on the line to Frankfort. However, none of these proposed lines were ever built, and in retrospect, the rumors of these lines seemed to have been part of a campaign to bring pressure on the Shelbyville City Council to allow the interurban cars to run through their city.

Many influential people in Shelbyville continued agitation against L&E. Many of these people had earlier been in favor of the line but had now turned against it. The reason for this seems to have been the result of various factors. Many became convinced that instead of bringing new business and prosperity to Shelbyville, the interurban would carry it away to Louisville. Those who championed this position pointed to Frankfort, Versailles, Paris, and Georgetown. When the interurban lines from Lexington reached these towns, they did not see a boom in business; instead, Lexington saw a growth in business, as people from the small towns used the interurban for the convenience of going to the "Big City."

Others who were anti L&E did so because they saw the interurban causing an increase in local property taxes, for the taxing authorities would view L&E's interurban line as having increased the value of their property. Others held that once Main Street was paved with brick, there would be demands by residents living on other city streets to have brick pavements put on their streets. This would force the city to borrow money or raise taxes. Others opposed the interurban, because they feared that it would bring the wickedness of Louisville into Shelbyville or allow Shelbyville's youth easy access to improper places located in Louisville.

The fight against L&E operating in the streets of Shelbyville climaxed in 1912. The year before, L&E had been absorbed by the Louisville and Interurban Railroad (L&I). In 1912, L&I decided to force the issue of operating through Shelbyville on Main Street. Thus, that year L&I bought a lot at Second and Main Street on the east side of Shelbyville and started to build a passenger and freight depot. Rehabilitation work was carried out on the Main Street track and overhead wires.

The city immediately sought an injunction to stop this work and sent its police force to arrest the workers. L&I fought back against the city in court and obtained a judgment against the city to cease harassment of the company. Shelbyville now changed its tactics, and instead of fighting L&I over laying rail on Main Street, refused to issue a building permit to the company for its new depot. Once again, it was back to the courts, and once again, L&I prevailed.

With the track and wire in place through Shelbyville, but with no station on the east side of town, L&I introduced streetcar service between the "Council Bluff" Station and Second Street. This streetcar service was initiated on August 19, 1912, and ran until December 20, 1912. Interurban car service through downtown Shelbyville finally was inaugurated on that day. Hereafter, for the rest of the life of the line, the interurban cars ran through Shelbyville to the new depot at Second Street where the interurban cars turned on a wye before heading back to Louisville. The interurban line, as completed, stretched 31 miles from the Louisville passenger station at Third and Liberty to the Shelbyville Depot. The main passenger stations along the line were located at Hegan, Mile Post 15.2 (from Louisville), where a spur track was located; Eastwood, at MP 17.2, which had a combination station and substation with nearby stock pen, team loading platform, and a wye; Simpsonville at MP 22.3, which had a freight/passenger station, platform, stock pen, and spur; and Scott Station with its combination station and substation, plus stock pens, team loading platform, and spur track.

For the next ten years, L&I's Shelbyville Line would earn a modest return on its investment. The line provided prompt and frequent service, while a night owl car allowed locals to attend places of entertainment in Louisville and return home the same night. Express and regular freight car service for moving Less Than Carload (LCL) packages was developed. Those going to Louisville to shop did not need to carry their purchases back home but could have them dispatched via the interurban. The farmer, in turn, could ship milk, eggs, fruits, and vegetables to the Louisville market. Thanks to L&I investing in stock cars and building a spur into the Bourbon Stock Yards, livestock could be shipped to the Louisville market for sale.

Starting in the early 1920s, improved roads, the omnipresence of the automobile, and labor strife among L&I's workers led to a decline in the use of the interurban by people along the line. Slowly the line began to sink toward insolvency. The Great Depression drove the final nails into the Shelbyville Line's coffin. Service was, at first, reduced by L&I to save money. Less service also made the line less convenient. The result of less service was the loss of more customers and less revenue to meet fixed costs. Trucks began hauling most of the freight that L&I had carried between Shelbyville and Louisville. To add insult to injury, the trucks ran, free of charge, down Shelbyville's Main Street, which L&I had paved and had to keep in repair. In addition, L&I had to pay Shelbyville $500 dollars per year in franchise taxes and pay property taxes on rails and wires within the city limits. The result was that in 1933 L&I announced that it would file a petition with the Kentucky Railway Commission to abandon its Shelbyville Line.

In 1934, L&I received permission from Kentucky to abandon its Shelbyville Line. The last day of service was May 15, 1934, with the last car departing Shelbyville for Louisville at 5:30 PM. Shortly thereafter, those citizens who had fought to have the interurban's tracks and overhead wires removed from Main Street had the satisfaction of seeing the rail and wire removed for salvage.

The citizens of Shelbyville, true to their relationship with the interurban, now complained about the lost revenue that the city was experiencing with the shutting down of the interurban line. The city stated that in order to make up for the shortfall in tax revenue brought on by the closing of the interurban line, it would have to increase taxes or cut services. It was on that note that Shelbyville's relationship with the streetcar and interurban car ended.

THE INTERURBAN CAR FOR SHELBYVILLE <CS>

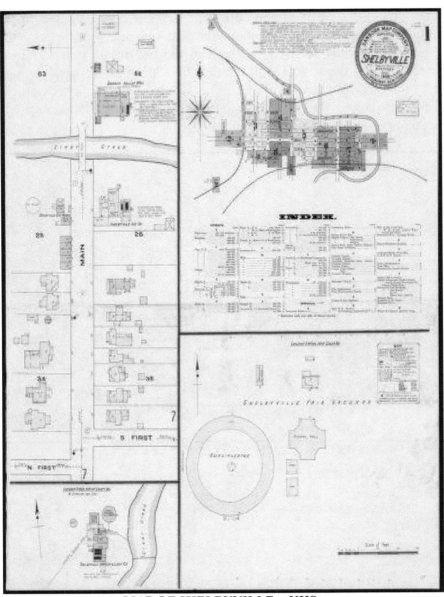

MAP OF SHELBYVILLE <KHS>

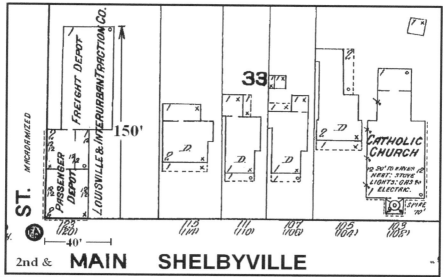

INTERURBAN PASSENGER AND FREIGHT DEPOT--SHELBYVILLE <CHB>

THIS CAR CARRIES A SIGNBOARD INDICATING IT IS GOING TO SHELBYVILLE. <EC>

THE TRACK IS AT LAST GOING DOWN ON MAIN STREET. <CS>

THE POWER POLES FOR SUPPORTING THE ELECTRIC CANTINARY ARE BEING RAISED ON MAIN STREET NEAR THE INTERURBAN STATION. <BF>

INTERURBAN CAR #120 IS SEEN RUNNING THROUGH SHELBYVILLE ON ITS WAY TO LOUISVILLE. <EC>

THE INTERURBAN CAR IS INBOUND FOR THE DEPOT IN SHELBYVILLE. <CHB>

ABOVE AND BELOW ARE BEFORE AND AFTER PHOTOS OF MAIN STREET IN SHELBYVILLE AFTER THE ARRIVAL OF THE INTERURBAN. <CHB>

MAIN STREET, LOOKING WEST FROM FIFTH, SHELBYVILLE, KY.

PHOTO BY CUSICK, FRANKFORT, KY.

Shelbyville Division.

STATIONS	C 102 A.M.	D 104 A.M.	C 98 A.M.	D 106 A.M.	D 110 A.M.	C 116 P.M.	C 118 P.M.	D 120 P.M.	D 122 P.M.	D 124 P.M.	D 126 P.M.	D 128 P.M.	D 132 P.M.	A 134 P.M.	D 136 P.M.
Louisville.............Lv.	4 45	6 00	6 20	7 15	9 15	12 15	1 15	2 15	3 15	4 15	5 15	6 15	8 15	10 15	11 15
Baxter and Lex. Rd... "	4 53	6 08	6 28	7 23	9 23	12 23	1 23	2 23	3 23	4 23	5 23	6 23	8 23	10 23	11 23
City Limits........... "	5 09	6 23	6 43	7 37	9 38	12 38	1 38	2 38	3 38	4 38	5 38	6 38	8 38	10 38	11 38
St. Matthews........ "	5 12	6 26	6 46	7 42	9 42	12 42	1 42	2 42	3 42	4 42	5 42	6 42	8 42	10 42	11 42
Beechwood (Junc.)... "	5 17	6 32	6 51	7 47	9 47	12 47	1 47	2 47	3 47	4 47	5 47	6 47	8 47	10 47	11 47
Middletown........... "	5 27	6 43	7 02	7 57	9 57	12 57	1 57	2 57	3 57	4 57	5 57	6 57	8 57	10 57	11 57
Hagan................ "	5 35	6 53	7 09	8 06	10 05	1 05	2 05	3 05	4 05	5 05	6 05	7 05	9 05	11 05	12 05
Eastwood............. "	5 40	6 58	7 15	8 11	10 11	1 11	2 11	3 11	4 11	5 11	6 11	7 11	9 11	11 11	12 11
Long Run............. "	5 44	7 00	....	8 14	10 14	1 14	2 14	3 14	4 14	5 14	6 14	7 14	9 14	11 14	12 14
Lincoln Ridge........ "															
Simpsonville......... "	5 53	7 09	....	8 23	10 23	1 23	2 23	3 23	4 23	5 23	6 23	7 23	9 23	11 23	12 23
Scott................ "	6 00	7 16	....	8 30	10 30	1 30	2 30	3 30	4 30	5 30	6 30	7 30	9 30	11 30	12 30
Fair Grounds......... "	6 04	7 20	....	8 34	10 34	1 34	2 34	3 34	4 34	5 34	6 34	7 34	9 34	11 34	12 34
Shelbyville...........Ar.	6 12	7 27	....	8 42	10 42	1 42	2 42	3 42	4 42	5 42	6 42	7 42	9 42	11 42	12 42

A—Saturday only.   C—Daily except Sundays and Holidays.
D—Daily.   Trains will stop on signal at all stations between City Limits and Shelbyville.
NOTE—This Time Table shows the time at which trains may be expected to arrive and depart, but their arrival and departure is not guaranteed.

The first decade of the 20th century saw the phenomenal growth of electric interurban railroads in the United States. Two interurban hubs developed in Kentucky; one was based out of Lexington and the other out of Louisville. The Lexington lines, operated by the Kentucky Traction and Terminal Company (KT&T), reached out to five Kentucky cities: Paris, Nicholasville, Versailles, Georgetown, and Frankfort. Running from Louisville, the Louisville and Interurban Railroad (L&I) had seven lines, two of which extended beyond Jefferson County. One of these lines went to LaGrange and the other to Shelbyville. From Louisville, a line operated by Interstate Public Service extended north to Indianapolis, Indiana, where a protrusion of interurban lines branched out to the west, north, and east.

An interurban line originating at Lexington reached Frankfort in 1907. Shelbyville was connected to Louisville by interurban cars in 1910. Between Frankfort and Shelbyville stretched an 11-mile gap without interurban tracks. This interurban gap soon became known as "The Missing Link." Much newsprint and talk were to be devoted to the necessity of laying track to close the gap between these two lines, yet little was done in the years immediately after 1910. The main problem was what gauge to build the track to, as each existing line was of a different gauge.

L&I had built their track to a five-foot broad gauge; KT&T operated over standard gauge of four feet 8.5 inches. Thus, if the Louisville Line was extended to Frankfort, the citizens of Frankfort would benefit from the necessity of goods and passengers having to transfer from one line to the other due to the fact that the Louisville cars could not run on the Lexington rails because of their wider wheel base. If the KT&T Line was extended to Shelbyville, KT&T cars could not run onto Louisville due to their narrow wheelbase. Therefore, Shelbyville would now reap the benefits that, in theory, Frankfort had obtained from the Louisville Line being extended to that city.

172

This difference in rail gauges also influenced the way the business leaders of Louisville and Lexington viewed the line. If the Louisville Line was extended to Frankfort, the city of Louisville saw itself gaining commercial business from Frankfort. Under this option, Lexington supposedly would see no gain in business from Shelbyville due to the cost of transfer at Frankfort. Frankfort, by having unbroken links with both Lexington and Louisville, would now spread its business between these two cities, costing Lexington some of the Frankfort trade. The extension of KT&T track from Frankfort to Shelbyville reversed the argument made by Lexington concerning the Louisville track reaching Frankfort. The businessmen of Louisville and Lexington held opposite points of view concerning the benefits of the extension of the KT&T Line to Shelbyville. Shelbyville would now become the transfer point between Louisville and Frankfort. Both cities would see gains only if the line originating in their central business district was extended and losses if the other city's line was extended.

The Shelbyville and Frankfort Realty Company finally broke this impasse in January 1917. The company came to the forefront to act as the promoter of an interurban line between Frankfort and Shelbyville. To build and operate the proposed line, the backers incorporated the Frankfort and Shelbyville Electric Company (F&SE), which planned to start construction on March 1, 1917, on a five-foot gauge track from Shelbyville to Frankfort. Cost of the line was estimated at $600,000. The Louisville Board of Trade endorsed the construction of the line "as a distinct advantage to the business interest of Louisville."

On March 31, 1917, F&SE announced that they had secured the necessary right-of-way in Franklin and Shelby Counties and terminal locations in both Frankfort and Shelbyville, and they were ready to start construction. With this, F&SE offered for sale 1,750 shares of preferred stock at $100 a share. An additional 50 shares were to be sold at a later date. Also to be sold upon completion of sale of the preferred stock was $250,000 in common stock and $600,000 in first mortgage bonds. The company stated that it would reserve $360,000 in stocks and bonds for sale to the citizens of Shelby County. The company's perspective stated that revenue for the first year of service was projected at $198,000 and operating expenses at $139,000.

This gave a first year profit of $59,000.

The F&SE interurban line, as laid out, was to run on the north side of State Pike, present day U.S. 60. The F&SE's Shelbyville terminal would be co-located with the L&I's terminal while the Frankfort terminal would be on Second Street near the St. Clair Street Bridge. The F&SE's rail line would pass through the Kentucky towns of Clay Village, Peytona, Graefenburg, and Bridgeport. The promoters also stated that the line would provide convenient service to the citizens of Bagdad (5 miles from the track), Jacksonville (8 miles), Hatton (4 miles), Lockport (12 miles), Benson (3 miles), Farmdale (4 miles), Alton (4 miles), Harrisonville (4 miles), Waddy (2 miles), Southville (7 miles), and Little Mount (10 miles). Two additional towns that were touted as using the F&SE Line were Bellknob and Clifton, two towns that I have been unable to locate. (#1) To those who know these villages and crossroads, most with less than 100 souls, the above will ring of promotional hyperbole taken to the utmost. In addition, most of these villages were served by either the Southern Railway or the Louisville & Nashville Railroad.

F&SE further announced that, unlike most interurban companies who laid their ties directly onto the earth, F&SE's Frankfort to Shelbyville Line would be ballasted from end to end with rock. Power for the line would at first be purchased from Louisville and Lexington, but as soon as possible, the company would build its own power plant. F&SE also promised that the cars that would operate its line would be "of the modern interurban type."

The United States' entry into World War I on April 6, 1917, caused investment money to dry up and the cost of construction material to skyrocket. As a result, F&SE announced that construction of the line would be postponed until 1918. With war production running at full blast in 1918, F&SE was forced that year to postpone construction until 1919. The company announced at this time that the Frankfort to Versailles interurban line would be in operation no later than January 1, 1920.

Talk of construction was to lay dormant until early 1919 when, with the war over and new wealth looking for investment opportunities, the promoters of the F&SE Line once again took to the stump. Now, they stated, was the time to start construction of the long delayed missing link. Completion of the missing link between Frankfort and Shelbyville would only increase the economic prosperity the region was enjoying. *The Courier-Journal* reported that "Louisville businessmen are taking active steps to assure success of the project." Louisville capitalists reportedly backed the line so as "to offset competition from Cincinnati for business in Central and Eastern Kentucky." It was estimated that 25,000 persons lived directly on this proposed line. Whoever wrote this population estimate added one zero too many; the correct number was 2,500. F&SE promoters promised that to insure that the people of Franklin and Shelby Counties would not miss out from the wealth to be generated by this line upon its completion, $100,000 in preferred stock was being reserved for them. That furthermore, on completion of the F&SE Line, it was "planned to have residents of the interested communities on the board of directors."

In May 1919, the interurban line, now named the Frankfort & Shelbyville Electric Railway Company (F&SERy), announced that it had taken options on steel rails, ties, and trolley wire. Three steel bridges were to be erected for convenience in the crossing of Guist, White Oak, and Benson Creeks. While the press release is not clear about the gauge the line was to be built to, the author assumes it was now to be 4 feet 8.5 inches, as KT&T was to supply the rolling stock. It was reported from Lexington that "the new line will mean as much to Louisville as it will to Lexington, people in Lexington having long favored such a route."

June 1919 saw F&SERy announce that it was ready to start building. The cost of the proposed line was put at $400,000. The company's literature proclaimed that upon construction of its line, land along its right-of-way would increase in value by at least $50 an acre. Bridgeport, Graefenburg, Peytona, and Clay Village, F&SERy stated, would see an influx of prosperous businessmen and professionals who would build homes in their communities to enjoy the country life and use the interurban to commute to work. Louisville's interurban system would then rival the interurban systems of Columbus, Ohio, Indianapolis, Indiana, and Detroit, Michigan. The filling in of the missing link by the F&SERy would bring thousands of new shoppers to Louisville. The markets of Central Kentucky would again belong to

175

Louisville. The F&SERy, the promoters stated, could not fail, as it would connect the state's largest city with the state's capital city. Such lines, F&SERy literature proclaimed, were always a financial success. The hills to the west of Frankfort would enjoy a housing boom as the convenience of the interurban opened them for settlement.

Later that month it was announced that the Shelbyville Chamber of Commerce was working on a subscription of $35,000 to speed construction of the line, and the Frankfort Chamber of Commerce was raising $65,000 for the same purpose. It was further stated that instead of F&SERy having a terminal on Second Street in Frankfort, it would now cross the St. Clair Street Bridge and use the KT&T Terminal at Main and Olive Streets.

On June 25, 1919, F&SERy announced that "Everything is in readiness to start construction as soon as the necessary capital is raised." The line, they reported, "offers no difficulties from an engineering and construction standpoint." The engineering and construction may have posed no difficulties, but the raising of the necessary funds to start construction remained elusive. The automobile was starting to make in-roads on existing interurban lines throughout the nation. Ridership on interurbans across the country was falling as jitneys and unregulated buses began to capture riders. Financial returns on interurban operations were low since cities and counties across the nation refused to allow them to raise fares to meet the influx of inflation brought on by the war. Venture capital thus stayed away from the Frankfort and Shelbyville Line. Unable to raise the funds to construct its line, F&SERy disappeared without having turned a shovel of soil.

The missing electric rail link between Frankfort and Shelbyville, that was to tie Lexington to Louisville, was to remain missing. The two cities were not to be linked by electric interurbans speeding along at 60 miles per hour. The 22-mile rail gap remained unclosed when, in 1934, both the Louisville to Shelbyville and the Lexington to Frankfort interurban lines ceased operations. Both were victims of the automobile, the Great Depression, and Southeast Greyhound Line, which closed the gap by offering bus service over The Midland Trail from Lexington, via Frankfort and Shelbyville, to Louisville. The gasoline powered automobile, bus, and truck running on public maintained roads had won.

#1–I expect that "Ballknob" was actually Bald Knob and "Clifton" was Cliffside.

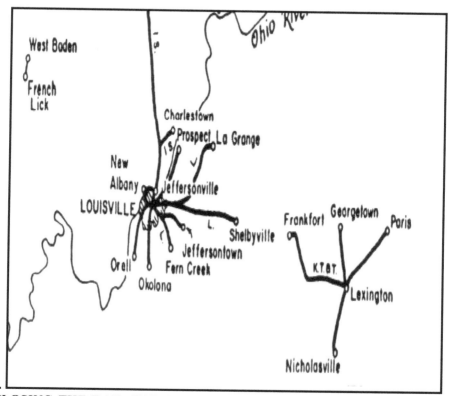

CLOSING THE RAIL GAP BETWEEN THE LOUISVILLE INTERURBAN LINES THAT ENDED AT SHELBYVILLE AND THE KT&T LINES THAT ENDED AT FRANKFORT, WHILE OFTEN TALKED ABOUT, WAS NEVER ACCOMPLISHED. <CHB>

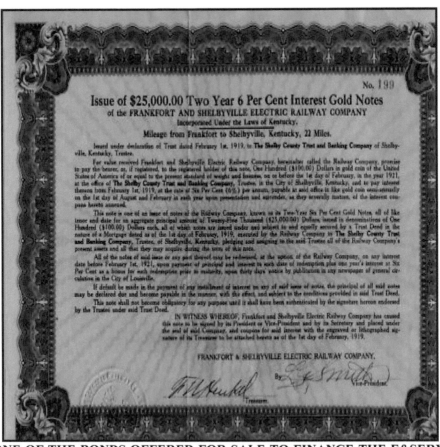

Issue of $25,000.00 Two Year 6 Per Cent Interest Gold Notes
of the FRANKFORT AND SHELBYVILLE ELECTRIC RAILWAY COMPANY
Incorporated Under the Laws of Kentucky.

Mileage from Frankfort to Shelbyville, Kentucky, 22 Miles.

No. 199

ONE OF THE BONDS OFFERED FOR SALE TO FINANCE THE F&SERY. NOTE THAT THE INTEREST WAS TO BE PAID IN GOLD. THE REQUIREMENT TO PAY BONDS OFF IN GOLD WAS HALTED BY CONGRESS ON JUNE 5, 1933. THEREAFTER, ALL BONDS WERE TO BE PAID OFF ONLY IN LEGAL TENDER, i.e. U.S. CURRENCY. <CHB>

The last three decades of the nineteenth century saw a new form of transportation arrive in Kentucky. This was the streetcar. At first, horse or mule-drawn, it was soon electrified and forever changed the face of many of Kentucky's cities. Until streetcars arrived on the scene, one had to live within walking distance of where one worked. This was true of rich and poor alike. True, the private, horse-drawn carriage existed, but it was more of an inconvenience than a convenience. The horse and its wagon could not be parked on the street for any length of time. A horse had to be watered and fed, plus sheltered from the elements. A horse had to be harnessed and un-harnessed to the wagon, a time consuming operation when this form of transportation was used. Horse waste products were a nuisance and had to be disposed of. In addition, horses could get sick and die. In 1872, North America suffered the Great Epizootic that killed hundreds of thousands of horses.

The advent of the streetcar increased the distance one could live from work. Whereas one could cover three miles walking in an hour, on a streetcar, one could cover 20 miles in the same time. A streetcar system quickly became the visual sign that a center of population was a city and not a village or town. A streetcar line at the turn of the 20th century proclaimed that a city, with such a system, was a forward-looking community with all the latest conveniences. If a city was to grow, it had to have a streetcar system and be tied to a railroad. A railroad provided the outside stimulus to allow growth; the streetcar made the growth possible.

Kentucky was to see many a charter issued for proposed streetcar systems, but only a few were built. The truth was that while many civic boosters saw a streetcar system as a way for their town to become a city, the cost of building a streetcar system demanded that a city already exist in the form of a number of close together towns or a central, concentrated population. These towns within cities were called neighborhoods. Only a large population wanting to travel to different places within the community each day made a streetcar system economically possible. A streetcar system called for enormous outlays of capital for rails, wire, and equipment before the first cent in revenue was earned. Once in operation, the streetcar line had a fixed operating cost that could not be reduced. Only in a large population area could sufficient patronage be generated to fill the cash box to cover operating costs. The result of this economic factor was that only seventeen cities in Kentucky developed streetcar service.

Two communities in Kentucky developed only horse-drawn streetcar systems, Richmond and Barbourville. Both developed their horse-drawn systems to transport people from the train station to their business districts. Richmond's service was short-lived, lasting from 1890 to 1898. Barbourville, using an ex-Louisville horsecar, represented a small town dependent on the railroad for survival. At Barbourville, the Louisville & Nashville (L&N) Depot was located over a mile from the courthouse. The L&N had chosen to build its tracks out of the flood plain of the Cumberland River in which Barbourville was located. With dirt roads that were often impassable, the town needed a streetcar line not only to grow but also to continue to exist. In all probability if the streetcar line had not been put in, Barbourville would have slowly moved to the site of the train station. The Barbourville horsecar system claims to have been the last such system operating in the United States when it closed in 1919.

From 1891 to 1893, Middlesborough operated what some claim was the first all electric streetcar system west of the Allegheny Mountains. It used battery-powered cars, thus doing away with overhead wires. While this saved money in construction costs, it posed weight penalties on the cars in the form of heavy batteries. The cars also had limited service availability, as their batteries had to be recharged at the car barn after so many runs. The line's length of two miles and the absence of any significant grade on the line allowed the use of battery powered cars. Due to the failure of Middlesborough to grow into the city that its promoters had envisioned, the streetcar system was abandoned as a result of insufficient patronage.

Eight of Kentucky's streetcar systems started as horse-drawn lines and then were converted to electricity. While initial investments in electric lines were higher than horse-drawn lines, they were cheaper to operate. Horses had to be cared for even when not working, and they could only work for four to six hours before they had to be rested.

Horsecar systems were developed in Paducah, Louisville, Northern Kentucky, Maysville, Georgetown, Frankfort, Lexington, and Ashland.

Louisville had a number of individual horse-drawn streetcar lines constructed immediately after the Civil War. These lines were slowly consolidated and then electrified by the Louisville Railway Company circa 1890. This company operated only within the city limits of Louisville. One other streetcar company served Louisville, the Interstate Public Service Company. It operated over the K&I Bridge to provide streetcar service between downtown Louisville and New Albany, Indiana. Both of these systems suffered declining ridership in the 1930's. The World War II years caused a substantial increase in riders, but as soon as the war ended, riders abandoned the system for the automobile. Within a few short years, streetcars were gone. Louisville's last streetcar service was on Derby Day, 1948.

Starting in 1865, Northern Kentucky developed numerous horse lines that were later consolidated and electrified. These consolidated lines operated in the 20th century as the Cincinnati, Newport & Covington Light and Traction Company (CNCL&TC), commonly called the Green Line. The Green Line served both Kenton and Campbell Counties. With the exception of one line that tied the two counties together, all of these lines terminated in downtown Cincinnati. One Northern Kentucky line that was not absorbed by the CN&C was the Ft. Thomas-Highland Heights Line. Developed by real estate speculators, this line ran from the end of the CN&C's Ft. Thomas Line to the present day site of Northern Kentucky University. The CN&C's Ft. Mitchell Line was the last streetcar line to operate in Kentucky. It ended services in 1950.

Paducah had the third streetcar system to open in Kentucky when horse-drawn service started in 1872. In 1890, the system was electrified by the Paducah Electric Company, and trackage was increased to 18.5 miles. The streetcars tied together Paducah's residential and business centers to the city's rail and water transportation hubs. Paducah was blessed with excellent rail and water transportation systems and this transportation network, coupled to the street railway system, allowed Paducah to become the dominant city in the Purchase Area. At the end of its life, the Paducah streetcar line was part of the Stone and Webster Company's nation-wide streetcar holdings. The end for the Paducah streetcars came in 1929 when gasoline buses ousted the electric streetcars.

Maysville boasted a one-track streetcar line, with passing track every half mile that ran eastward from the Chesapeake and Ohio Railway train station past the Louisville & Nashville Railroad Depot. Maysville, unable to expand to the north due to the Ohio River or southward due to steep hills, could only grow east and west along the narrow strip of land between the river and hills. The streetcar made possible a linear growth of Maysville. Without the streetcar, Maysville would have just been another small river town like Augusta or Vanceburg instead of the dominate city between Covington and Ashland. Streetcar operations in Maysville lasted from 1862 until 1936 when buses took over the service.

Georgetown had two separate train stations, the Frankfort and Cincinnati Railroad Depot and the Southern Railway Depot, that were located at the west and east ends of town. Located in between them was the business district and Georgetown College. Thus, Georgetown was a natural for a small horse-drawn line. The line opened in 1890 and looped the central part of the city, stopping at the two railroad stations. In 1902, the line was electrified by the Georgetown & Lexington Traction Company, and its services were extended to Lexington. In 1911, the Georgetown Line became part of the Kentucky Traction and Terminal Company operation. City streetcar service in Georgetown ended in 1922 while interurban service to Lexington ceased in 1934.

For a short time in 1893, Frankfort had a horse-drawn line that was converted by the Capital Railway Company into an electric line later that same year. Over-extended financially, the electric railway went into receivership in 1897. In 1907, the line came under the control of the Frankfort & Versailles Traction Company, and then in 1911 became part of Kentucky Traction & Terminal Company. The Frankfort streetcar line was never a real money-maker, but it allowed Frankfort to expand into South Frankfort, out Owenton Road, and up Main Street Hill toward Lexington. There is also a good possibility that without the streetcar system that allowed Frankfort to grow to accommodate an expanding state government, Kentucky's State Capital might have been moved to Lexington or Louisville at the beginning of the 20th century.

The Lexington streetcar system started operations in 1882 as a horse-drawn system but was soon electrified. The electrified line's purpose was to expand the residential land area of the city and quickly transport those arriving by train at the Queen & Crescent (Southern Railway) Depot on Broadway to downtown business establishments. Much of Lexington's commercial business was derived from people in Central and Eastern Kentucky who traveled to Lexington via the Louisville & Nashville Railroad, the Chesapeake & Ohio Railway, and the Southern Railway. So successful were the streetcars in filling downtown with people that, in 1938, they were banished from Lexington due to congestion on Main Street and their place taken by buses. The slow death of downtown Lexington started at this time.

In 1890, Ashland and Catlettsburg were joined together by a horsecar line that ran between the two cities and also provided city service within Ashland. While the horsecar line paralleled the Chesapeake & Ohio Railway's track, for just the cost of a nickel, it provided much more frequent service. In 1893, the horsecar line was electrified and then shortly thereafter was taken over by the Ohio Valley Electric Company. This company provided service from Huntington, West Virginia, via Ashland, to Ironton, Ohio, thus tying these industrial areas together and laying the framework for the foundation of the tri-state area's economic interdependence. The Great Depression, with its adverse effect on local heavy industry, led to the closing of the Ashland line in 1937. Thus, there is no longer a public transportation system in the area that allows a worker, without private transportation, to seek employment throughout the tri-state area.

The remaining street railway systems developed in Kentucky were electric lines from the beginning to the end of their lives. The Henderson Traction Company is typical of the companies that leaped directly into the electric era. With its six miles of track, the company served its community with 16 cars starting in 1887. The cars delivered riders not only to work but also to the ballpark and the fair grounds. The city's boosters considered themselves to be just as up-to-date as Evansville, Indiana, their neighbor across the Ohio River. Rising costs and declining ridership put the Henderson Line out of business in 1923. At this time, tracks and wire were reaching the end of their life and needed replacement, and the money to renew them just was not there.

Bowling Green's Park City Railway Company operated a picturesque city line that tied together Western Kentucky State Normal School, Ogden College, the downtown area, the Louisville & Nashville Depot, and the Barren River packet boat landing. Opened in 1898, the line lasted until World War I. Operating but three miles of track, the line just could not generate enough money to pay its operating costs, much less the fixed cost.

The Owensboro City Railroad was unusual in that not only did it move passengers, but also it delivered coal to the city from the Fern Hill Coal Mine west of the city limits. Like the Paducah, Louisville and Northern Kentucky streetcar systems, the Owensboro streetcar system allowed the city to grow inland from the Ohio River. The Owensboro City Railroad, with its 8.5 miles of track, tied the Louisville & Nashville Railroad and the Illinois Central Railway Depot, located to the south of the business district, to the city's river port landing. Streetcar service in Owensboro lasted from 1885 to 1934. Again, fixed costs versus declining revenue doomed the system. It is interesting to note that the Ohio River cities that developed streetcar systems soon outdistanced their rival, non-streetcar-served cities. In fact, these non-streetcar-served Ohio River cities have municipal boundaries that are even today defined by what is a convenient walking distance for residents to the downtown business area.

Paris developed a local streetcar system in 1902, but this system was soon lost as it, like the Ashland system, was amalgamated into a larger system. The Paris city line became part of the Bluegrass Traction Company that provided services from the Bourbon County Courthouse to the Fayette County Courthouse. Local streetcar service ended circa 1914. In 1911, Blue Grass Traction became the part of the Kentucky Traction and Terminal Company that ceased operation between Paris and Lexington in 1934.

The Somerset Water, Light and Traction Company's line, organized to connect downtown Somerset with the Cincinnati, New Orleans and Texas Pacific Railroad (Southern Railway) Depot, most probably should never have been built. Opened in 1905 with two cars and three miles of track, the line was soon in receivership. It never made a profit but was important for tying Somerset's central business district to the railroad station and railroad shops at Ferguson, Kentucky. While the Somerset Line did not make a profit, it provided a necessary service that allowed others to make a profit. What on its own may not be economically viable often becomes a necessity when viewed as part of a total economic system. Such was the Somerset Line until 1925 when it was made redundant by the automobile. The streetcar line allowed Somerset to grow to become the dominate city in the region.

Starting in 1893, Winchester Railway, Light and Ice Company operated 2 miles of track in that city. The line tied the Lexington & Eastern Railroad Depot and the combined Chesapeake & Ohio Railway and Louisville & Nashville Railroad Depot to the courthouse and business district. The Winchester company's name reflects that street railway companies were often more than just a transportation company. Many of the electric lines had to build their own power plants to obtain the electricity to operate the cars. It was then an easy step for these companies to start selling their excess power, at first to commercial customers and then residential customers. Excess electrical power not used at night could be used to manufacture ice for sale during the day to commercial and residential establishments. Up until the 1940's, ice was an important item in preserving foods throughout much of Kentucky. For many years, the icebox reigned supreme in Kentucky homes over the more expensive refrigerator. Any child who has missed the treat of being given a sliver of ice from the iceman or milkman on a hot summer day has missed one of the great pleasures in life. The Winchester Line ceased operations in 1921, unable to afford to repair the city streets upon which its cars ran.

The period 1890 to 1920 was a golden age for streetcar operations in Kentucky and the United States. By that year, there were well over 1,000 streetcar companies in the United States serving more than 2,000 cities. These companies owned over 26,000 miles of track, operated some 6,000 streetcars, and employed over 280,000 men and women. Some 30 years later, in 1950, most would be gone. Interestingly, beginning in 1980, many American cities would start to re-establish local streetcar service.

A 1915 survey of the United States streetcar systems undertaken by the U.S. Department of Labor provides a snapshot of wages and hours worked by a streetcar operating crew. The record shows that in Frankfort, Kentucky, cars were operated by one man, a motorman. That company employed ten men in this position and had five on the extra board. These five men worked only when extra cars were needed or a regular worker was off sick or late for his assignment. Once the man working the extra board replaced someone late or absent due to unexcused sickness, he moved to the regular employment column while the regular worker went to the bottom of the extra board to begin his climb upward to regular employment again. The average pay for a motorman was $.184 per hour, with wages based on seniority running from $.16 to $.20 per hour after five years of good service. The average Kentucky motorman's pay was $.19. The average workweek for the Frankfort motorman was 60 hours, with the motorman working between 8.5 and 11 hours per day depending on the line over which he was operating. The average Kentucky motorman worked a 63.5-hour week.

Not only did streetcar lines have to pay taxes on their rail laid in the street, but they had to maintain the surface of the street from one to three feet outside their rails. Any motor vehicle was then allowed to travel on this section of the street maintained by the streetcar company free of charge. In fact, the driver of the car on this section of the street most probably complained about the streetcar traveling down the street ahead of him. When the streetcar left town, these same people complained about the higher taxes they had to pay to maintain the streets on which they drove. Interestingly, one could generally tell where the streetcar tracks were located within a street as the track was normally laid in a right-of-way made of brick. Brick was much easier to remove and reset than concrete or asphalt when a section of street rail needed work done on it or had to be replaced.

One problem that the streetcar and interurban companies were unable to overcome was a bias by all news media outlets to blame any collision between an interurban or streetcar with a pedestrian or roadway vehicle as the fault of the operator of the streetcar or interurban. The headline in the newspaper always read, no matter who was at fault, "Streetcar hits _____." One newspaper picture I came across showed a streetcar lying on its side after being broadsided by a truck. True to form, the newspaper headline over the article recounting the incident read, "Streetcar Strikes Truck." Yet another problem was the average Kentucky citizen. These individuals were always tripping or slipping when getting on or off the streetcar, falling off after illegally riding on the outside of the car, and walking in front of the streetcar. These events were always the fault of the streetcar company.

An additional 16 towns had local streetcar companies chartered but not built. These were Madisonville, Hopkinsville, Grayson Springs, Glasgow, Lebanon, Harrodsburg, Stanford, Lancaster, Mt. Sterling, Irvine, Beattyville, London, Pineville, Louisa, Prestonsburg, and Ft. Jefferson in Ballard County. The Ft. Jefferson Line was part of a real estate scheme in 1905 to build a new city where the Westvaco plant now stands. The city of Ft. Jefferson never prospered beyond some artist's sketches. The proposed Hopkinsville Line was unusual since it was the only line the Commonwealth of Kentucky proposed to help finance. Their financial help was to pay to extend the line out to Western State Hospital.

Kentucky's electrical operated cars were referred to as being either a trolley or a streetcar. Generally, a trolley had a single truck with two axels rigidly attached to the body of the car; the truck was located at the center of the car. On a single truck car, the car's body could only extend some ten feet beyond the truck. Any greater extension of the car body caused a nauseating swaying and bouncing ride. The streetcar was a double truck car; it had a set of double axel trucks at each end of the car. These trucks were not attached to the car's body. The car body rode on the trucks via a pin that dropped into the center of the truck. The result was that when a double axel car made a turn, the body of the car would continue forward before starting to turn. The car's body thus swung in an arch that extended far beyond the rails, and woe to the motorist who did not leave enough room between his automobile and the streetcar as it made its wide sweep around a corner.

Both the horsecar and streetcar were plagued by problems of ventilation, illumination, and heating. Ventilation was needed to remove the smells coming from the bodies of the passengers, particularly when the cars' windows were closed due to rain or cold. Heating was needed to allow operations to continue during the winter months. Illumination was needed to allow passengers to see to board, walk within the car, and de-board. It was only near the end of streetcar operations within Kentucky that most of these problems were solved.

One final type of electric owned public transportation vehicle that operated in Louisville and Covington needs to be mentioned, the trolley bus. Trolley buses drew their power from two overhead wires, one providing power and the other acting as ground. The trolley bus ran on rubber tires and was not confined to the rails within the street. It could maneuver around objects and pull to the curb to load and unload passengers. Trolley bus operations within Kentucky started in Louisville in 1936 and ended in Covington in 1958.

It needs to be noted that streetcar companies in Kentucky did not vanish due to a conspiracy by General Motors Bus Division in cooperation with tire and gasoline companies. The problem was that street railway companies were regulated like a utility. The law, as interpreted by the regulators, allowed the street railway companies to collect sufficient fares to cover their operating costs, pay off bonds, provide a fair dividend to investors, and cover taxes. Street railway companies were not allowed to accumulate capital to upgrade or expand their property. Such up-grades and expansions had to be paid by issuing more stock or borrowing money. A run-down streetcar company seeking additional funds was not looked upon favorably by investors. Therefore, street railways found themselves in a downward spiral as they were unable to borrow funds to upgrade their services, and local and state government refused to subsidize their operations. The solution was to get rid of streetcars and purchase buses for which financing was available.

This government bias against streetcars and interurbans is clearly visible by reviewing issues of *Kentucky Progress Magazine* from the 1930s. This semi-official state publication, from its conception in 1929 to its demise, never once touched the subject of street rail transportation. The magazine seemed determined that its pages remain unsoiled by accounts of transportation modes not based on concrete roads or airport runways.

It is interesting to note that Frankfort, Paducah, Owensboro, Louisville, Lexington, and Northern Kentucky, after removing the streetcar to improve traffic flow in downtown areas, have today taken to operating buses disguised as streetcars to bring people back to downtown. Those seeking to see a remnant of Kentucky's lost streetcar past need only go to Louisville's Union Station, now TARC's headquarters building, or Devou Park in Covington. Here, at each of these locations, a streetcar from the local system is preserved.

Will streetcars return to Kentucky in the 21st century? If some have their way, the answer is "YES." Two cases can be made for the return of streetcar service. One involves Louisville where a streetcar service would loop from the museum sport district on the riverfront to the hospital complex and Union Station on Broadway. This would be an excellent mover of an urban population. The other proposed system would tie the riverfront entertainment areas of Covington, Newport, and Bellevue to Cincinnati's riverfront sports complex: Paul Brown Football Stadium, the Great American Baseball Park, and Riverfront Coliseum.

LOUISVILLE RAILWAY HORSECAR #102, BUILT IN 1865 AND USED UNTIL 1901, SURVIVES AT TARC HEADQUARTERS LOCATED IN THE FORMER LOUISVILLE & NASHVILLE RAILROAD'S UNION DEPOT. <CHB>

CINCINNATI, NEWPORT & COVINGTON RAILWAY PARTY CAR IS PRESERVED IN COVINGTON'S DEVOU PARK BEHRINGER-CRAWFORD MUSEUM. <CHB>

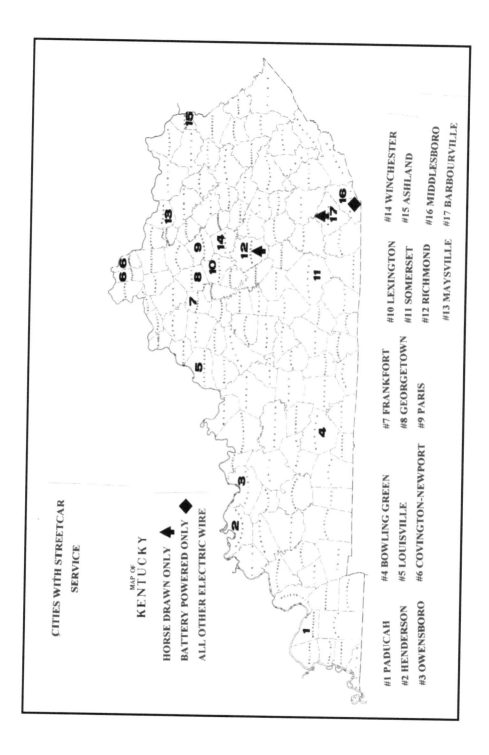

CITIES WITH STREETCAR
SERVICE

MAP OF
KENTUCKY

HORSE DRAWN ONLY ◄

BATTERY POWERED ONLY ◆

ALL OTHER ELECTRIC WIRE

#1 PADUCAH
#2 HENDERSON
#3 OWENSBORO

#4 BOWLING GREEN
#5 LOUISVILLE
#6 COVINGTON-NEWPORT

#7 FRANKFORT
#8 GEORGETOWN
#9 PARIS

#10 LEXINGTON
#11 SOMERSET
#12 RICHMOND
#13 MAYSVILLE

#14 WINCHESTER
#15 ASHLAND
#16 MIDDLESBORO
#17 BARBOURVILLE

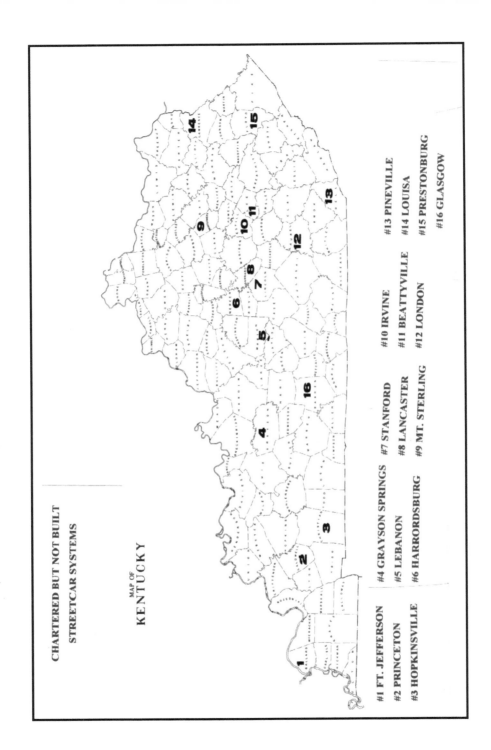

CHARTERED BUT NOT BUILT
STREETCAR SYSTEMS

MAP OF
KENTUCKY

#1 FT. JEFFERSON
#2 PRINCETON
#3 HOPKINSVILLE

#4 GRAYSON SPRINGS
#5 LEBANON
#6 HARRORDSBURG

#7 STANFORD
#8 LANCASTER
#9 MT. STERLING

#10 IRVINE
#11 BEATTYVILLE
#12 LONDON

#13 PINEVILLE
#14 LOUISA
#15 PRESTONBURG
#16 GLASGOW

THE ASHLAND & CATLETTSBURG LINE

UNITING BOYD COUNTY

With the coming of the Chesapeake and Ohio Railway (C&O) to Boyd County in 1875, the economies of Ashland and Catlettsburg, Kentucky, began to expand. Ashland became the hub of C&O passenger train service, which reached north to Detroit, Michigan; west to Cincinnati, Ohio; southwest to Louisville, Kentucky; south to Elkhorn City, Kentucky; and east to Newport News, Virginia.

Ashland also became a center for iron and steel production and soon replaced Catlettsburg as the major city in Boyd County. Catlettsburg, however, remained the county seat of government and hosted federal and state offices. Citizens of Ashland involved in legal matters found themselves having to travel to Catlettsburg, the area's judicial seat, to file or adjudicate legal matters. Ashland's central business district soon provided a far larger selection of goods than was available in the stores at Catlettsburg. When Catlettsburg's citizens contemplated a major goods purchase, they had to travel to Ashland to buy in a competitive market. Unfortunately, for the citizens of these two communities, the cities were situated six miles from each other. Travel between the two cities was by horse-drawn omnibus, private buggies, or by C&O passenger trains.

None of these modes of travel was convenient. Use of a horse-drawn vehicle for travel meant a trip over rough roads. The train, while providing a fast, smooth ride, did not provide fast, frequent service. To a few farsighted entrepreneurs, the solution to this problem was the development of a streetcar line to tie the two cities together and provide a local public transit system within Ashland.

In October 1888, a number of Boyd County businessmen met to organize a horsecar line to serve Ashland. Their first purchase was an inactive streetcar charter issued in 1873 for the construction of a horsecar line in Boyd County. Having acquired the inactive horsecar line charter, the businessmen incorporated themselves as the Ashland and Catlettsburg Street Railway Company (A&CSR) in October 1889. While the Ashland and Catlettsburg Street Railway Company was laying its tracks, the cities of Ironton, Ohio, and Huntington, West

Virginia, were also developing streetcar lines.

The A&CSR horsecar line opened for service on May 20, 1890. When it opened, the line consisted of two loops within the city of Ashland: Loop #1 served the central business district and ran from the ferry at 13th Street to Montgomery Street, then eastward on Montgomery to 17th Street where it turned on Greenup Street and then ran back to the ferry. Loop #2 tied the residential areas to downtown. It ran down Winchester from 22nd Street to 8th Street where it turned south to Central Street. At Central, it went east to 11th Street where it made a dogleg to Bath Street. It then went east on Bath to 16th Street where it turned south to Hilton Street. Then it was down Hilton to 22nd Street for a turn north on 22nd to Winchester Street. Loop #1 crossed Loop #2 twice at Central and twice at Winchester Street. The success of the two horsecar lines led their owners to electrify their lines in 1893.

Conversion of the A&CSR to electrical power took place on February 12, 1893. The Ashland city line was rebuilt and equipped with track of four-feet 8.5-inch gauge. During the conversion of the A&CSR to electrical power, the streetcar line was extended from Ashland to Catlettsburg. In its journey between the two cities, the electric rail line paralleled C&O track. From Ashland to the outskirts of Catlettsburg, the trolley tracks lay to the south of the C&O main line. At the outskirts of Catlettsburg, at Pikes Crossing, the trolley line crossed at grade the double mainline tracks of the C&O and then ran on into downtown Catlettsburg. When the A&CSR started to build across the C&O track at Pikes Crossing in 1891, the C&O obtained an injunction preventing the streetcar company from crossing their track on grade. After a court battle, the injunction order was permanently set aside on 21 April 1896 and the C&O was instructed to allow the ACSR to build across its track. The crossing was thereafter protected by a C&O employee station in a tower overlooking the crossing. He manually lowered a gate, preventing crossing of the C&O track when a train was observed approaching.

The first A&CSR revenue run between Ashland and Catlettsburg took place on January 1, 1895. The company announced that cars would run every 15 minutes from Ashland to Catlettsburg, from 6:00 AM to 10:00 PM. In 1896, A&CSR reported that its president was Willis L. Ringo and his office was located at 110 16th Street in Ashland. The company stated that it owned 15 passenger cars (indications are that six were open summer cars and seven were closed winter cars), one work car, and one power station with two generators. The total operating track of the line covered 6.1 miles. A carbarn and terminal were erected at 1001 Winchester Avenue in Ashland. The carbarn still stands today but now houses a truck rental firm. Streetcar tracks are still visible in the floor of the building.

The ACSR operated its cars on a time schedule over single track. In order to operate both east and westbound cars over this track, passing tracks were located every mile or so. Eastbound cars had the right-of-way over westbound cars. Thus, a westbound car would take the passing track until the eastbound car had passed.

In late 1899, the street railway companies of Huntington, Ironton, and Ashland-Catlettsburg were merged together by Zachary T. Vinson and Johnson M. Camden as the Ohio Valley Electric Company (OVEC). The stated goal of OVEC was to provide through electric railway service from Huntington to Ironton via Catlettsburg and Ashland. On December 13, 1900, OVEC was reorganized as Camden Interstate Railway Company (CIRC). A passenger ferry was inaugurated at Ashland by CIRC to carry passengers between its Ohio and Kentucky lines.

Six days later on December 19, 1900, the banks of the Ohio River were covered in a heavy fog. Today it is unsure just what happened, but what is known is that two CIRC city cars had a head-on collision on a stretch of single track outside of Ashland. In the resulting crash, twelve persons received injuries described as varying from serious to minor. What is not known is if the eastbound car was running ahead of schedule or the westbound car had failed to take a passing track. Frank Friel, editor of the *Ashland Independent,* was riding in the southbound car. Just before the collision, he reported a voice told him to go to the rear platform. Once at the rear platform, that voice ordered him to step off the car. This he did only seconds before the collision. Other incomplete CIRC accident records show that John Steed and Oliver Hood were killed in 1912 while walking on CIRC track, as were Edward Kirk in 1913, Columbus Sears in 1914, and Walter Trusty in 1915.

In 1906, a new streetcar line was opened in Ashland, the Ashland Street Interurban Railway Company, renamed in 1907 as the Ashland Interurban Railway Company. This 1.2-mile line connected with CIRC at 29th and Winchester Streets. The line was built by Park City Land Company and ran south from Winchester to Monroe Street where a subdivision was being developed. This line was leased to CIRC on May 9, 1909.

In order to encourage uses of the line on Sundays and holidays, CIRC built two amusement parks, Clyffeside Park in Ashland and Camden Park in Huntington. Clyffeside Park was developed on the east side of Ashland and contained a lake for boating, a casino used for dancing, plays, and movies, a picnic grove with bandstand, and various rides including a roller coaster. Clyffeside Park survived until the early 1920s when it was closed and sold off for commercial development. Clyffeside's name continues in existence as a block sign on CSX track where the park once stood, while a mural of the park graces the floodwall at the Ashland Amtrak Depot.

In October 1916, the Camden Interstate Railway Company was reorganized as the Ohio Valley Electric Railway Company (OVERC). This reorganization made little difference in day-to-day service but did result in the streetcars being repainted. CIRC had operated its cars painted in yellow. OVERC ordered the cars repainted in "Pullman green" with cream trim.

In 1917, an event in Ironton did lead to a change in OVERC service. That year the Portsmouth Street Railroad & Light Company, an interurban railway, finally reached Ironton from the west. It was now possible for a citizen of Ashland to take the ferry to Coal Grove and ride to Portsmouth, Ohio, by interurban car. To accomplish this feat, one had to change cars at Ironton from one line to the other. This service would last until 1929.

Another event that took place circa 1920 was the folding of OVERC into the Consolidated Power & Light Company that was controlled by Appalachian Electric Power Company, part of American Electric Power Company, a subsidiary of the Middle West Utilities Company. Middle West Utilities was controlled by Samuel Insull.

On January 10, 1919, an OVERC car crossing the Big Sandy Bridge was struck by a C&O train. The car had just entered Catlettsburg when a C&O train, performing switching service, backed into the OVERC car. A number of individuals were reported injured and the car was demolished.

In 1924, with costs rising faster than revenue, OVERC looked into revamping its organization to save money. During the first 30 years of streetcar and interurban service in the United States, no thought had been given to the weight of individual cars nor to the number of men employed on each car. In a company-wide survey, OVERC found that its 66 cars were of various designs, weighed between 39,000 and 58,000 pounds, and required the services of a motorman and conductor. The differences in car weight meant that the heavier cars did more damage to the line than those of less weight. In addition, the heavier cars required more power to attain running speed than those of less weight. OVERC, therefore, sought to replace its Kentucky and West Virginia cars with lightweight, one-man operator cars. The three Birney cars providing service in Ironton were not replaced. The new cars, designed by Kuhlman, weighed 34,000 pounds, were 47 feet in length, could seat 48 passengers (12 in the smoking compartment and 26 in general seating), and needed only one man to operate. When the 40 new cars went into service, OVERC's operating costs were reduced 40 percent.

In 1925, OVERC introduced a new concept in public transportation to Ashland. The gasoline bus made its first tentative entrance on the streets of Ashland and Huntington. OVERC acquired buses to extend their services to the new suburbs growing up around Ashland and Catlettsburg. Bus service did not require investment in a right-of-way; rather the government provided and kept in repair the streets the buses rolled over. Gradually the bus began to replace the streetcar on OVERC routes in Ashland and Huntington. Buses were also used to extend service into new areas of development. From an investment point of view, the bus enjoyed a number of advantages over the streetcar. Whereas the owner of a streetcar line had to pay property tax on his company's right-of-way, he also had to maintain a portion of the street over which his cars ran. The streetcar line owner thus contributed both directly and indirectly to maintenance of streets and roads over which it ran, while the bus ran free of direct cost in maintaining this same pavement.

On December 30, 1927, OVERC was sold to the Central Public Service Commission (CPSC), which continued to operate the electric railway system under the banner of OVERC. The start of the Great Depression in 1929, however, marked the beginning of the end of OVERC and streetcar operations in Ashland-Catlettsburg, Ironton, and Huntington. On August 31, 1930, streetcar service in Ironton was shut down and the franchise sold to Blue Ribbon Line. This company, using CRSC's franchise, provided bus service between Ashland and Ironton. Local bus service between Hanging Rock, Ironton, and Coal Grove was taken over by Employees Bus Company.

On July 1, 1933, in order to raise additional capital, CPSC sold off OVERC's remaining bus lines to Fred W. Samworth, who reorganized these bus operations under the name of Ohio Valley Bus Line. The infusion of new capital into OVERC only prolonged the slow death of the Ashland-Catlettsburg and Huntington streetcar lines. Declining ridership, increased maintenance costs, the inability to change fare structure, and failure to meet bond payments resulted on November 6, 1937, in the closing of OVERC's interurban service between Guyandotte, Huntington, Kenova, Catlettsburg, and Ashland and its streetcar lines in Ashland and Huntington. The last OVERC streetcar run, Guyandotte to Huntington, was made by William Jordan who had worked as a motorman for OVERC for 49 years. Most of the surviving OVERC streetcars and interurban cars were scrapped, but fourteen of the lightweight cars were sold to the Lehigh Valley Transit Company of Allentown, Pennsylvania, where the cars were used until 1952.

In 2011, public transportation in Ashland is provided by the Ashland Bus System owned by the city of Ashland. This public owned bus line now provides service within the Ashland and Catlettsburg area and connecting bus service to West Virginia.

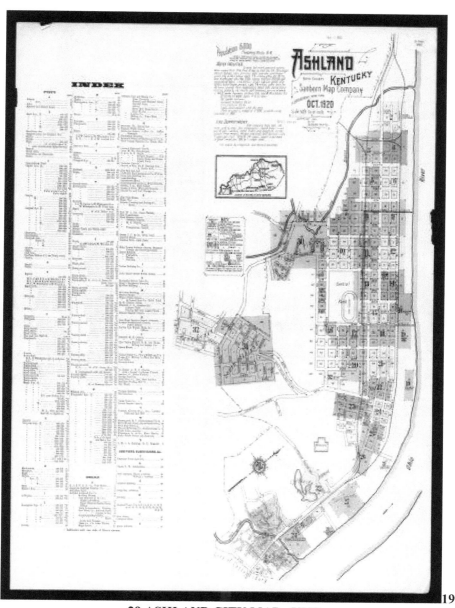

19

29 ASHLAND CITY MAP <KHS>

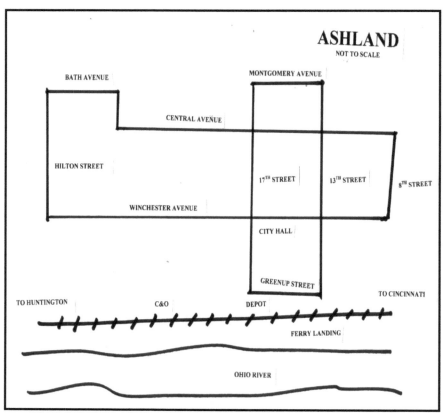

MAP OF THE ASHLAND CITY STREETCAR SYSTEM <CHB>

THE FORMER ASHLAND STREETCAR BARN ON WINCHESTER AVENUE IS NOW A GARAGE FOR HERTZ RENT A CAR. <CB>

LAYING STREETCAR TRACK IN WINCHESTER AVENUE. <CHB>

A CITY CAR RUNNING ON WINCHESTER STREET <CHB>

A CAMDEN SUMMER CITY STREETCAR IN ASHLAND <CHB>

AN ASHLAND & CATLETTSBURG STREET RAILWAY CAR <CHB>

ON THIS PAGE AND NEXT ARE VIEWS OF CITY STREETCARS OPERATING WITHIN ASHLAND. <CHB>

Winchester Ave., looking East from Broadway, Ashland, Ky.

Winchester Avenue, East from 15th St.,
Ashland, Ky.

205

ABOVE AND THE NEXT PAGE: OVERC PURCHASED 40 OF THESE CARS IN 1924 FOR BOTH CITY AND INTERURBAN SERVICE. AS INTERURBAN CARS, THEY HAD A TWO-MAN CREW AND AS CITY CARS, A ONE-MAN CREW. IN KENTUCKY, THE SMOKING COMPARTMENT WAS RESERVED FOR COLORED PASSENGERS IN COMPLIANCE WITH KENTUCKY'S JIM CROW LAWS. SINCE WEST VIRGINIA HAD NO JIM CROW LAW, THE COMPARTMENT WAS USED IN THAT STATE FOR SMOKING. <CHB>

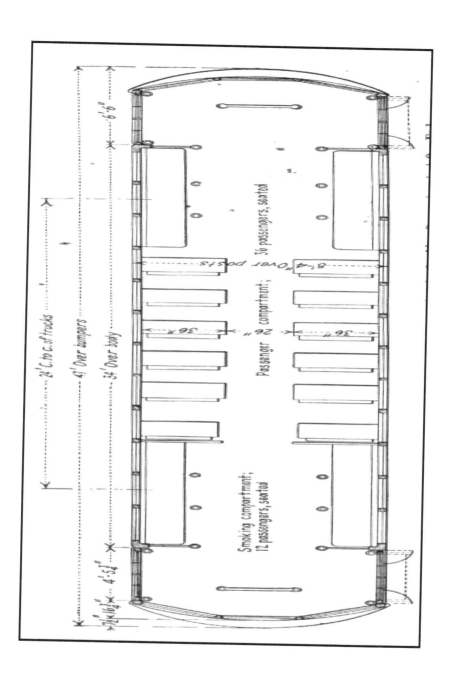

Smoking compartment;
12 passengers, seated

Passenger compartment; 36 passengers, seated

8'4" Over posts

26"

36"

36"

6'6"

24' C. to C. of trucks

41' Over bumpers

34' Over body

4'5¾"

7½" 16¾"

BARBOURVILLE

A HORSECAR LINE

There were two horsecar lines in Kentucky that never made the transition from horse power to electric power. These were the lines in Barbourville and Richmond. The Richmond Line did not last long enough to become an electric line while the Barbourville Line soldiered on long after every other horsecar line in the United States had been electrified.

Horsecar lines needed minimal investment to be started. Basically the owner just put wooden rails down in the dirt street, purchased a car and horse barn, and bought five or six donkeys or mules. While animal-pulled trolleys are generally called horsecars, they were, in most cases, actually pulled by donkeys or mules. Normally three spare animals had to be owned for each animal that was working. Animals get sick and can only work so many hours per day, thus the need for extra animals if service was provided from early morning until evening. Animals also need to eat; the average horsecar animal ate 10 to 12 pounds of grain per day plus eight to ten pounds of hay or grass. Most horsecar lines operated from 6:00 AM to 9:00 PM and therefore required three changes of pulling animals.

There was one other problem about the animals used to pull the horse cars--they put out an extremely large quantity of manure and urine each and every day, manure that had to be moved elsewhere for disposal before it overwhelmed the stable. When people talk about the Good Old Days when streets were of dirt, they often fail to mention that a lot of that dirt was actually the droppings and urine from animals, deposits that added to the texture and smell of the streets. Those who complain about modern day smells should have lived next to a stable on a hot, muggy day.

The Barbourville horsecar line, under the name of Barbourville Street & Railroad Company, was incorporated in 1890 by a number of Barbourville businessmen. Its first president was Silas B. Dishman. Barbourville, located on the northern bank of the Cumberland River, has been the county seat of Knox County since 1800. In 1890, Barbourville was incorporated as a city, and with the opening of the coal fields of Southeastern Kentucky, began to grow.

The Cumberland River at Barbourville is not navigable, for Cumberland Falls lies downstream from the city. It is assumed that Barbourville was located adjacent to the Cumberland River for the convenience of obtaining water and disposing of waste products. This location, however, put Barbourville in the center of the Cumberland River flood plain. Thus, about every decade or so, Barbourville would experience the waters of the Cumberland River overflowing its banks.

The Louisville & Nashville Railroad (L&N), when it built east from Corbin, Kentucky, for the Southeast Kentucky Coal Fields and local timber reserves, located its right-of-way above the Cumberland River flood plain. The result was that when the L&N came to Barbourville in 1888, it located its depot .5 miles north of the courthouse and its surrounding businesses. Those arriving and leaving Barbourville by train then had to either walk the half mile to and from the depot or hire a buggy. It was to provide easy access between downtown Barbourville and the L&N Depot that the Barbourville Street & Railway Company was organized.

It is reported that Mr. Dishman built the Barbourville horsecar line for $3,200 and that it cleared a 10 percent profit during its first year of operation. The line, as built, ran from the L&N Depot down Depot Street to Broadway. It then followed Broadway to Knox Street and continued on this street to Courthouse Square. From Courthouse Square, the line ran up North Main Street and over to the carbarn at Wall Street. With only one car on the line, bought from Louisville City Railway Company, there was no need for a passing track, so the line was single tracked from the car barn to the L&N Depot. Unlike other horsecar lines, the Barbourville horsecar was propelled by one animal while most lines used two. It appears that the car was turned at the end of the track simply by unhitching the donkey or horse and moving it to the other end of the car. Although proof is lacking, there are claims that another passenger car was bought and a freight car also was used on the line.

The schedule for the running of the Barbourville Street Railway Company called for it to arrive at the L&N Depot before the L&N train departed. In 1893, four passenger trains, #23, #24, #80 and

#81, called at the depot each day. Train #23 ran from Corbin, Kentucky, to Norton, Virginia, with a departure from Barboursville at 5:20 PM. Train #24 left Norton at 4:35 PM for a pull from Barboursville at 11:40 PM. Train #81 ran from Corbin to Shawanee, Tennessee, highballing out of Barbourville at 3:52 AM. Train #80 ran from Shawanee to Corbin with a departure of 9:00 AM from Barbourville. Fare for a ride on the horsecar either to or from the depot was $.05 during the day and $.10 at night. In 1916, traffic on the L&N had increased and six passenger trains a day stopped at the depot: #11, #12, #21, #22, #23, and #24. Trains #11 and #12 ran between Corbin and Middlesborough (time table spelling) with departures from Barbourville at 6:43 AM and 1:52 PM. Trains #21, #22, #23 and #24 ran between Corbin and Norton. Trains from Corbin were #21 and #23, which pulled at 4:10 AM and 10:18 PM from Barbourville and Trains #22 and #24 from Norton that left Barbourville at 10:18 PM and 11:42 AM.

While Silas Dishman was President of Barbourville Street & Railway Company, he and his associates did not operate the line. The horsecar line was put up for lease every year with the highest bidder getting the rights to operate the line. The company supplied the horsecar, barn, and tracks. The bidder was responsible for providing the animal power and the car operator. Thus during the Barbourville horsecar's life, it was operated by a number of different locals including Bob Vermillion, Bill Davis, Dan Williams, Henry Bowman, Ike Golden, Andrew Mitchell, and George Tye. The last operator of the line was Ike Golden who was known as Uncle Ike to one and all.

During the life of the Barboursville horsecar line, the famous, the notorious, and the ordinary rode it. Toward the end of its life, riding the horsecar became a requirement of all those visiting the area. Among those who rode on the car was Governor James D. Black who was burned when the car jumped the rail and, while turning over, threw the Governor against the heating stove. Others who rode it were Charles Fairbanks, Theodore Roosevelt's Vice Presidential running mate during the 1904 Presidential campaign, and Caleb Powers, a local attorney.

The second decade of the 20th century brought changes to Barbourville. Coal and lumber money had brought prosperity to the city. People were buying cars and trucks. Citizens began to demand that the streets be paved. In 1919, with World War I ending, the city fathers finally bowed to the will of the citizens and began a street improvement program by covering streets in gravel. With ridership down and the necessity of laying new rails in the gravel streets, the decision was made to close down the Barbourville Street & Railway Company. In July 1919, the Barbourville horsecar, at this time operated by Clarence and Charles Mitchell, made its last run to and from the L&N Depot. It is claimed that this last run by the Barbourville Street & Railway Company marked the end of horsecar operations in the United States. The wheels and axle from this car survive at the Knox County Museum in Barbourville, a museum well-worth visiting.

Of interest is the fact that Pineville, the county seat of Bell County located 17 miles east of Barbourville, was also separated from its L&N Depot. At Pineville, the L&N ran on the north side of the Cumberland River, but the courthouse and business district were on the south side, .5 mile from the depot. The L&N Depot was reached by a wagon bridge over the river. In 1890, it was reported that a horsecar line would be built to connect the courthouse to the depot, however, this line was never built.

BARBOURVILLE STREET RAILWAY SYSTEM, BARBOURVILLE, KY.

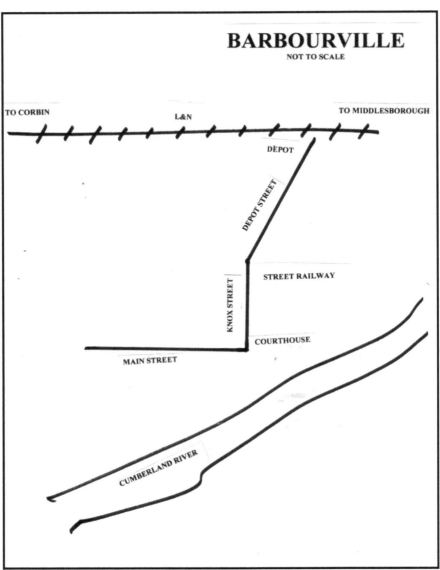

A MAP OF THE BARBOURVILLE HORSECAR LINE <CHB>

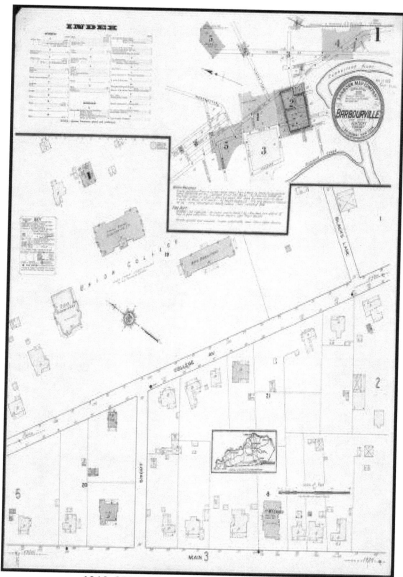

1919 CITY MAP OF BARBOURVILLE

THE BARBOURVILLE HORSECAR AT THE L&N DEPOT LOADED WITH PASSENGERS FOR TOWN <CHB>

HORSECAR TRACK IN THE STREET AT THE COURTHOUSE <CHB>

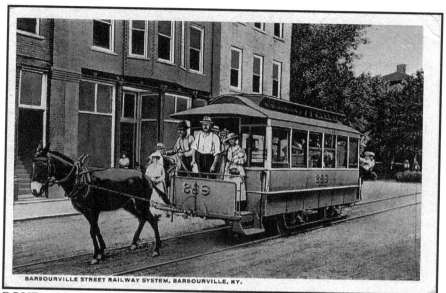

BARBOURVILLE STREET RAILWAY SYSTEM, BARBOURVILLE, KY.

ABOVE AND BELOW, THE HOSRECAR OPERATIONS WITHIN THE STREETS OF BARBOURVILLE <CHB>

Barbourville Street Car System,
Barbourville, Ky.

Bowling Green has always considered itself a progressive city. It has looked upon itself as the center of trade, culture, political influence, and education for South-Central Kentucky. Its location at the headwaters of the Green-Barren River system meant that it controlled the shipment of goods in and out of the region. In 1860, Bowling Green added to its importance by becoming the junction of the Louisville and Nashville Railroad (L&N), from Louisville to Nashville, Tennessee, and to Memphis, Tennessee. Bowling Green thus grew from a small rural community in 1850 to a regional commercial center by 1890, thanks to the L&N and the city's location at the head of steamboat traffic on the Barren River.

During the 1880s, Russellville, Glasgow, and other nearby communities jockeyed to supplement Bowling Green as the mecca for commerce in South-Central Kentucky. Bowling Green, in order to consolidate its position and show that it was more than just a country town, set out to build for itself a modern public transportation system in the form of a mule car line.

The Bowling Green mule car line was organized as the Park City Railway Company with the first dirt being turned on the construction of this line in April 1889. In that month, a force of African-Americans, under the direction of Dan Reagan, began construction of the mule car track from the L&N Depot, located at Main and Adam Streets, to the Morehead House, some 2,050 feet to the east at Main and State Streets. In overall charge of the project was Colonel H. H. Crump, a civil engineer.

The mule car track was built to standard gauge, 4 feet 8.5 inches, to allow freight cars from the L&N to be moved over its track. The line's operating equipment consisted of four mule cars and twenty mules. The location of the car barn and stable is unknown, but one would suspect it was near the L&N Depot. The work in carrying out the building of the line was apparently done within a two-month period, Colonel Crump and Mr. Reagan only starting work on the line after all the material had been delivered. The company was under pressure from the city of Bowling Green to cause the least disruption to vehicular traffic on Main Street while building the line. The mule car track was in place by the end of June 1889, and mule car service started the next month.

The mule car line proved to be an immediate success with both citizens and visitors. It was quickly proposed to extend the mule line to the Warren County Fairgrounds, located at Broadway and Laurel Streets, and to the Fairview Cemetery. Both of these locations were considered good generators of traffic on Sundays and holidays when businesses were closed. The existing mule line was single track with no turning track at the end of the line. A passing track, however, was located at the Bowling Green Public Square. The mules at the end of the line were simply unhitched from one end of the car and repositioned at the other end.

Immediately after the mule line was put in operation, questions were raised about converting the line to electric operation. Company officials reported that they were investigating both electric battery operated cars and cars running off overhead electric wires. The battery cars apparently were preferred, as they would not necessitate the construction of overhead wire, and the existing cars could be converted to battery power by placing batteries under the seats. Park City Railway Company claimed that battery-powered cars would only have to be taken out of service for two short periods each day to recharge their batteries. However, in 1895, the mule line was converted to overhead electric operations, not battery powered, and the track extended to the Fairgrounds and Fairview Cemetery. The first electric passenger car service started on September 1, 1895; the line was now four miles in length. Construction of the electric streetcar line was made possible by the sale of stock in the company during that year.

The line now reached beyond the L&N Depot to the Public Landing on the Barren River at the end of Church Street. At the Public Landing, the street railway connected with the boats of the Evansville and Bowling Green Packet Company. Located at the wharf were the icehouse and carbarn. The manufacturing of ice was always a good way to use the excess electricity produced by an electric rail line's power plant. Sharing the wharf area with the power plant was the Lexington Brewing Company. The streetcar power plant was located on Portage Road between Ada and Gertrude Streets.

In 1895, Bowling Green joined the ranks of Louisville, Lexington, and Paducah in having an electric streetcar system running on its streets. Park City Railway Company not only operated streetcars carrying passengers but pulled freight trailer cars through the city with a freight motor. The company's equipment that year consisted of four passenger cars, one freight motor, and seven freight trailers. Both passenger and freight service provided a steady cash flow, however, it was not enough to cover both operating costs and interest on construction loans.

On December 10, 1896, a receiver was appointed to manage the Park City Railway Company's streetcar line. The receiver, however, was unable to generate any more money than the line's original owner, and the line sank toward bankruptcy. Finally, in 1898, Park City Railway Company was declared bankrupt. To settle claims against the company, the streetcar equipment and rail line was sold on the courthouse steps on February 28th. Park City Railway was bought by the Bowling Green Railway Company, a subsidiary of Westinghouse Corporation.

A few farsighted businessmen had begun to realize at the end of the 19th century that the real profit in operating an electric street railway was not in providing public transportation, but in selling surplus electric power produced by the street railway company's power plant. Thus, the Bowling Green Railway Company's first order of business was to build a new and larger power plant at Dellifield, to the west of Bowling Green on the Barren River, and to extend the line's tracks farther out into the country.

Under ownership of the Bowling Green Railway Company, the streetcar track was expanded to its greatest length, 7.5 miles. Equipment in 1900 consisted of six passenger cars, one freight motor, seven trailers, and three freight cars. In 1908, Bowling Green Railway Company stated that it owned nine motor cars and seven freight trailers; it is uncertain if the freight motor was retained. The seven freight trailers were used to haul goods from decks of steamboats calling to unload at the Public Landing into downtown Bowling Green or from the L&N Depot to the riverfront wharf. It is thought that the trailers were also used to move goods between businesses within the community. Records are unclear if there was an exchange of cars between the Bowling Green Railway and the L&N.

Bowling Green Railway, as it existed in 1910, consisted of three rail lines centered on Bowling Green's Public Square. These lines ran from the Public Square to the Warren County Fairgrounds with its ballpark; to the Fairview, St. Joseph, and Mt. Mariah Cemeteries; and to the Public Landing on the Barren River.

The streetcar line to the fairgrounds left the Public Square and ran up State to Twelfth Street, then onto Broadway where it turned and ran out to the fairgrounds. It entered the fairgrounds via Fairground Alley. The line to the Fairview Cemetery left the Public Square, also on State Street, but ran down State to near Sixth Street where it turned onto a private right-of-way that led to Fairview Avenue. The line then ran out Fairview to just past High Street, where it again entered a private right-of-way until it reached the three cemeteries.

The line to the Public Landing was financially the most important of the three lines and was the main generator of traffic. This line left the Public Square and ran down Main Street to Adams Street. It crossed under the L&N railroad tracks via the Sixth Street Underpass. It then ran over Boat Landing Road to the Public Landing.

The line to the Public Landing was later changed after a physical brawl and a legal suit against the L&N. The street railway company wished to relay its track to the Public Landing so it would cross the L&N at grade. This action, it was claimed, would remove the present streetcar route from an area of blight to an area teaming with vitality. However, with the L&N track at Bowling Green being one of the busiest in Kentucky, the L&N took a dim view of this plan. On-grade railroad crossings always led to a collision between a train and a vehicle, with the railroad being sued for damages. The L&N legal department could only begin to visualize the size of the lawsuits if one of the L&N trains hit a streetcar while it was crossing the railroad track. The L&N first tried to use physical force to stop the building of the on-grade crossing, then legal arguments. The L&N lost both actions. The resulting street railway route now left the Public Square and ran down Main to Adam Street, turned on Adam to Potter, where it ran for one block. At Church Street, it turned left and continued to Power Street. At Power it followed that street to the Public Landing. It should be mentioned that not all streetcar rides to the Public Landing were directly concerned with business. Bowling Green was dry, but the Public Landing was in the county where alcohol sales were legal and so it became the male area of entertainment.

In its annual report starting in 1910 and continuing each year until 1914, Bowling Green Railway proclaimed that the Fairview Line would be extended and a new line built northward. These proposed new tracks would have increased the company's track miles from 7.5 to 10.5 miles. These track extensions were never undertaken.

At the beginning of the 20th century, Bowling Green Railway Company seemed to have a bright future ahead of it. The street railway was an essential part of the city. It had allowed the city to expand beyond walking distance to work. Attendance at baseball games had increased due to the ease of travel to the ballpark. The streetcar line provided transportation for those attending burials at the Fairview Cemetery and even transported the coffins. Local social events were planned around the availability of the streetcar transportation network. Summer nights were made bearable by a ride in an open-air streetcar. In wintertime, travel across town was warmer in a drafty streetcar than on foot, fighting the cold wind blowing down the streets.

During the first decade of the 20th century, the streetcar line was operating a mixture of open and closed streetcars. Open summer cars operated with no sidewalls thus allowing a cool breeze to reach all. This fact, however, also allowed one to board and exit anywhere along the length of the car. This meant the conductor had to be fast on his feet to insure that all riders paid their fares. All cars at this time were two-man cars with a motorman and a conductor.

Circa 1910, enclosed streetcars were converted to Pay As You Enter (PAYE) and reconfigured to one-man operation, the motorman. Fares were now collected as passengers boarded the front of the car, "Pay As You Enter." Exiting the car was via the rear door of the car. These PAYE cars reduced the cost of streetcar operations by almost 50 percent by eliminating one salary position. The PAYE cars would

220

allow the Bowling Green streetcar line to survive for a few more years.

In 1915, Bowling Green Railway Company found itself in deep financial trouble. It had lost its main source of revenue with the ending of steamboat operations from Evansville, Indiana, to Bowling Green. Income from passenger rail operations was not enough to cover daily expenses and maintenance charges, much less meet mortgage payments coming due. A bond issue in the amount of $20,000 (payable in gold) was due that year. Gold, however, was in short supply as there was a demand for gold by the European Powers to finance the cost of World War I. The result was that in 1915 the company was put up for sale and was purchased by Southern Traction Company for $20,500. The carbarn was relocated from its Barren River riverfront to Eighth and Kentucky. Southern Traction Company soon found that fares were too low to cover the increased operating costs being brought on by inflation due to the war in Europe. Pleas to the Bowling Green city government to allow the streetcar company to increase its fare were met with deaf ears. The result was that Southern Traction defaulted on the bonds it had sold to raise money to purchase the line. The Potter-Matlock Trust Company, holder of the bonds, sued for its equity.

In 1916, Southern Traction Company was placed in receivership. The receiver tried to increase business on the line by discounting tickets to ride. Normal fare was ten cents, but twelve tickets could be purchased for 75 cents or six cents per ride. The hemorrhage of money, however, increased, as after the war, the citizens of Bowling Green went on an automobile buying binge. Trucks now moved goods while citizens rode in Model T Fords. In 1921, Southern Traction Company was operating six cars: two convertible cars, two summer cars, and two enclosed cars.

While the American love of cars was reducing the streetcar line's income, the American love with lawsuits dealt the line a fatal blow. In 1921, a judgment was entered against Southern Traction Company as the result of an accident involving a pedestrian. The plaintiff, upon winning the case, found himself not richer, but instead, the owner of Southern Traction Company. The new streetcar line owner immediately suspended service and closed the line. Its tracks were taken up and overhead wire removed for sale as scrap. No buyers were found for the company's streetcars so they were burned to recover any metal in them. In 2011, public transportation in Bowling Green is provided by GO-BG Transit.

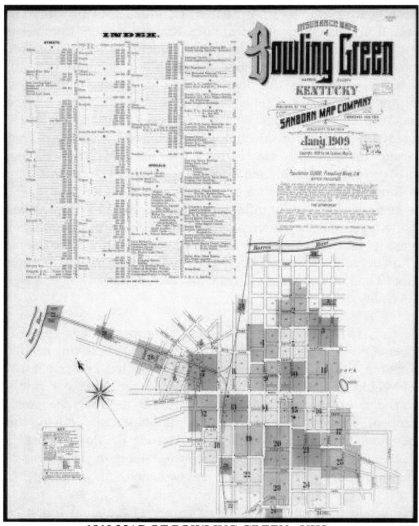

1910 MAP OF BOWLING GREEN <KHS>

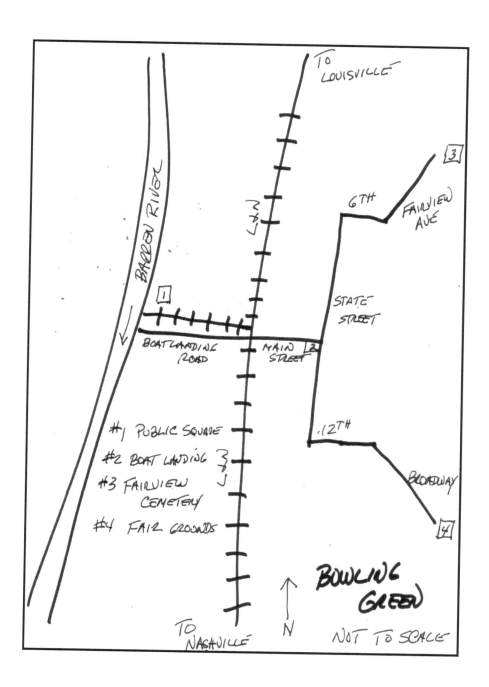

TO
LOUISVILLE

3

6TH

FAIRVIEW
AVE

L&N

STATE
STREET

1

BARREN RIVER

BOAT LANDING
ROAD

MAIN
STREET

2

#1 PUBLIC SQUARE

.12TH

#2 BOAT LANDING

#3 FAIRVIEW
CEMETERY

BROADWAY

#4 FAIR GROUNDS

4

BOWLING
GREEN

TO
NASHVILLE

N

NOT TO SCALE

BOWLING GREEN'S STREETS AT THE BEGINNING OF THE 20TH CENTURY LACKED A COVERING OF BRICK OR CONCRETE, THUS THE STREETCAR ENABLED THE CITIZENRY TO TRAVEL ABOVE THE MUD. <CHB>

FOLK ART PAINTING OF A PARK CITY HORSECAR <CHB>

PUBLIC SQUARE, BY NIGHT, BOWLING GREEN, KY.

A GOOD WAY TO BEAT THE NIGHTTIME HEAT WAS TO RIDE THE STREETCAR. <CHB>

THE BOWLING GREEN CARBARN <CS>

THE GROUND IS SNOW COVERED AND MUDDY, BUT THOSE ON THE STREETCAR HAVE DRY FEET. <CS>

Evansville and Chaperhone Boats, Bowling Green, Ky.

TWO PACKET BOATS WAIT AT THE PUBLIC LANDING. <CHB>

A PARK CITY HORSECAR WAITS FOR PASSENGERS. <CHB>

A STREETCAR PREPARES TO LEAVE THE PRIVATE RIGHT-OF-WAY AT THE FAIRGROUNDS FOR RUNNING IN THE CENTER OF THE PUBLIC ROAD. <EC>

A STREETCAR ROUNDS PUBLIC SQUARE ON ITS WAY TO THE
CEMETERY. <CS>

FRANKFORT

BRIDGING THE KENTUCKY RIVER

In the decades following the Civil War, Frankfort, the Commonwealth's capital city, remained a walking city. Residents walked to shop, work, attend school or church, and to socialize. Visitors and residents alike traveled on foot, for there was no public transportation within the city. This meant walking in dusty streets in the summer, muddy streets in the fall and spring, and streets full of slush in the winter. Horse-drawn buggies were available, but for use within town; they were often more trouble than they were worth. Considerable effort was required to harness the horse to the buggy and then reverse the process when finished. In addition, horses could not be left unattended all day at the curb. This was true not only in Frankfort, of course, but throughout the state except for some large cities that had horse-drawn omnibuses or the new horse-drawn streetcar.

In 1884, Frankfort took its first steps toward a horse-drawn streetcar line when a bill was introduced in the Kentucky House of Representatives to incorporate the Frankfort Street Railroad Company. For unknown reasons, this measure did not pass. Two years later, in 1886, legislation was adopted to give Frankfort a horse-drawn streetcar system. That year Edward P. Bryan, John Starks, Dallas Crutcher, James A. Scott, W. L. Collins, and S. I. M. Major incorporated the Frankfort, Bellepoint and Leestown Street Railway Company. The line was to start at Main and St. Clair Streets and extend to the towns of Bellepoint and Leestown. However, the only line open was within the downtown area of Frankfort.

The same year Frankfort's horse line was proposed, an event took place in Richmond, Virginia, that eventually changed the face of the American city. In 1886, Frank J. Sprague perfected the electric-powered street railcar. Within months, electric streetcar lines were begun throughout the United States. The presence of an electric streetcar system symbolically differentiated a city from a town. Frankfort, the capital city of the Commonwealth, set out to have an electric streetcar system.

The year 1890 found Frankfort citizens W. H. Posey, J. W. Pruett, John T. Buckley, John Meagher, Fayette Hewitt, and Pat McDonald incorporating the Capital Railway Company to provide electric streetcar service. The new company's charter provided for service within Frankfort and to any point five miles beyond the city's limits. On August 3, 1893, with the necessary funds raised, work started on the building of Frankfort's electric streetcar system. Portions of the horsecar line were incorporated into this electrified system. The Frankfort electrified streetcar line opened for service on March 28, 1894. Capital Railway Company provided transportation from the front of the Capital Hotel at Main and Ann Streets outward in four directions.

As built, the Frankfort streetcar line employed both open-air and closed cars. The former was a joy to ride in the summer during a Kentucky heat wave; however, a shower or a rainstorm left the passengers exposed to the elements. Canvas side curtains could be lowered in rain, but normally a shower had come and gone by the time the curtains had been dropped and secured. Then, once the sun came out, the humidity in the cars approached that of a steam bath, and the process had to be reversed. In winter, the canvas sides were replaced with removable wooden frames containing a glass window. Though stuffy, the closed cars kept rain and snow off the passengers. The enclosed cars, however, could be stifling hot in the summer and freezing cold in the winter. A major problem with the convertible summer/winter cars was judging when the seasons would change, especially in Kentucky where it is an art to predict when winter is over and summer has ended.

In bad weather, the floors of the cars were little better than the unpaved streets, because the passengers tracked in the elements on their shoes and boots. Herbert Jackson who lived in Frankfort during this period recalled, "The streets were but dirty roads. They would be oiled and sanded once a year. No matter how you tried not to step in the oil, you got oil on your shoes. This, much to the annoyance of all, was tracked all over town."

Left out of the streetcar route was Bellepoint, west of the Kentucky River. Real-estate developers constantly lobbied for the streetcar line to reach there, but this extension was never constructed.

The problem with building a streetcar route to Bellepoint was obtaining permission to use the Louisville & Nashville Railroad (L&N) Bridge and building a bridge to cross Benson Creek into Bellepoint. Prospective revenue, which could be generated by a line to Bellepoint, would not begin to cover fixed costs.

Within a few years, it was apparent that the builders of the Frankfort line had overextended, and there were no funds for expansion. In fact, revenue was far below fixed costs. Unable to meet its bills, the line was ordered sold by the court on April 26, 1897. No bid was received for the line, so the enterprise, renamed the Frankfort and Suburban Railroad, continued to operate under a receivership. Such an overextension of capital in building local streetcar lines plagued many such enterprises throughout the United States.

Streetcar service in Frankfort operated from 6:00 AM to 11:00 PM, with an average headway between cars of fifteen minutes. During the morning and evening rush hours, more frequent service was provided. Attempts to raise the five-cent-per-trip fare were defeated by the Frankfort City Council. Management of the line complained that citizens begrudged the company a nickel for a twenty-minute ride to the fairgrounds, where without hesitation they paid a dime for a three-minute merry-go-round ride.

The ringing of the streetcar bell provoked a number of complaints from the local citizenry. They complained that the too-frequent bells scared the horses. On the other hand, if a streetcar struck a citizen, that victim was sure to state he did not hear the streetcar because the bell was not rung. Others complained that the streetcar track in itself was a hazard, because its gauge was the same as the width of most wagons. The result was the wooden wheels dropped into the groove intended for the streetcar wheel and then when the wagon driver tried to maneuver out of the tracks, the result was a broken wheel.

Yet, for others, the streetcar provided a cooling ride in the summer. The gentle swaying and clanking helped to bring on sleepiness. Others found cheerful the sight of a lighted streetcar cruising the city, the car's illuminated interior a beacon to those returning home at night. It was also a joy to the work-weary, for they did not have to expend additional energy walking home. Moreover, the streetcar meant an increase in the number of eligible women a gentleman could court, for the whole city was now within fifteen minutes of his house. Most people saw the Frankfort streetcar as a convenience since they did not have to tread the city's dirty, manure-spotted streets in rain and snow. Safety and comfort was only a nickel away when out and about in the Capital City.

In a reminiscence, Nettie Glenn of Frankfort told how on Halloween the children would soap the tracks on Shelby Street as the streetcar climbed the hill to Todd Street. When the streetcar encountered the soap, its wheels spun in place. The boys then ran out and pulled the trolley pole free of the electric line, killing the lights on the car and rendering the car powerless. Older boys might place a carbide mixture on the tracks. As it ran over the mixture, the streetcar would set off a series of loud explosions. A more dangerous stunt was to hop onto the outside rear of the car for a free ride; the nickel thus saved could go for candy or soda.

As Ms. Glenn also pointed out in her reminiscence, the Frankfort city streetcars were governed by Kentucky's Jim Crow traditions. Consequently, Black citizens rode in the back of the car, Whites in the front. The actual line of demarcation between the races on local cars was flexible, depending on the number of each race on board. White patrons, to be sure, always received preferential seating.

With the building of the New Capitol Building in South Frankfort, it was proposed to reroute the streetcar line so passengers could be dropped off nearer to the seat of government. However, the cost of extending a nearby street defeated this plan. Another proposal called for the cars to loop around the Capitol. This proposal also failed, as it was felt that the streetcar track and overhead wires would detract from the beauty of the Capitol, an odd objection since one of the advantages given for choosing the site in South Frankfort had been the very presence of the streetcar line.

Existing hotels and restaurants were all clustered around the site of the Old Capitol on the Public Square in North Frankfort. The streetcar system had allowed these establishments to remain viable when the seat of government was relocated a mile from its former site.

Without the streetcar line to South Frankfort, the 1880s proposal to tear down the existing structures on the Old Capitol grounds would most probably have been carried out.

In 1908, the conductors of the Frankfort streetcar system considered going on strike to protest the new method of fare collection. Prior to that time, the conductor started his run with "X" amount of money. At the end of the day, money over this amount was considered the fare collected. Such a system was subject to abuse by the conductors. To provide an accounting trail, a fare collector indicator was installed in each of the cars. This was a box containing a counter and a bell. As the conductor accepted the fare, he was to pull a cord connected to this box for each fare. When the cord was pulled, the counter advanced, and a bell rang. Passengers, however, could not distinguish the fare-register cord from the stop-request cord. The result was that passengers mistakenly pulled the fare-register cord causing additional fares to be registered. Since the conductor was responsible for turning in a nickel for each fare rung up, he found himself liable for fares not collected. The conductors tried unsuccessfully to persuade passengers to pay the additional fare when they pulled the cord by accident. Conductors claimed they themselves had to pay between fifty and seventy-five cents out of their own pocket per day to cover the shortfall. To correct this problem, the streetcar company promised to install electric push buttons to record the fares.

In 1902, an interurban line opened between Georgetown and Lexington. The next year service was extended from Lexington to Paris. Between 1905 and 1907, Central Kentucky Traction Company built a line between Versailles and Lexington, and the Frankfort and Versailles Traction Company opened a track between these two towns. In 1907, the Frankfort and Versailles Line, the Versailles and Lexington Line, and the Capital Railway Company were consolidated under the Central Kentucky Traction Company whose board of directors included two citizens of Frankfort, J. I. Noel and M. J. Meagher.

In 1905, Central Kentucky Traction placed an order with the American Car Company for two wooden Brill Grooveless Post Cars. These cars were forty-four feet long, eight feet wide, and weighed eighteen tons. Seating was provided for thirty-three Whites and seventeen Blacks in two compartments separated by a hardwood partition with glass in the upper panel. The segregated compartments were identical in quality of furnishings: the woodwork was cherry, the ceiling birch veneer, and the seats upholstered in spring cane.

In 1908, Central Kentucky Traction placed an order with J. G. Brill Company for two additional wooden interurban cars that were almost duplicates of the 1905 order. The cars were fifty-five feet long, weighed over twenty-six tons, and were equipped with forty seats for Whites and sixteen for Blacks. A baggage compartment, ten feet by eight and one-half feet and located at the rear of the car, was used for both carry-on packages and consigned goods. For the convenience of those riding between Frankfort and Lexington, the interurbans were outfitted for "Read-Wyl-U-Ride" service, which consisted of a rack containing the *Lexington Herald.*

The year 1911 saw Central Traction placing an order for a double truck baggage/refrigerated motor freight car from the American Car Company. Later that year, Kentucky Traction Terminal Co. (KT&T) ordered a baggage/refrigerator motor freight car. In addition, KT&T purchased a portable electric substation from McGuire Cummins Company of Chicago. The line's larger, faster interurban cars were at first painted black but then later added red and white lettering.

December 1908 saw Frankfort newspapers proclaiming the start of two new interurban lines from Frankfort. The first line was the result of a meeting between the Chambers of Commerce of both Frankfort and Lawrenceburg and Central Kentucky Traction Company to develop an interurban line from Frankfort to Lawrenceburg. It was announced that the two chambers had obtained easements from the property owners for the right-of-way. A preliminary engineering survey had set the cost of constructing the line at $375,000. Central Kentucky Traction intended to start construction of the line in the spring, once the necessary capital had been raised. At the same time, the Louisville and Eastern Railroad, which provided interurban service from Louisville to Shelbyville, announced that it would build an interurban line from its station in Shelbyville to Frankfort to connect with Central Kentucky Traction. Neither of the companies, however, was able to raise the requisite funds to construct the proposed lines.

In 1913, the Shelbyville and Frankfort Electric Railway Company was formed to bridge the gap between these two cities and thus allow interurban service to Louisville. A survey was carried out and options for the right-of-way obtained. The citizens of Bridgeport were said to be expecting transformation into a suburb of Frankfort, many of the "better class" supposedly preferring life in the country around Bridgeport. Cost of the line was estimated at three hundred thousand dollars. Once again, the company was unable to secure funding. Another attempt in 1916 likewise failed.

The desire to build interurbans was not just to foster the convenient transportation of people and goods. There was another reason: to increase the value of land. The *Lexington Herald,* in 1908, stated that interurbans "mean increase in population, business and land value" in the towns they connect. The interurban "increases the value of agricultural land" it passes. The newspaper continued, "Land ordinarily doubles in price within five years after the establishment of an electric line." This increase in value was due to the fact that, unlike the steam railroad, an interurban passenger or box freight motor would stop wherever flagged. Since the value of the farmland rose as a result of the interurban's touching it, the type of farm products produced on land next to an interurban had to change in order to produce a value in comparison to the land value. "It means one can no longer be employed in farming that gives $100 to $200 per acre. One can no longer keep a cow that produces only 200 pounds of butter per year or raise a steer that weighs 500 pounds at the end of a year." Farmers near the interurban line had to start using modern scientific methods or see their property sold to others because of the increase in cost to maintain these lands. A better class of farmer was also found along the interurban, one who "appreciated the convenience of the interurban that allowed him to mix with friends oftener." In addition, the interurban allowed the farmer's children to find employment in the city and town during those times of year when their help was not needed at home.

In 1904, the Paris-Lexington and the Georgetown-Lexington lines were renamed Blue Grass Traction Company. Then in 1910, the Lexington Interurban Railroad built a line from Lexington to Nicholasville. These three interurban lines, Central Kentucky Traction, Bluegrass Traction, and Lexington Interurban, merged in 1911 to form the Kentucky Traction and Terminal Company (KT&T). The KT&T titled itself the "Blue Grass Route." Included in the merger were the Kentucky city streetcar lines of Georgetown, Paris, Lexington, Winchester, and Frankfort. Among those serving on the KT&T Board of Directors was Charles E. Hoge of Frankfort. KT&T was a subsidiary of the Philadelphia-based Kentucky Securities Corporation, which also owned Blue Grass Park and the Lexington Ice Company. Kentucky Securities was, in turn, owned by Middle West Utilities, which also owned Kentucky Utilities (KU). KU and KT&T were considered one and the same, although they were actually two separate corporations. The two companies had so integrated their operations that they looked like one company.

A favorite destination for many Frankfort people was Blue Grass Park (originally called the Belt Way Park). Located on twenty acres on South Elkhorn Creek just to the west of present-day Keeneland Race Track, the park boasted all kinds of rides, including a roller coaster, plus dancing, concerts, swimming, ball games, picnicking, boating, and penny arcades. In 1907, more than 450 "electric parks" nationwide were operated by streetcar and interurban companies who gleaned fifty million riders from these attractions. How better to increase ridership, especially on a Sunday or holiday? Yet, KT&T closed Blue Grass Park in 1925, when Joyland Park, located on Paris Pike, opened on the outskirts of Lexington.

A terminal building and interurban storage area for the KT&T was established at the northeast corner of Main and Olive Streets in Frankfort next to the Capital Hotel. Many salesmen coming to Frankfort found the location of the terminal next to the hotel a blessing. Food, drink, and a room were only one hundred feet away. Just beyond, at the corner of Ann and Main, one could catch a streetcar to any point in town.

The rails of the interurban route from Frankfort to Lexington were located within the center of East Main Street out to the Frankfort Cemetery. Beyond the Frankfort Cemetery, the track moved to a private right-of-way along the south side of the road. The tracks turned on a private right-of-way at Versailles Road and ran to the city of that name.

The corner of Cheapside and Main Street in Lexington was the KT&T terminal point; the interurban cars did not turn at Lexington but continued onto Paris. Another KT&T line ran between Georgetown, Lexington, and Nicholasville. Total trackage operated by KT&T was 91.7 miles, including 1.1 miles of city streetcar line in Winchester. (The connecting KT&T interurban line from Lexington to Winchester was never built.) Hourly service was provided between Frankfort and Lexington by KT&T from 6 AM to 8 PM, with "night owls" running at 9:30 and 10:45 PM. The trip took ninety minutes.

On February 21, 1910, the Frankfort streetcar line suffered its most serious accident. That Monday morning Frankfort was blanketed under one of the Kentucky River winter fogs that often cut visibility to one hundred feet or less. The fog had flowed out of the valley and covered the hilltops. On schedule, an interurban car departed the Central Kentucky Traction Depot in Frankfort at 8:20 AM and headed up Main Street Hill for Versailles and Lexington. Inward bound from the Green Hill Cemetery for downtown Frankfort was a local streetcar with a conductor, motorman, and ten passengers.

Normally, the interurban and the streetcar met at the passing track at the Feeble Minded Institute located at Glenns Creek Road and Main Street, but occasionally the meeting was at the next passing track up the line at the Kentucky Normal School for Colored People (Kentucky State University). The interurban ran on a timetable, and it was the responsibility of the streetcar to stay out of its way. If the streetcar could not make the Feeble Minded siding by 8:35 AM, it was to wait at the passing track beyond the Normal School. The interurban car waited at the siding until 8:35 AM and then started up the single track toward Versailles. Just beyond the Feeble Minded Institute, the interurban car saw the streetcar come out of the fog one hundred yards away. Both motormen cut their current and applied brakes, but it was too late. With a loud crash, the two cars came together. Due to its extra height, which allowed high-speed running, the interurban car rode up and over the streetcar.

The collision of the streetcar and interurban occurred at less than ten miles per hour. Weight and inertia, however, had their way. The heavy interurban crushed the front of the streetcar, trapping Owen F. Graves, the streetcar motorman, against the front of the passenger

237

section with its cowcatcher. Graves, who had not deserted his post but had held to the hand brake, was pinned into the streetcar and had to be cut out of the wreckage. At King's Daughters Hospital, both of his legs were amputated. Of the passengers, "Boss" Hockensmith suffered the gravest injury. Riding on the rear open platform, he was thrown violently forward into the passenger compartment and suffered severe cuts and bruising to his head, arm, and shoulder. Four others escaped injury, including the conductor, Charles Lawrence. The much-heavier interurban sustained only minor damage, and its passengers received no injuries requiring treatment. As soon as the track was cleared, the interurban proceeded to Versailles and Lexington.

The exact cause of the accident is not known. Lawrence, the conductor of the streetcar, claimed his watch showed 8:33 AM right before the accident. The conductor of the interurban stated that he remained at the siding until 8:35 AM by his watch, as required by the timetable. Thus, the question was which of the conductors' watches had the correct time, as shown by the official clock at the interurban station. No record apparently exists to answer this question.

Yet another memorable accident to strike the Frankfort streetcar line occurred four years later. On July 18, 1914, Harry Rice was motorman of city car Number 17. At Ann and Broadway the city tracks crossed those of the Louisville and Nashville Railroad (L&N). Running north to the ballpark, Rice failed to see an L&N train, the Louisville Express, entering the station on the outer track as the Lexington Express was departing the station on the inner track. The impact of the resulting crash turned the streetcar on its side. Rice suffered injuries to his back and legs. The sole passenger on board was not injured.

This incident led to considerable public concern about the safety of the streetcar railroad crossing. As a result, the L&N crossing guards were ordered to be more careful in guarding the crossing. KT&T motormen were instructed to take great care in crossing the railroad tracks and to be prepared for train movement in any direction, at any time, on any track. In addition, a trolley hood was installed on the overhead power line extending over the railroad tracks. The hood would prevent the streetcar trolley pole from disengaging the overhead wire while crossing the L&N track. When the trolley pole disengaged from its power source, it would cause the streetcar to stop.

KT&T intensified its safety campaign. Students taking part in a safety contest were awarded KT&T safety pins, and over two thousand posters with safety messages were distributed throughout the community. Among the messages carried on the posters were "Don't Play on the Tracks," "Don't Hang on Behind the Cars," "Don't Put Your Arms or Head Out the Window," "Don't Cross Immediately Behind a Standing Car," and "Stop, Look, Listen." Another series of posters showed how to board and deboard from a streetcar.

In 1913, Frankfort's streetcar conductors were assigned an extra duty as a result of the successful nationwide campaign to make the general public more aware of germs and their transmission. Conductors were ordered to enforce the anti-expectoration law. Thus, when a conductor saw someone spitting on the floor, he was to order the offender to stop. According to an agreement worked out with the Frankfort Police Department, if the spitter refused, the conductor was to halt the car and call a policeman to arrest the criminal. It was hoped that this policy would lead to the end of this "abominable practice" in public places.

The years 1916 and 1917 were not friendly to KT&T's financial books. First, the Commonwealth of Kentucky announced it was reevaluating all railroad property. KT&T found its net worth of real property increased from $1.2 million to $1.64 million, and its taxes rose correspondingly. Then in 1917, coal shortages, caused by strikes in Eastern Kentucky, adversely affected the streetcar and interurban operations. Starting in September, schedules were shortened and time between runs increased. Curtailed electrical power production and brownouts became common. On a number of occasions, there was insufficient power in the lines for the cars to operate. On September 17, the power generator ran completely out of coal. For most of that day, until new supplies arrived, the cars shut down. The resumption of coal mining in October allowed stocks to be replenished and electric production returned to normal.

The year 1918 found KT&T in a dispute with the Frankfort City Council over a proposed streetcar fare hike. KT&T sought to raise its fare to $.06 a ride due to wartime inflation. Following a bitter battle, the city council authorized a penny increase in fare only because KT&T threatened to stop service. At the same time, approval was granted by the Kentucky Railroad Commission to raise interurban fares from $.025 per mile to $.03. Soon, permission was given to raise interurban fares to $.036 per mile. The Frankfort city fare increase for KT&T was short lived, for in 1922 the city rolled back the fare to $.05.

In June 1923, Frankfort was without streetcar service. The city had entered into a street improvement program and was letting contracts to pave streets in the downtown area. This meant KT&T would have to relay its track to meet the new street level. In addition, the city wanted KT&T to pay part of the paving charge. The streetcar company objected to this additional cost, especially since the city had lowered permissible fares the year before. To fill the need for local transportation, a bus company commenced operations. The Frankfort Bus & Truck Line operated two buses. Initially, they charged five cents per ride but, within five days, this was raised to ten cents. KT&T quickly pointed out that even the bus company, which had no investment in track or overhead wire and did not have to help maintain the streets, was unable to operate at a nickel per ride. "How," KT&T then asked, "can the streetcar line operate at five cents per ride?" The city apparently relented and decreased its demands on the street railroad, for the cars were back in operation in July and the buses gone. However, at this time, the line to the Hemp Factory and Old Stagg Distillery also ceased operations. While the distillery remained in production during Prohibition, its work force had been cut by over 50 percent, while at the same time, the output of the 'hemp" factory had declined with a corresponding reduction in its workforce. With few workers to transport, the streetcar line out Leestown Road was unprofitable and KT&T sought to close it. The exact date of this line's closure is unsure but took place circa 1923.

Starting in 1919, the automobile and improved roads began to make serious inroads on KT&T's Frankfort city and interurban revenues. In response, the size of the interurban car's crew was cut to one person. New equipment costing $375,000 was ordered. In 1922, out went the old, heavy, wooden interurban cars that weighed 18 tons each. In their place, from the Cincinnati Car Company came ten lightweight metal cars, each weighing 12.5 tons. (These curved-side cars were to revolutionize the streetcar and interurban fleets throughout the country during the 1920s.) Later, two additional cars of this type were ordered. The new cars, which began service in February 1922, had yellow bodies with black lettering edged in silver. The interior of the coaches was divided from front to rear into "White," "Colored," and "Smoking/Baggage" sections. Both the "White" and "Colored" sections featured seats covered in Pullman Plush Green. The smoking section had wooden benches and a unisex toilet. With the new cars, the time to travel to Lexington was cut by fifteen minutes. Providing speed and comfort, the new cars breathed life back into KT&T.

At the same time it ordered new passenger cars, KT&T purchased three lightweight freight motors. These freight motors, built by Cincinnati Car Company, weighed 15.5 tons and were 40 feet long and 11 feet high. The interior of the car for carrying the goods was 34.75 feet by 5 feet 10 inches. These cars operated with a single motorman. Previous cars had carried one or two helpers to load and unload the goods. Management decided to reduce the size of the motor freight crew since most goods carried on the cars could be moved by one man.

The conversion to one-man cars also necessitated a change in the interurban's single-ended passing tracks. The car taking the siding had to back out onto the tracks. This two-man operation meant stopping the car, getting off to throw the switch for the siding, running the car into the siding, and throwing the switch back to the mainline so the inbound car could pass, then reversing the procedure to get back on the track. KT&T's solution was to turn the spur into a passing track with spring switches. Outbound cars would automatically switch to the passing track. Once the inbound car passed the spring switch at the other end of the siding, the switch would allow the outbound interurban to regain the main line.

The Frankfort Freight terminal was open daily (except Christmas) from 7:00 AM to 6:00 PM. The local agent accepted goods and levied the charge for shipping them; he also received goods and notified customers of their arrival. In Frankfort, unlike other cities served by the KT&T, one did not have to pick up or deliver goods to the station. The Frankfort station had a contract with a local teamster for delivery anywhere within the city at an additional cost.

The Frankfort streetcar line, at the same time the new interurbans were added, had its old wooden cars replaced by seven modern cars. Photographic evidence suggests that these "new" cars were, in fact, part of Lexington Railway Company's 1905 American Car Company order. The cars were twenty-nine feet long and rode on a single truck. Originally operated as a two-man crew car of conductor and motorman, they had been rebuilt for one-man operation. These cars had become surplus with KT&T's order for twenty-seven single-truck, curved-side cars from Cincinnati Car Company. Some of the older surplus cars were passed on to Frankfort. In 1924, two additional curved-side cars were purchased from Cincinnati Car Company and assigned to Frankfort. Owen Caplinger later spoke of this period as a golden age of trolley service. "The cars," he recalled, "ran all the time, beautiful cars." KT&T was proud of these "new" cars and had sign boards mounted on the roofline to carry messages showing this pride. Typical messages carried were "Rapid, Comfortable Service," "Permanent 17 Hour Service," "Our Pride, Your Comfort," "Shop By Street Car," "No Parking Worries Here," and "This Car a Community Asset."

The rebuilt and new cars assigned to Frankfort were called Safety Cars and PAYE (for "Pay As You Enter") cars. They were referred to as Safety Cars, as they were built of metal and had deadman controls. A PAYE car had a one-man crew. Where formerly the motorman had operated the car and the conductor collected the fare, the motorman now collected the fare. One now paid the motorman a nickel when boarding the car through the front door. Exiting the car was via the rear door, which could be pushed open by the passenger only when the car had stopped. This system cut down on delays during the heaviest boarding-alighting periods, normally in downtown rush hours.

With the introduction of the new interurban cars, the schedule of the interurbans was changed. To equalize the distance each car had to travel, the routes were now Frankfort-Versailles-Lexington-Nicholasville and Georgetown-Lexington-Paris. These routes were forty miles and thirty miles long, respectively, compared to the former route lengths of fifty-six and twenty-four miles. The adoption of this routing allowed the schedule to be maintained with one less interurban car. Yet the acceleration, speed when running, and braking power allowed headway to be reduced to one hour instead of every ninety minutes. Elapsed time for the run from Frankfort to Lexington was one hour, seventeen minutes. This gave an average speed of sixteen miles per hour when stops were included, which compares favorably to 1929's calculated average speed of thirty-three miles per hour of the twenty-two fastest interurban lines in the United States.

KT&T was now operating in Central Kentucky fifty-seven city cars, fourteen interurbans, and three motor freights. These operated over 91.3 miles of track of which 16.5 were in paved streets. Of this, 12.73 miles of track were in Franklin County. Yet even as KT&T was being revitalized, an action was taking place that, in time, would destroy the streetcar and interurban system. Tax monies, part of which had been paid by KT&T, were used to pave the first stretch of highway in Kentucky. That year, 1923, the first concrete highway was poured in the state when a seven-mile stretch of Winchester Pike was paved in Fayette County.

For a time after the introduction of the new interurbans, revenues increased; however, by the late 1920s they were again on the decline. Average daily ridership between Frankfort and Lexington had been 1,509 in 1912. Patronage slipped to 1,297 in 1921 and dropped to 726 in 1924; average passenger load per trip fell from fifty to twenty-two over these years. Still, many Franklin Countians used streetcars and interurbans to go shopping or to go to work, school, and church. Students attending the University of Kentucky or Transylvania College relied on it. Gentlemen used it to carry themselves and their dates to the theater in Lexington. Families took it to spend the day at Bluegrass Park or Joyland. The sportsman used it to reach the racetrack.

The introduction of new interurban cars, because of their reductions in required crew size and electrical power, allowed fares in 1922 to be lowered to three cents per mile. One-way fares from Frankfort to Versailles dropped to $.50; to Lexington, $.90; to Georgetown or Nicholasville, $1.30; and to Paris, $1.50. A book of forty round-trip tickets cost $22.

Not only did the interurban carry passengers, it also carried goods. It served as the package delivery service of its day. A person could travel to Lexington to shop on Main Street and return home unburdened by packages. Merchants would take purchases to the KT&T freight depot on Main near Georgetown Road. There the packages would be sorted and put in the baggage compartment of the passenger car for delivery to Frankfort.

There were a number of proposed extensions of KT&T's tracks from Frankfort to Owenton, Lawrenceburg, and Shelbyville. The line to Shelbyville from Frankfort was promoted by both Lexington and Louisville with strong support from Frankfort. Numerous surveys were made, public meetings held, and articles printed, but the connection was never made. The main stumbling point was that the KT&T track was built to railroad standard gauge while the Louisville Interurban was built for a wider-gauge track. The promoters were always at odds over the gauge to be used in building the line. Lexington wanted it built to KT&T gauge and Louisville to its own broad gauge. The traveler going from Frankfort to Shelbyville instead had to be satisfied with a thrice-daily jitney service from the Capital Hotel to the Interurban Depot in Shelbyville. The proposed line to Owenton, which would have been an extension of the line to the ballpark, was never more than a line on a map as was the Lawrenceburg Line.

With the onset of the Great Depression in 1930, KT&T streetcar and interurban revenue fell. At the same time, labor strife increased as the workers demanded higher pay and shorter hours. KT&T, however, continued to provide excellent service and kept both the Frankfort city and the interurban cars well maintained. In fact, KT&T in 1931 placed second in a national rating of excellence in car maintenance based on the mean failure rate of cars per miles run. This failure rate included both mechanical problems and accidents. Total mileage racked up by KT&T cars that year was 1,925,568 miles.

On January 13, 1934, KT&T's workers went on strike. Apparently, the Frankfort city streetcar workers had voted against the strike but went out on strike as the union as a whole had voted in favor of it. Two days after the strike was called, KT&T asked to be placed in receivership, as they did not have the money on hand to meet notes coming due February 1. On January 17, James Hulett, representing Frankfort KT&T employees, informed James B. Hall, the KT&T receiver, that the Frankfort city streetcar workers had broken with the union. Hulett stated that the workers were ready to start up citywide streetcar service. This action was met with praise by the citizens and merchants of Frankfort as the lack of public transportation was a great inconvenience. Unfortunately, Kentucky Securities Corporation saw the strike as a way to close down what was now a marginal operation within their organization. Hall stated that he was asking permission of Judge Cochan to permanently close all KT&T rail operations on the grounds that they were money-losing operations. Counterarguments were made of maintaining KT&T in operation for the good of the public. On January 22, Judge Cochan ruled that KT&T could abandon all of its routes with the exception of the Lexington city routes. This pronouncement by Judge Cochan was followed the next day by the announcement that Orville M. Harrod and H. A. Gretter had formed the Capital Transit Company to provide citywide bus service. This bus service started on January 28, 1934. Two buses were used but were soon joined by a third. Fares were eight cents or two tokens for fifteen.

Thus died Frankfort's streetcar and interurban service. Only a few pictures remain to remind us. It is amazing to think that from 1905 to 1934 citizens of Franklin County could, on an hourly basis from 6:00 AM to 8:00 PM, catch an interurban and be whisked to Versailles, Lexington, Nicholasville, Paris, or Georgetown. They could also catch a jitney three times a day to go to Shelbyville to ride the interurban to Louisville and onto Indianapolis, Indiana.

With the closure of the line, Frankfort streetcars were taken to Lexington. Here they joined their sister cars in revenue service until 1938, when buses replaced streetcars in Lexington. With no demand for streetcars in other cities, the cars were sold for scrap.

During its existence, the streetcar line defined Frankfort and continued to do so for many years thereafter. Long after the streetcar system was forgotten by Frankfort's citizens, developers continued to build along its route and ignore other areas adjacent to the city. The east side of Frankfort grew as housing and businesses moved out of the Kentucky River Basin. The west side of Frankfort would not see development until the 1960s. It would start its real growth only in the 1980s. North Frankfort saw its growth along the east side of Fort Hill and Thornhill as a working class neighborhood developed. The west side of these hills did not grow until the 1960s, while residents of Bellepoint, where the streetcar never reached, habitually identified themselves as citizens of Bellepoint, not of Frankfort. This is likely a result of never having experienced the unifying factor of the streetcar.

The abandonment of KT&T's interurban line was a loss for the public who fell increasingly in love with cars. It is equally true, however, that the line deserved public support. Government insisted on taxing the physical property of KT&T to include right-of-way and equipment as well as the revenue it received. Government had also required that KT&T maintain that part of the public road on which it ran, but allowed others to use that same part of the road free of charge. Instead of taxing the line out of existence, the government should have supported it.

Today, unless a citizen of Frankfort owns a car, he or she can no longer visit the cities served by KT&T. It is also evident that KT&T was the artery that carried the lifeblood of shoppers to the retail stores of downtown Frankfort and Lexington. One interurban could carry sixty shoppers downtown and did not need a parking space. Two automobiles, which required the same amount of road space as an interurban, could deliver only eight people downtown, and automobiles required valuable land for parking. Government had no problem in subsidizing parking for the car but could not see abandoning taxes on the streetcar and interurban lines to help preserve them. The true demise of downtown Frankfort and Lexington started with the abandonment of KT&T. Those who lived in Frankfort and did not have a car could no longer visit Lexington, Versailles, Georgetown, and Nicholasville at their convenience. True, there were still some steam trains to these places, but passenger service was far from an hourly service. Buses, with their fume-spilling engines, now tried to serve downtown Frankfort as it became congested with automobiles. This private bus service lasted until the mid-1970s.

The merchants of Frankfort, who saw the streetcar as an impediment to the flow of automobile traffic, and the automobile-free flow as a source of sales, never asked the fundamental question, "Do people buy goods or do cars buy goods?" If this question had been asked, the fate of KT&T might have been different. It is interesting that when Frankfort, circa 1985, funded the Frankfort Transit System that offered public bus transportation to the central business district, the merchants of downtown Frankfort could only complain of the four automobile parking slots lost. The downtown bus stop was thus moved two blocks from downtown, from which point the stores are not even visible. Thus is it any wonder that the riders of the buses bypass downtown Frankfort and instead shop at the outlying malls where the bus stops adjacent to their buildings.

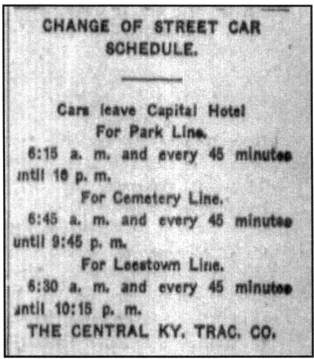

CHANGE OF STREET CAR SCHEDULE.

Cars leave Capital Hotel
For Park Line.
6:15 a. m. and every 45 minutes
until 10 p. m.
For Cemetery Line.
6:45 a. m. and every 45 minutes
until 9:45 p. m.
For Leestown Line.
6:30 a. m. and every 45 minutes
until 10:15 p. m.
THE CENTRAL KY. TRAC. CO.

A 1907 STREETCAR SCHEDULE FOR FRANKFORT. NOTE THE SOUTH FRANKFORT LINE IS NOT IN OPERATION BECAUSE IT IS BEING USED TO HAUL CONSTRUCTION MATERIALS TO THE NEW CAPITOL BUILDING. <CHB>

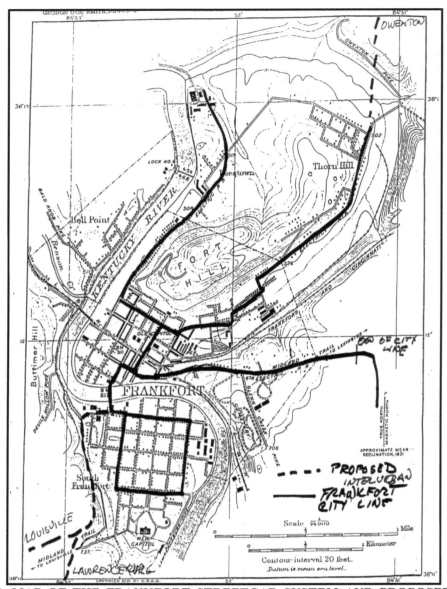

A MAP OF THE FRANKFORT STREETCAR SYSTEM AND PROPOSED INTERURBAN LINES OUT FROM FRANKFORT <CHB>

248

THE DEPOT, SHOWING C. & O. TRAIN, FRANKFORT, KY.

IN THE FOREGROUND IS ANN STREET WITH THE STREETCAR
TRACKS PASSING BY THE UNION DEPOT. CALLING AT THE STATION
IS A CHESAPEAKE & OHIO RAILWAY PASSENGER TRAIN. <CHB>

View on Shelby Street, Frankfort, Ky.

BOTH SHELBY AND SECOND STREET LACK BRICK OR BLACKTOP
PAVING. STREETCAR TRACKS RUN DOWN THE CENTER OF BOTH.
<BF>

Y. M. C. A. BUILDING, FRANKFORT, KY.

A STREETCAR PASSES IN FRONT OF THE YMCA AS IT HEADS ACROSS THE BRIDGE FOR DOWNTOWN FRANKFORT. <CHB>

THREE STREETCARS POSE AT SECOND AND SHELBY STREET WITH SIGNS ADVERTISING A FREE SHOW AT COVE SPRING PARK. <CHB>

THE CRC CARBARN SHOWING THEIR FREIGHT MOTOR SITTING IN THE CARBARN DOOR AND AN OPEN CAR ALONGSIDE THE BUILDING <CHB>

ONE OF F&SR'S ENCLOSED CARS HEADS DOWN ANN STREET PAST THE MASONIC LODGE. <CS>

A SUMMER CAR OF THE F&SR WITH FIVE PASSENGERS ENJOYING THE BREEZE DURING A HOT SUMMER DAY <EC>

A F&SR CAR HEADS UP ANN STREET TOWARD THE WYE AT ANN AND MAIN STREETS. <CCM>

Quarry and Rock Crusher of Devils Hollow Stone Co., Frankfort, Ky.

THE ABOVE TWO PHOTOS SHOW STREETCAR TRACK IN TAYLOR AVENUE. THESE TRACKS CARRIED BUILDING SUPPLIES FOR THE NEW (1910) CAPITOL BUILDING FROM THE L&N YARD IN BENSON VALLEY. <CHB>

THE ABOVE TWO PHOTOS WERE PART OF THE EVIDENCE
INTRODUCED INTO COURT BY THE F&SR AS DEFENSE OF ITS
OPERATIONS. THE PHOTOS SHOW THAT THE ONLY WAY A PERSON
COULD HAVE COME INTO CONTACT WITH THE SIDE OF THE
BRIDGE WAS BY LEANING DANGEROUSLY AWAY FROM THE CAR.
<BGRM>

A CRC STREETCAR IS ENTERING THE COVERED BRIDGE FROM BRIDGE STREET ON ITS WAY INTO TOWN. <CCM>

IT IS CIRCA 1914 AND MAIN STREET IS BEING TORN UP TO PUT IN NEW STREETCAR TRACKS. <CCM>

F&SR CAR #28 WITH ITS SAFETY NET RAISED. THE SAFETY NET WAS SUPPOSED TO PREVENT PEOPLE FROM BEING RUN OVER BY THE STREETCAR. THE SAFETY NET WOULD CATCH AND HOLD THE PERSON ABOVE THE TRACK. <EC>

KT&T CAR #29 AT ANN & MAIN STREET INBOUND FROM GREEN HILL CEMETERY. <CHB>

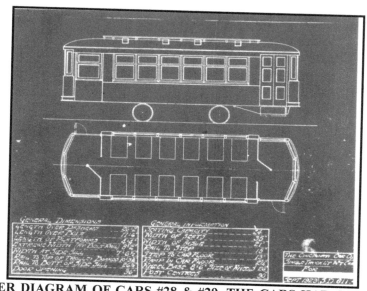

BUILDER DIAGRAM OF CARS #28 & #29. THE CARS HAD OPERATOR CONTROLS AT EACH END SO THEY DID NOT HAVE TO TURN AT THE END OF THE LINE. <EC>

INTERIOR OF CAR #28 LOOKING AT ONE OF THE MOTORMEN OPERATING POSITIONS. THE LARGE WHEEL IS FOR SETTING THE HANDBRAKE. <EC>

FROM CIRCA 1938 TO 1950, ONE OF THE KT&T CITY CARS SERVED AS A DINER ON HOLMES STREET ACROSS FROM LYONS LUMBER COMPANY. <CCM>

<BF>

A F&SR STREETCAR IS SEEN ENTERING THE GROUNDS OF THE BUFFALO TRACE DISTILLERY WHICH AT THIS TIME WAS OPERATING AS OLD FIRE COPPER DISTILLERY. <CCM>

A VIEW FROM WILKINSON BOULEVARD INTO OLD FIRE COPPER DISTILLERY. THE BOURBON BARRELS ARE BEING ROLLED ACROSS THE F&SR TRACK. <CCM>

How Can a Street Railway Company Pay Double Price For Everything It Uses and Still Exist On the Same Old 5 Cent Fare?

READ ABOUT THE PUPPY THAT BECAME A DOG.

Once upon a time there was a man who bought a little Pup. He was a poor man and had to be economical. "This Pup," he said, "can live and grow fat on Five cents worth of meat per day." Therefore he gave the animal that much meat.

The months went by and the Pup grew into a big Dog. He was so big that he gobbled up the Five cents worth of meat at a mouthful and barked in an attempt to persuade his master to give him more.

But the owner said "Five cents worth of meat was enough for you when you were a Pup and Five cents worth must be enough for you now."

After a time the cost of meat doubled, but the owner continued to give his Dog Five cents worth and no more.

As a result of this treatment the Dog grew thin and weak and after a while he dropped down in a corner of the yard and died.

"Gosh!" exclaimed the late owner, "I didn't think that a Dog that was getting Five cents worth of meat would starve to death."

Moral Number 1—What nourishes a Pup may starve a Dog.

Moral Number 2—Pup fares will not nourish a Street Railway Dog.

—From Electric Traction.

260

ABOVE AND BELOW, THE END OF THE TRACK THAT CARRIED BUILDING SUPPLIES FROM THE L&N TRACK AT BENSON VALLEY TO THE SITE OF THE NEW (1910) CAPITOL BUILDING. <CCM>

In 1890, the Capital Railway Company was organized to operate a streetcar system in Frankfort. In 1911, Capital Railway was absorbed by Kentucky Traction & Terminal Company (KT&T), which provided interurban service in Central Kentucky. As built, the Frankfort streetcar system consisted of four routes. The common meeting point for these routes was at the front of the Capital Hotel at Ann and Main Street, which was located to the rear of the Louisville and Nashville Railroad's (L&N) Union Station located on Broadway between Ann and High Streets. During its life, the depot also served the Chesapeake & Ohio Railway (C&O), Frankfort & Cincinnati Railroad (F&C), and Kentucky Highlands Railroad. To this day, the railroad tracks still run in an east-west direction in the center of Broadway but now carry the trains of R J Corman Central Kentucky Lines.

Of the four streetcar lines, one ran west on Main then turned south to cross the Kentucky River via the St. Clair Street Bridge to serve South Frankfort. The second line went east up Main Street, crossing over the L&N tunnel to serve the Frankfort Cemetery and the Kentucky Feeble Minded Institute. The remaining two routes went north on Ann and split at Mero Street, one line turning west to serve the lumber mills, hemp factory, and what is now Buffalo Trace Distillery. The other line diverged east on Mero to the Kentucky State Penitentiary and then north out Holmes Street and Owenton Road to the ballpark.

At Broadway, the streetcar line crossed three railroad tracks. Farthest north was the track leading into the L&N and F&C Yards. The middle track was the mainline track, while the other track was a passing track serving the Frankfort Depot. The depot had been built in 1908 by the L&N to replace a station built on the same site in the 1850s by the Louisville, Cincinnati & Lexington Railroad.

The streetcar line crossed the railroad track at Ann and Broadway. This was considered a dangerous crossing because at times train traffic at the depot was heavy. Trolley motormen were instructed to exercise caution in crossing the railroad tracks, and the L&N

employed a guard to protect the intersection during train movements. To protect its cars, the streetcar company had also installed a hood over its power line to prevent the trolley pole from disengaging from the wire as it crossed Broadway and losing power while crossing the railroad tracks.

Due to the physical layout of the depot, passenger trains often blocked Ann Street while loading and unloading passengers. Often two of the tracks would be occupied by trains, and occasionally all three tracks would see movement on them. This was a result of the F&C mainline and the L&N Frankfort freight yard track branching off to the north at the depot.

The L&N schedule called for Train No.17, the Louisville Express, and Train No.18, the Lexington Express, to meet at Frankfort. The Louisville Express departed the station at 10:06 AM and the Lexington Express at 9:55 AM. While the Lexington train was in the depot, its rear coaches would block Ann Street, and the engine of the Louisville Express would extend across Ann Street. While these two trains were generally on time, they did occasionally run late. As there was only single track to the east and west of the station, the meet had to be made in Frankfort unless one train was far behind schedule. On July 8, 1914, Train No. 17 was late into Frankfort.

Train No.18, bound eastward for Lexington, had entered the station and taken the passing track next to the station. Upon stopping, the train, as usual, blocked the trolley crossing at Ann Street. Delayed by this blocking was KT&T Car #17, operated by Henry Rice, outward bound for the ballpark. Only one passenger was on the car, Harry True, age 13, who was heading for his home.

With his streetcar behind schedule, Mr. Rice, the motorman, waited impatiently for the train to clear the tracks. For some reason many people calculate each second they have to wait for a train to clear a street crossing as taking a minute. Due to the late arrival of Train No.17, J. M. Burton, the L&N crossing guard, had walked east to High Street to throw the switch to allow Train No.18 to enter the mainline as soon as Train No.17 cleared.

Generally, both Train No.17 and Train No.18 were in the

station at the same time. Thus, both trains would foul Ann Street at the same time. On this day, however, Train No.17 was late as it entered the depot using the outer track, just as Train No.18 was preparing to leave.

As soon as Rice, the streetcar motorman, saw Train No.18 start to move, he prepared to continue on his run. As the last car of Train No.18 cleared the streetcar tracks, Rice started his car forward. He was unaware that Train No.17 was entering the station on the adjacent siding track. As Mr. Rice crossed over the outer passing track, to his left he saw Train No.17 bearing down on him on that track. Luckily, Bully Thompson, the engineer of Train No.17, had slowed almost to a stop, but despite the warning shout from his fireman, it was too late to avoid hitting the trolley car.

With a crash, the engine pilot went under KT&T Car #17, turning it over on its left side. Rice was violently thrown across the car and came to rest with portions of the car's interior falling on him. This equipment pinned him in the car causing major injuries to his back and legs. Surprisingly, young True suffered no injuries. Rice was freed from the car by nearby citizens and L&N employees and was taken to King's Daughters Hospital where he eventually recovered.

As it toppled, KT&T Car #17 landed so as to foul both the mainline and the inner passing track. While the left side and bottom of the car were heavily damaged, surprisingly the glass in the right side of the car was not broken. With no crane available to lift the streetcar, a chain was hooked on to it and connected to an L&N engine. In this manner the streetcar was dragged clear of the two passing tracks. The car continued to foul the mainline until that evening when an L&N crane was brought in, and Car #17 was put back on the streetcar track and towed to KT&T's Frankfort carbarn for repair. Train No 17, though delayed for 45 minutes due to the collision, continued on its way to Louisville, none the worse from the collision.

Needless to say, from that day forward, until streetcar service ended in Frankfort on January 13, 1934, KT&T instructed its motormen not to cross the railroad track until they were certain no train was moving on any of the three tracks in any direction. These instructions were thereafter followed religiously by KT&T motormen. At a railroad crossing, anytime is train time, on any track.

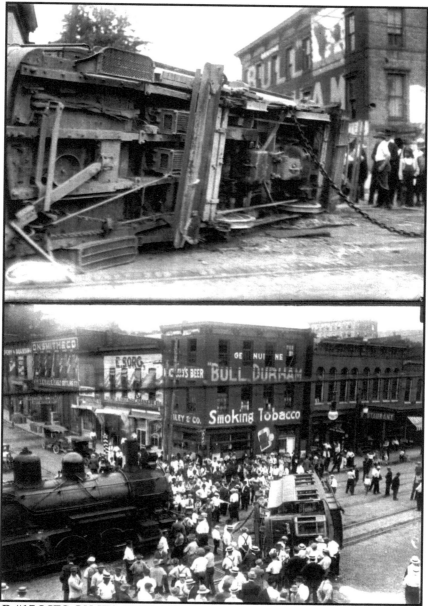

CAR #17 LIES ON ITS SIDE AFTER BEING HIT BROADSIDE BY AN L&N LOCOMOTIVE AT ANN & BROADWAY ON JULY 18, 1914. <CCM>

GEORGETOWN

HORSECAR TO INTERURBAN

Georgetown developed around Royal Spring and by the early 19th century, it was a thriving village dependent upon wagons to transport its goods. In 1834, the Lexington & Ohio Railroad provided an outlet to the world via Payne's Station located 6 miles south of Georgetown. Then on 14 October 1879, the Cincinnati Southern Railroad (CSRy), later Southern Railway and today Norfolk Southern Railway, reached Georgetown on its way to Chattanooga, Tennessee. January 1, 1885, saw the Louisville Southern Railroad (LSRR), Louisville to Lexington with a branch from Versailles to Georgetown, reach Georgetown where it shared use of the Cincinnati Southern Depot. Finally, on June 1, 1885, the Kentucky Midland Railroad (KM), later Frankfort & Cincinnati Railroad, reached Georgetown during its construction from Frankfort to Paris. Before the coming of the Cincinnati Southern Railroad to Georgetown, horse-drawn omnibus service had been provided from Georgetown to the Louisville & Nashville Railroad (L&N), successor to the L&O, at Payne's Depot, and to the Kentucky Central Railroad Depot in Lexington.

It should be noted that coal hauled by wagon from Payne's Depot to Georgetown sold for $.22 a bushel, but with the coming of the CSRy, its price dropped to $.10 a bushel. Contemporary news reports note that before the arrival of the CSRy, coal merchants only sold coal by the bushel; however, since the coming of the CSRy, they only sold coal in ton loads.

Kentucky Midland (KM) located their depot in the valley of a creek some 20 feet lower than Georgetown's central business district while the CSRy/LSRR Depot was located a mile east of the courthouse. Equally distant between both depots was Georgetown College. In 1888, local citizens organized the Georgetown Street Railway Company to operate a horsecar line that tied the two railroad depots together and took citizens and visitors alike to the Scott County Courthouse and Georgetown College. The horsecar line apparently owned two horsecars and ran over 2.5 miles of tracks. In truth, the horsecar line used mules to pull its cars. The line was leased to William Powell and J. C. Cantrill who commenced service on

September 6, 1890.

The route of the horsecar line was east on Jackson Street to Main Street, then west on Main to Chambers Street, and finally north to the KM Depot. The horsecar would be turned at the KM Depot to run south on Chambers back to Main. At Main, the car turned west to Broadway. There the line swung south along that street to Jackson where the route turned east to the CSRY/LSRR Depot, completing the loop.

In 1895, Georgetown Electric Street Railway Company was formed to convert the horsecar line to electric power. Overhead electric lines were in place by June 1, 1895, but service using electric powered cars did not start until June 12, 1895. On that day, 1,500 passengers were carried on the 15-minute loop run. The route down Chambers Street was abandoned since the Frankfort & Cincinnati Railroad (F&C), successor to Kentucky Midland, now stopped at the CSRy Depot. The F&C track crossed CSRy track at the depot. The Georgetown Electric Street Railway Line had two cars, with John Cole assigned as motorman to Car #1 and Jack Wright to Car #2.

In 1901, Georgetown Electric Street Railway Company was reorganized as Georgetown & Lexington Traction Company (G&LT). The new company built an 11.5-mile electric interurban line that connected Georgetown to Lexington along present day US 25 at a cost of $250,000. Service to Lexington started in June 1901 with cars leaving Georgetown on the hour for Lexington and cars arriving in Georgetown from Lexington on the half hour. G&L advertised that Freight Motor #14 carrying baggage, parcels, express, and freight would leave Lexington for Georgetown at 10:00 AM., Noon, 2:00 PM, and 4:00 PM and would leave Georgetown for Lexington at 9:00 AM, 11:00 AM, 1:00 PM, and 3:00 PM. With advance notice by applying to the management of the company, one could arrange for freight movements, excursions, and trolley parties.

The interurban line within Georgetown followed the local streetcar route. The interurban depot was located on Main Street while the company's powerhouse and carbarn were located near Royal Spring.

In 1904, Georgetown & Lexington Traction was reorganized as Blue Grass Traction Company, and interurban service was extended from Lexington to Paris. In 1911, Blue Grass Traction Company became part of Kentucky Traction & Terminal Company (KT&T) that provided service to Nicholasville, Versailles, and Frankfort. KT&T also operated the local streetcar systems in Lexington, Winchester, and Frankfort.

In the years immediately after World War I, the private automobile became omnipresent in Georgetown. By 1922, ridership on the local Georgetown streetcar system had declined to a shadow of its former self. At the same time, ridership was decreasing while the cost of operating the streetcar line was increasing. KT&T found itself stymied by the Georgetown City Council because they refused to let KT&T raise the fare from a nickel to a dime. The result was local streetcar service in Georgetown was suspended by KT&T in 1922, never to return. The interurban line, however, would continue to move passengers and Less Than Carload (LCL) packages until January 1934. By 1934, KT&T had lost almost all of its passenger and package traffic to the automobile and the truck. With mortgage payments due at the end of the month and no money in the company treasury, KT&T went into receivership and interurban service ceased on 13 January 1934. Public bus service was then provided for a number of years between Georgetown and Lexington by Southeastern Greyhound. The streetcar and interurban track remained in the streets of Georgetown until 1941 when it was removed as part of a national wartime scrap drive.

In 2011, Georgetown has no public passenger train or bus service. It seems strange that in 1911 the citizens of Georgetown had available more forms of public transportation to more parts of Kentucky than do the citizens of Georgetown in 2011.

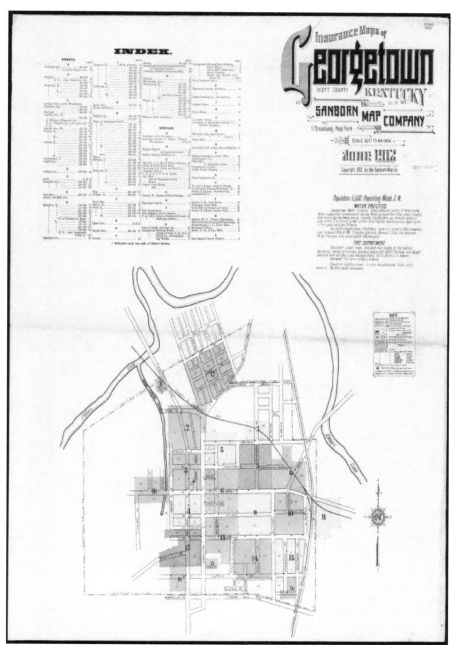

1912 MAP OF THE CITY OF GEORGETOWN <KHS>

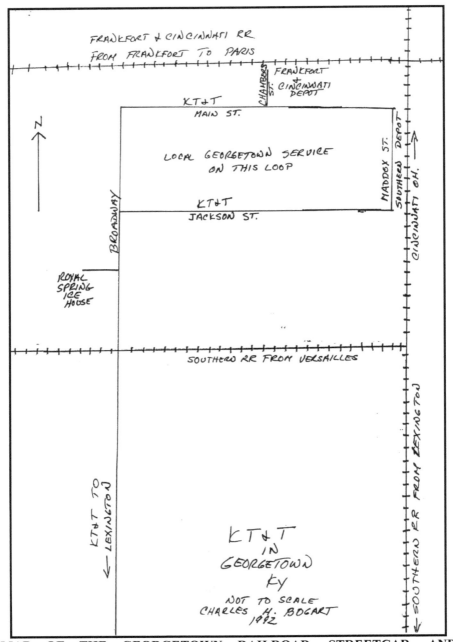

MAP OF THE GEORGETOWN RAILROAD, STREETCAR, AND INTERURBAN RAIL LINES <CHB>

GEORGETOWN'S FIRST HORSE-DRAWN STREET RAILWAY CAR. IT
RAN FROM THE KENTUCKY MIDLAND DEPOT TO THE CINCINNATI
SOUTHERN DEPOT. <CHB>

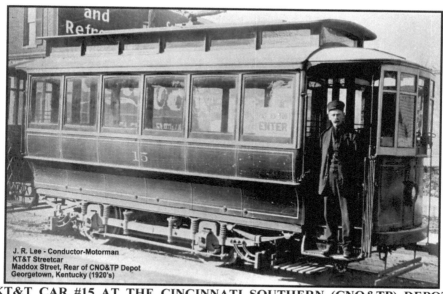

KT&T CAR #15 AT THE CINCINNATI SOUTHERN (CNO&TP) DEPOT
<CS>

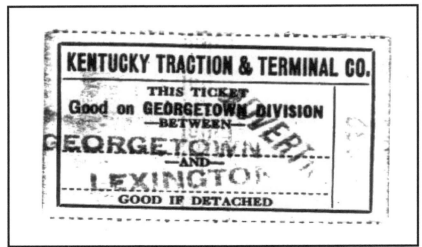

A KT&T INTERURBAN TICKET FOR A RIDE FROM GEORGETOWN TO
LEXINGTON <CHB>

A KT&T STREETCAR RUNS OVER A ROAD OF DIRT AS IT SERVES
DOWNTOWN GEORGETOWN. <EC>

HENDERSON

AN INTERURBAN LINE FEEDER

Henderson, Kentucky, during the 19th century and for most of the 20th century, was in competition with Evansville, Indiana, and Owensboro, Kentucky, to be the leading city within the Western Kentucky Coalfields. This meant that as soon as one of the other cities added a modern innovation to its community, the other had to follow or be viewed as being non-progressive. The condition of a city's streets was one method of defining a city as being progressive. Unfortunately, in visiting Henderson, early pedestrians always found the surface of Henderson's dirt streets to be either a gooey, muddy cesspool, fouling shoes and clothes, or covered with wind-driven dust that clung to clothes and skin and irritated the eyes.

Henderson, like other cities of this era, tried a number of methods to keep its streets clean by employing street cleaners to pick up horse droppings, spraying water and oil to keep down the dust, and pulling spreaders and rollers along the streets to smooth out the ruts. These actions, however, still left the citizen on foot as he or she moved about town visiting, conducting business, or seeking pleasure. In 1886, Henderson, with a population of 8,000 and trying to get its citizens above the dirt of the streets, granted a 30-year charter to Henderson Street Railway (HSRy) to operate a horse-drawn street railroad within the city. Henderson was only marginally large enough to support a horsecar line, but the streetcar line promoters were confident that Henderson would grow to become the major city of the area.

On September 19, 1887, the first real steps were taken to get people up and out of the mud and dust of Henderson's streets. On that day, workers of HSRy, under the direction of David and Paul Banks and E.G. Sebree, began to lay track in the dirt surface of Green Street near its intersection with Washington. Before the year was out, horse-drawn streetcars were carrying the citizens of Henderson from their homes to downtown and back. These horse-drawn cars partially freed the citizens of Henderson from having to walk in the mud or dust of their streets. These cars also made Henderson co-equals with Owensboro and Evansville in having the latest in modern conveniences.

The horse-drawn streetcars had one major drawback. They were powered by horses. This meant that HSRy had to maintain three sets of horses for each car, as the horses could only work a four-hour day and remain healthy. In addition, the speed of the cars was not much greater than a person walking, and the cars did not subtract from the liquid and solid waste being deposited on the surface of the streets by animals.

In 1894, with the horse-drawn streetcars being a financial success and Henderson's population having increased to 11,000, the investors in HSRy set out to convert their line to electricity. With a new franchise to operate on the streets of Henderson, HSRy changed its name to Henderson Electric Street Railway (HESRy) and then to Henderson City Railway (HCRy). The modified city franchise that allowed HCRy to convert its line to electricity also added some additional responsibilities for the streetcar line operators. HCRy would be responsible for oiling and watering the dirt streets on which they traveled to keep down the dust. During snowstorms, HCRy was also responsible for plowing not only the right-of-way of its track but also that part of the street next to its track. As HCRy proclaimed that the electric cars would run over the streets at speeds of up to 12 miles per hour, some members of the city council became concerned that this high speed would create a vicious dust storm in the wake of the cars. The result was speed restrictions of five miles per hour within the downtown area. All cars also had to ring a gong when traveling through intersections and be so controlled that they could stop within ten feet. As the cars only had handbrakes for stopping, this stopping requirement would have imposed impossible speed restrictions on the operation of the cars. This stopping distance requirement was ignored by the operators of the streetcars to the great delight of the brotherhood of attorneys, who could prove the streetcars were operating at a reckless speed each time a client was involved in a collision with a streetcar.

Upon completion, HCRy's electric streetcar line was six miles long. It was built to standard gauge, 4 feet 8.5 inches, with rail of 40-pound-weight. This rail soon proved to be too light for the traffic carried and was upgraded to 50 pounds. Trolley lines from downtown served the fairgrounds, Atkinson Park, and the baseball park. The company's carbarn and powerhouse were located at South Main and Jefferson Streets and housed the 16 single-truck trolley cars owned by the company. An adjacent building at the site served as the powerhouse for producing the electricity to propel the cars over the tracks. The last horsecar ran over Henderson's streets in 1896.

In 1904, HCRy purchased five new 18-foot long single truck cars from St. Louis Car Company, #100 to #104, due to a demand from the city of Henderson that it operate modern cars. While HCRy's streetcars were well-patronized, the company was unable to recover enough money from their 5 cent fare to meet mortgage payments, pay salaries, maintain the equipment, and pay property and franchise taxes. In 1907, the streetcar company was forced into receivership when its workers went on strike for higher pay. The strike lasted six weeks. After the strike, HCRy was reorganized as Henderson Traction Company (HTC) and money was raised to upgrade track and equipment. The Elm Street Line, whose track had deteriorated to being almost unusable, was re-laid with 70-pound rail. HTC's 1908 annual report stated that it owned nine closed cars and three open summer cars plus one trailer. It operated six-and-one-half miles of track and manufactured its own power, using one steam engine and two generators.

During 1907, HTC sought to buy new equipment, but the internal financial resources to accomplish this did not exist. HTC therefore undertook to rebuild Cars #100 to #104 into one-man cars. Since all Henderson city cars were double-ended, this posed a problem. A one-man car necessitated all passenger boarding at the motorman station. However, every time the car changed directions, the motorman had to switch ends. HTC developed a rear door locking mechanism that only the operator could lock and unlock. This allowed boarding and exiting being switched from one end of the car to the other, depending on direction. HTC also rebuilt the sides of its cars with steel panels giving them a modern appearance. The result was that HTC operated in the black from 1908 to 1911.

In 1912, national politics touched HTC in the form of political advertisements. The Bull Moose Party of Theodore Roosevelt adorned six cars with signs showing a Bull Moose, a Big Stick, and proclaiming "Let's Put Them Back To Work." The Republican Party adorned other cars with signs carrying the message of "Working men are busy, capital is busy, everybody is busy, wages are good, and times are good under Taft. Why Change?" Interestingly, the winner of the race, Woodrow Wilson, had no political signs posted on the Henderson streetcars.

The year 1912 also saw HTC put in new tracks from Main Street to Union Depot. Union Depot served the Louisville & Nashville Railroad, the Louisville, Henderson & Texas Railroad, and the Illinois Central Railway. The existing HTC 50-pound track had been showing its age by giving a rough ride, or as the local newspaper called it, a "bump-the-bump ride." In truth, the rail had become warped and rolling in contour from heavy use. The old rail was replaced with an 80-pound steel rail. In addition, HTC purchased three new one-man streetcars from Chicago, Illinois. These cars were praised as being "of the latest design" and "would provide the added capacity to handle the crowds going to the Fairgrounds and Baseball Park."

Throughout its life, the Henderson streetcar system had a major problem on its route up and down Fourth Street. At Fourth and Elm Street, the streetcar, when southbound within a seven-foot distance, crossed over and under the rails of the Louisville & Nashville Railroad (L&N). The L&N viaduct provided but a clearance of 13 feet 9 inches above the track of the streetcar while the L&N demanded a 19 feet 6 inch clearance over its adjacent on-grade track. They wanted a 19 feet 6 inch clearance over their on-grade track so a brakeman could safely stand upright on top of a boxcar while going over the streetcar track. Why telltales could not have been positioned on the L&N track to either side of the streetcar's overhead wire to provide warning to the brakeman to lie down on top of the boxcar is lost to posterity. Throughout the existence of streetcar operations on Henderson's Fourth Street, various devices would be installed to allow this quick six-foot upward transition of the overhead wire within a lateral distance of seven feet, yet would allow the trolley pole with its trolley wheel to remain engaged to the wire. All too often, the trolley pole came loose from the overhead wire causing the streetcar to coast to a stop. On one occasion, the motorman forgot to turn his controller to the off position when he got off his car to reset the trolley pole against the overhead wire. The result was that once the trolley pole re-engaged

276

the overhead wire, the streetcar took off with the motorman still standing in the street. It is claimed that a new running speed record was set that day by that un-named motorman that has yet been equaled, as he caught up to and boarded his car.

In 1919, Henderson Traction Company became a subsidiary of Evansville & Ohio Valley Railroad, owners of Evansville, Henderson & Owensboro Railroad, Evansville Suburban & Newburgh Railway Company, and Southern Indiana Gas & Electric Company. With this reorganization, Henderson Traction Company ceased to generate its own power and instead began to purchase its electricity from the Henderson Municipal Power Plant. It was becoming apparent that the real profit to be made from electricity was not using it to power streetcars but to provide electrical power to homes and businesses.

As per all streetcar operations in the United States, the years between 1916 and 1929 were to prove the undoing of the Henderson streetcar system. Starting at the turn of the 20th century, citizens in all towns across the United States began to demand paved streets on which to run their automobiles. With paved streets, automobile ownership grew. Then with the start of World War I, inflation began to build within the country causing increased costs for operators of streetcar lines. The city council of Henderson, like many other American city councils, refused to provide financial relief to the streetcar company through higher fares. In addition, the Henderson streetcars operated on a single-track in the center of the street with a passing track in strategic locations. The streetcars running in either direction in the center of the street now interfered with the increased automobile traffic running over Henderson streets. The increase in automobile traffic over the city's streets also made potential streetcar passengers leery of boarding and offloading from a streetcar into the center of the street.

At some point around 1918, the Henderson streetcars were equipped with a Johnson Fare Box that was situated next to the motorman. The fare box collected not only coins but also tokens and automatically signaled if the correct fare had been paid. These fare boxes could only be opened using a special key that was held in the company auditor's office. Thus, the motorman was no longer responsible for handing over actual money to the company and making up any difference between the calculated collections for fares recorded and actual money handed in. The motorman was still responsible for the $30 in coins he carried to make change for passengers not having the correct fare.

During the winter of 1917-18, ice and snowstorms seriously disrupted Henderson streetcar service and caused additional expense to HTC by forcing it to hire extra workers to clear the streets that were then used by those owning private cars and horse-drawn vehicles. For a two-week period in 1918, HTC shut down its streetcar line over a dispute with the city council concerning the company's responsibility in maintaining the streets in which its tracks ran. HTC contended that the street maintenance the city wanted it to undertake was solely for the benefit of private vehicles.

The year 1919 saw the start of a decline in the population of Henderson. By 1923, the city could only count 13,000 residents, a decrease of 4,500 souls from the city's 1918 wartime high. The economic hard times and the declining population that affected Henderson following World War I devastated the streetcar company. Starting in 1920, the streetcar line began to operate at a sustained loss.

In August 1923, Henderson City Council directed that Main Street be paved. No longer would Henderson's streets be at the mercy of Mother Nature. The paving of the streets would necessitate taking up the existing streetcar track and laying new track. HTC was not taking in enough revenue in fares to cover existing costs, much less undertake the laying of new rail. The result of the city's street paving program was that the streetcar company filed for bankruptcy and ceased operations that year. Public transportation for the citizens of Henderson returned in 1957 with the establishment of Henderson Area Rapid Transit (HART), which continues to operate in 2011.

From 1912 to 1928, Henderson was also served by the interurban cars of the Evansville & Ohio Valley Railway, ex-Evansville, Henderson & Owensboro Railway. The cars ran between Henderson and Evansville by using the transfer ferry *"Henderson."* More details of this operation are found in the chapter on interurban service between Henderson and Evansville.

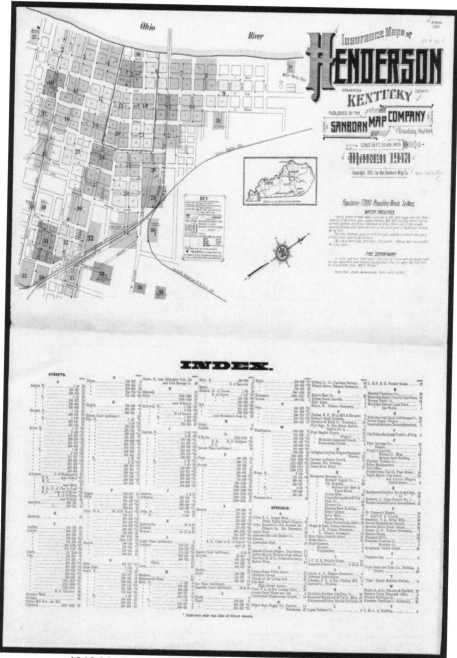

1913 MAP OF THE CITY OF HENDERSON <KHS>

FOUR STREETCARS CAN BE SEEN ON MAIN STREET DURING RUSH HOUR. <WF>

TWO STREETCARS PASS EACH OTHER IN DOWNTOWN HENDERSON. <CHB>

SECOND STREET, LOOKING EAST, HENDERSON, KY.

A LONE STREETCAR RUNS THROUGH DOWNTOWN HENDERSON. <CHB>

THE LOCAL STREETCAR FRANCHISE IN MOST CITIES CALLED FOR THE STREETCAR COMPANY TO WASH DOWN THE STREETS. HERE THE LOCAL WATER CAR IS SEEN GOING ABOUT ITS DUTIES BUT WRAPPED WITH AN ADVERTISEMENT FOR A LOCAL BUSINESS. <CHB>

An OPEN AIR CAR PREPARES TO LEAVE THE HENDERSON CITY CARBARN. <CHB>

A VIEW OF THE INTERIOR OF THE HENDERSON POWER PLANT <CHB>

AN UNKNOWN HENDERSON MOTORMAN POSES ON THE STEPS OF HIS CAR. <CHB>

Lexington, located in the heart of Bluegrass country, quickly found itself at a disadvantage as it tried to grow from a town into a city. Lexington was not located on or near a navigable stream. All goods coming into or being shipped out of Lexington had to move by wagon, which was a slow, costly process. Thus, the city was always at the forefront of transportation improvement. Lexington was an early supporter of internal improvements. At first, its citizens sought improved roads and stage coach routes but later moved to support canalization and railroads. In 1880, Lexington was served by four railroads: Kentucky Central, Kentucky Union, Louisville & Nashville, and Cincinnati Southern. In 1874, within the city limits of Lexington, local businessmen had already developed an omnibus service.

Thus, as the 1880s arrived, Lexington viewed itself as a leader in transportation. It was only natural that its citizens would embrace the horsecar, as the horsecar was nothing more than an omnibus running on rails. Yet in early 1882, it was not local businessmen who incorporated the Lexington City Railway Company but three out-of-towners, John Cross and Charles Diver of Little Rock, Arkansas, and Charles Skinner of Cincinnati, Ohio. Before the first rail went down, the Lexington City Railway Company was reorganized as the Lexington Street Railway Company.

Moving with speed, the investors soon had four miles of track laid in the streets and fifteen cars running. The track was built to a 4 feet 10 inch gauge and consisted of 30 pound rail, i.e. each yard section of rail weighed 30 pounds. The line's 15 cars, purchased at a cost of $450 each, were actually pulled by two mules, but the line rejoiced in the loftier claim of being a horsecar line. On 12 August 1882, the first horse car pulled by two mules started through the streets of Lexington. The initial routes established were the Green Line that ran to the Fair Grounds (Red Mile Race Track) and the Red Line that ran from Eastern State Asylum to A&M College (University of Kentucky). Later routes ran to the Lexington Cemetery and through various neighborhoods. The fare was originally $.10 but was later reduced to $.05.

The Lexington horsecar line proved to be a double-edged sword for its promoters. Lexington Street Railway had been built as cheaply as possible to maximize the profits of the promoters. The line, however, proved to be a rousing success. In fact, the line attracted so much business it could not handle it all. During a four-day period in September, the horsecar line carried 16,000 passengers to the Fairgrounds for the State Fair. Unfortunately, not enough animals had been purchased to work the line. One might say fifteen cars, each with two mules, meant the need to have 30 mules; however, this is not the correct answer. If the mules were worked more than four hours each day, they soon broke down and became unfit for work. Just like a human beings, the mules also needed an occasional day of rest, and like humans, they also got sick. The line needed 120 mules, at a minimum, to maintain service.

The *Lexington Herald* reported that the problem with the Lexington Street Railway was that its management did not know how to operate the line effectively. "Such a thing as following a schedule was not thought of. When a car managed to arrive at one end of its trip, it was turned around and an effort was made to reach the other end of the line. Sometimes it was successful, but more often prospective passengers became tired of waiting and made the trip on foot. Instead of minutes, the wait was often stretched into hours, and in many cases, the car failed to show up at all. The road was equipped with the lightest possible rails, lighter probably than any ever used elsewhere in any city. The cars had more the appearance of toys, and the mules which drew them were scarcely larger than Shetland ponies."

The reason the Lexington Street Railway was constructed seems to have been based on real estate speculation. Property within walking distance of downtown Lexington had all been developed and was rising in value. Beyond walking distance of downtown was considerable undeveloped land. The horsecar turned this undeveloped land into valuable land. The middle class could buy town lots beyond the developed area but still be able to travel to work in a reasonable time by riding the horsecar. It also appears that the builders of the horsecar line hoped to turn a fast profit by quickly selling the line after it went into operation but before its many deficiencies surfaced. While the horsecar line did set in motion a mini real estate boom within the

Pralltown and Woodland Park area and allowed the McGarvey and Goodloe Subdivisions to prosper, the horsecar line found no immediate buyer.

In 1883, the horsecar line was extended to Woodland Park, not only to attract homebuyers to the area, but also to serve the 110-acre park located there, which was owned by the Chautauqua Association. The park contained not only facilities to hold events but housed the local semi-professional baseball team's playing field. Woodland Park was later purchased by the city and today is part of the Lexington Urban County Park System.

Those who invested in the Lexington Street Railway Company put up $30,000. Total construction of the line was estimated to be $40,000. To make up the $10,000 shortfall, the three owners sold $50,000 in stock and $40,000 in bonds. The stock was being watered down to insure maximum profit for the three organizers of the horsecar line. However, there is some evidence that during the first year of operation, Lexington Street Railway Company and its horsecar line not only paid its cost but earned money. It must be stated, however, that the main reason for building the line was to sell building lots and for the line to then be sold off at a profit to another entrepreneur. In 1885, the endeavor to sell the Lexington Street Railway Company succeeded, and the line was purchased by R. B. Metcalfe.

With the sale of the Lexington Street Railway Company to R. B. Metcalfe, another set of investors arrived in Lexington and in 1886 organized the City Passenger Railway Company. This company proposed to build an electric operated trolley line in competition with the Lexington Street Railway. This company was soon reorganized as the Central City Passenger & Transportation Company (CCP&T). It appears that the owners of CCP&T had no real plan to build an electric trolley system but instead hoped to force Metcalfe to buy their charter to maintain his monopoly. Metcalfe, however, refused to purchase CCP&T.

In 1889, Lexington was served by six railroads: 1) Louisville & Nashville Railroad from Louisville with three daily round trip trains; 2) Newport News & Mississippi Valley Railroad from Ashland, Kentucky, with three daily round trip trains (Chesapeake & Ohio

286

Railway); 3) East Tennessee, Virginia & Georgia Railway from Louisville with two daily round trip trains (ex Louisville Southern Railroad); 4) Kentucky Union Railway to Beattyville, Kentucky, with two daily round trip trains; 5) Kentucky Central Railroad to Covington and Maysville, Kentucky, with five daily round trip trains; and 6) Queen & Crescent Route (Southern Railway) with ten daily through trains from Cincinnati, Ohio, to Chattanooga, Tennessee.

In 1890, Lexington had two passenger depots. One was the Queen & Crescent (Q&C) located a mile from downtown Lexington at Broadway and Magazine Street. Trains using the Q&C Depot ran through the station. Lexington's other depot was located on Vine Street at the rear of the Phoenix Hotel. This depot had two tracks and did not allow the run through of trains. Every train that pulled into the Vine Street Depot had to back out from the depot. From the previous paragraph, it becomes apparent that Lexington's Vine Street Depot served daily as the termination point for fifteen passenger trains and the originating point for fifteen passenger trains. The result was daily chaos as trains tried to load and unload their passengers. A train that arrived late caused a cascade of delays. The solution to this bottleneck was a belt railroad that tied all the rail lines to the depot via a large loop. The charter of Central City Passenger & Transportation Company (CCP&T), however, was the solution to this quandary. While CCP&T owners had not turned over the first spade of dirt, the company's charter was still intact. CCP&T's charter, after mentioning the line could use "animal or electricity" to operate its cars, contained the provision "or other power." "Other power" obviously covered steam. CCP&T's charter would thus allow building of a belt railroad, centered upon the two Vine Street Depots, upon which steam-powered trains could run in and out of downtown Lexington. In 1907, the two depots were consolidated into Lexington Union Station, also located on Vine Street.

In 1888, Passenger & Belt Railway Company (Belt Railway) was formed, and it purchased the charter of Central City Passenger & Transportation Company. Belt Railway set out to not only build their steam belt railroad but also build an electric trolley line that would be in direct competition with the Lexington Street Railway horsecar line. Lexington Street Railway's charter was very restrictive in what the line could do, their charter not allowing for any service but that which was animal powered. Metcalfe, however, refused to sell Lexington Street Railway to Belt Line due to hostility toward some of its directors. Economically, however, it was a losing battle and Metcalfe eventually had to sell on March 20, 1890, but not to Belt Railway. That year Metcalfe sold Lexington Street Railway to an outsider at less money than Belt Railway had offered. In truth, however, he sold his line to Belt Railway, for the purchaser was a dummy corporation set up by Belt Railway. The last horsecar clopped through Lexington on 4 September 1890.

At the end of its operation, Lexington Street Railway was operating four horsecar lines: 1) Lexington Cemetery to Woodland Park via Main Street; 2) Kentucky Association Racetrack to the Fair Grounds; 3) Courthouse to the University of Kentucky; and 4) the "U" shaped North Broadway into Main Street, over Main to Limestone, and then out North Limestone. While all four lines served the Vine Street Depots, the line out South Broadway to the Fairgrounds appears not to have been extended the .5 mile needed to reach the Queen & Crescent Depot.

Once Belt Railway had control of the Lexington Street Railway, they moved to take up its track. Starting in July 1890, they began to put in their own rail; in went heavy steel T-rails for the line's track. The track was laid to standard gauge, 4 feet 8.5 inches. At the same time, electric lines were strung from the 1889 built powerhouse to poles along the trolley car routes. A car barn to house the cars was constructed on Loudon Avenue near Limestone Street. The first car, #8 purchased from Pullman, ran on the electric line on July 29, 1890. The first revenue service was offered on September 1, 1890. Lexington civic boosters now stepped forward and claimed that Lexington had the "first electric street railway system in the country" as opposed to a city that had but one street rail line operated by electricity. They also claimed that the Lexington electric street rail system was the first to use "heavy steam road 'T' rail." The electric trolley aficionados can argue this point among themselves. After being stripped of their wheels and axles, the old horsecars were offered for sale as outbuildings. While some of the old car bodies were bought by individuals, most were disposed of as fuel into the company's power generating station.

Five streetcar routes were built centered around the Fayette County Courthouse on Main Street. At Main and Cheapside, a Transfer Station was built, as this was the one point common to all lines. The Transfer Station was an old car body placed in the middle of the street with the trolley track jogging around it. The shelter provided some protection from inclement weather. However, in 1911, with an increase in automobile traffic on the streets of Lexington, the Transfer Station became viewed as a hindrance to private transportation and not a refuge for those seeking shelter from rain or snow. Thus, that year Lexington City Council ordered the Transfer Station removed as a "public nuisance." The Transfer Station was replaced by a small safety zone providing no shelter.

The five electric rail lines ran simpler routes to the old horsecar lines. Interestingly, the Fairgrounds Line was not at this time extended out to the Queen & Crescent Depot. Streetcar lines ran to the Lexington Cemetery, Woodlawn Park, University of Kentucky, Kentucky Association Racetrack, and Eastern State Hospital.

In 1899, Belt Railway was reorganized as the Lexington Railway Company and plans were announced to extend the car lines, but nothing came of this proposal. In 1901, however, agreement was reached with the Georgetown & Lexington Traction Company (G&LT) to allow that company to run its interurban cars to Main and Cheapside. The G&LT, using standard gauge track, entered Lexington via Georgetown Road, following the route of the Lexington Railway Company to the Transfer Station. Later that year G&LT was reorganized as Blue Grass Traction Company and built a line out Limestone Street to Paris Pike. Once again, the interurban shared track, for part of the distance, with the Lexington Railway Company.

In 1905, Lexington & Versailles Traction Company (L&VT), which ran on standard gauge track, was granted rights to run from the Transfer Station to the Fairgrounds using the streetcar track. L&VT's cars went out Broadway, past the Fairgrounds to Angliana Avenue where they turned for Versailles. This new track provided the city line access to the Q&C Depot. In 1907, Versailles & Frankfort Traction (V&FT) Company extended L&VT track to Frankfort. L&VT and V&FT were both subsidiaries of Central Kentucky Traction Company. In 1905, Blue Grass Traction Company, Central Traction Company, and Lexington Railway Company were brought under the control of Lexington & Interurban Railway (L&I).

L&I planned to build interurban lines out from downtown Lexington to Nicholasville, Richmond, and Winchester. Only the Nicholasville Line was built, opening for service in 1910. In 1911, L&I was bought out and became Kentucky Traction & Terminal Company (KT&T). KT&T, besides owning the city lines in Lexington, owned the trolley lines in Frankfort, Georgetown, and Winchester.

In 1913, KT&T reported that it owned 30.3 miles of city track and 61.43 miles of interurban track, 15 interurban cars, 4 freight motors, and 50 city cars operating in Lexington, Georgetown, Frankfort, and Winchester. During that year, the four Lexington city car lines carried 4,697,272 passengers while the interurban trains running into and out of the city carried 1,610,272 passengers. Total car mileage for the four city street lines was 1,095,074 miles and for the interurban lines, 811,213 miles. In carrying out this service, KT&T employed 398 men, and within Lexington owned 27 buildings of various types, including a substation, powerhouse, ice plant, depot, and carbarn.

In 1913, KT&T completed an upgrade of its track within the city of Lexington. They reported that all the new ties were of oak, placed two feet center to center, and the rails placed on them were of steel weighing 80 pounds. "The rebuilt track was laid in streets surfaced in brick. The space between the rails, and for eighteen inches on the outside of the rail, was paved with vitrified brick paving blocks. On the inside of each rail was laid a special cut Missouri red granite block, which passes underneath the head of the rail. The brick was bonded with cement filler." City streets paved in asphalt were rebuilt as above "with the exception that special cut row of granite blocks was placed on each side of the rail and the space between these blocks and on the outside of them were surfaced with asphalt to conform to the remainder of the street."

It should be noted that KT&T interurban service also provided "Less Than Carload" (LCL) carriage of goods via its freight motor cars. KT&T's LCL service was the UPS of its day. The freight motors moved various goods, including ice and milk, from their producers to retailers or from retailer to customer. When the lady of the house came to Lexington to shop via the interurban car, she did not have to carry her purchases back with her to the interurban depot. At the end of the business day, the stores delivered their out-of-town customers' purchases to the KT&T Depot on Main at Merino Street. The goods taken to the KT&T Depot were there loaded onto the freight motor for next day delivery to the buyers' hometowns. All goods for forwarding from Lexington over KT&T were due at the KT&T Depot by 5:00 PM. The LCL cargo would then be taken to the consignee's depot that evening for pickup the next day. LCL goods would also be brought from outlying stations into KT&T's Lexington Depot. On the Nicholasville Line, the freight motor left Lexington at 9:00 PM and returned from Nicholasville, with any LCL cargo bound for Lexington, at 10:15 PM.

The years 1914 to 1920 would not be kind to KT&T; inflation brought on by World War I would rob the company of profit. Automobiles would become the common means of transportation for the middle and upper class. The Lexington Motor Car Company of Lexington started production of their "Lexington" automobile in 1908. The company would build some 500 cars here before moving to Connersville, Indiana, in 1910.

In 1922, KT&T operated over 91.33 miles of track of which 16.5 miles were on paved streets. KT&T owned 49 one-man cars, 8 two-man cars, 3 freight motors, and 14 service cars. City fare was $.07 while interurban fare was $.036 per mile. If one bought a book of tickets, city fare became $.0625 and interurban fare $.03 per mile.

In 1923, with costs rising and the user base of KT&T shrinking, KT&T's response was to order twenty-seven lightweight city cars from the Cincinnati Car Company, #200 to #226. The cars were 26 feet 2 inches long and could seat 28 passengers. The new cars used less electricity to power them and were operated by one man, the motorman. The new cars were equipped as Pay As You Enter Cars (PAYE). All passengers boarded the cars via the front door and deposited their money in the fare box that sat beside the motorman. The motorman's only involvement, if fare collecting, was to make change, issue transfers, and insure the correct amount of money went into the fare box. Passengers exited from the car via the rear door. These cars would later be fitted with magnetic brakes. Lexington, as a result of this Cincinnati Car Company purchase, became famous within the traction industry for operating a total system based on only one type of car. Experts of the era constantly pointed out the savings KT&T was able to realize by operating only one type of car, particularly in car parts it had to stock.

Also during the 1930s, Lexington received four Cincinnati Curved Side Cars from the closure of Ohio River Electric Railway of Pomeroy, Ohio; four from the defunct Buffalo & Lake Erie Traction Company of Erie, Pennsylvania; and four from Maysville Street Railway of Maysville, Kentucky, after it ceased operations. It appears, however, that only Cars #28 and #29 from Ohio River Electric Railway actually ran in Lexington.

It must be noted that Kentucky was a firm adherent to the Jim Crow Law that required separate but equal accommodations for "Colored." Kentucky's legislature would not vote to adopt the 13th Amendment to the United States Constitution, which in 1865 abolished slavery, until 1976. "Colored" persons were expected to ride in the rear of the car. The interurban cars had a separate compartment marked "Colored," but on local trolleys, this was a space assigned by race, expanding and contracting depending on the composition of the passengers.

For a short time, the use of lightweight cars and one-man crews caused a positive cash flow for KT&T, but all too soon, the operation began drifting back into the red. The start of the Great Depression in 1929 pushed KT&T firmly into the red. Management began to seek ways to close down street and interurban operations. KT&T itself was a subsidiary company first of Kentucky Securities Company, then International Utilities Company, and then in 1930 of Middle West Utilities Company, which was part of the Samuel Insull Empire. Money was not made by operating public transportation companies but by producing and selling electricity to residential, commercial, and industrial establishments. When the Insull Empire went into receivership in 1932, KT&T was one property the trustees wanted to get rid of.

During the life of the streetcar in Lexington, the various companies operating these lines had gone through four bitter strikes taking place in 1890, 1901, 1913, and 1934. The first three strikes produced major worker management confrontations, and the 1913 strike led to major riots. The 1934 strike was instituted on 13 January by the Amalgamate Association of Street Electric Railway and Motor Coach Employees of America. The strikers' demands for higher pay and shorter hours were greeted with joy by KT&T's management. Here was the leverage to abandon KT&T and cease interurban and trolley operations in Lexington. The court partially agreed with KT&T management's request. KT&T was allowed to shut down the interurban lines and end city service in Frankfort, the only other local line operating, but not in Lexington. Not only would the city lines have to continue to operate, but KT&T would have to retain in operation portions of the interurban line in Fayette County. The main segment of interurban track that had to be operated led to Joyland Park.

Joyland Park was a typical interurban amusement park built in 1926 on Paris Pike to replace Blue Grass Park, which had been located on Versailles Road at South Elkhorn Creek. Joyland Park featured rides, a swimming pool, dance pavilion, and midway. The park would remain in operation until 1963 and now lies buried under commercial establishments serving I-64/I-75.

With the demise of KT&T, Lexington Railway System was formed in 1935 to operate the trolley lines within Lexington. The Lexington Railway moved quickly to convert all the streetcar lines to bus lines. The result was that when car #206 made its run from the Fayette County Courthouse to the carbarn on April 21, 1938, it marked the last time a trolley car would operate in revenue service in Lexington. The twenty-seven Cincinnati Curve Side Cars did not find a buyer among other streetcar operators, and most were stored for some time at the carbarn before being sold for scrap or summer homes on the Kentucky and Dix Rivers. In 1956, Lexington Railway would become Lexington Transit Corporation. Then in 1972, the city of Lexington formed LexTran, the current city bus operator.

The Cincinnati Curved Side Interurban Cars owned by KT&T were, with the exception of two, sold to Cleveland, Ohio. KT&T #311 became a gasoline station, *Two Carrs*, located at North Broadway and

Russell Cave Road until torn down circa 1955. The other, Car #305, was used until 1938 to provide city service to Joyland Park on Paris Pike. It was scrapped circa 1944. During WWII, most of Lexington's street track was taken up for scrap drives. Some small portions of track reportedly remain buried under asphalt in parts of Lexington. Until recently, a series of depressions in Limestone at Colfax Street, near the University of Kentucky, showed where paved over ties had finally rotted causing a series of mini dips in the street.

Today Lexington has a local public transportation system, LexTran, and an airport that allows people to fly to the far corners of the world, but it lacks a public transportation system that ties it to nearby towns. It is strange but true that the Lexingtonians of 1911 had greater access to local, area-wide public transportation than those living here in 2011.

A complete roster of Lexington streetcars can be found in William Ambrose's book *Traction in the Bluegrass*.

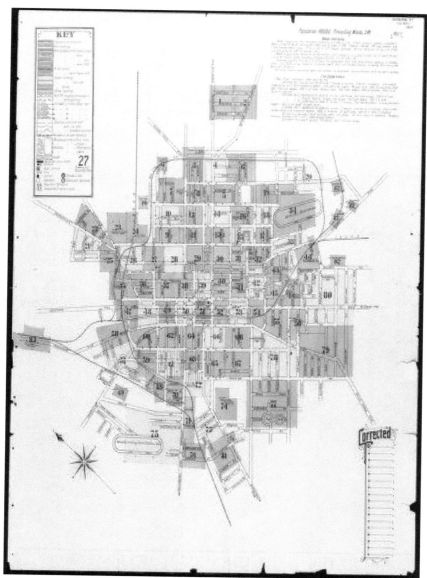

MAP OF THE CITY OF LEXINGTON <CHB>

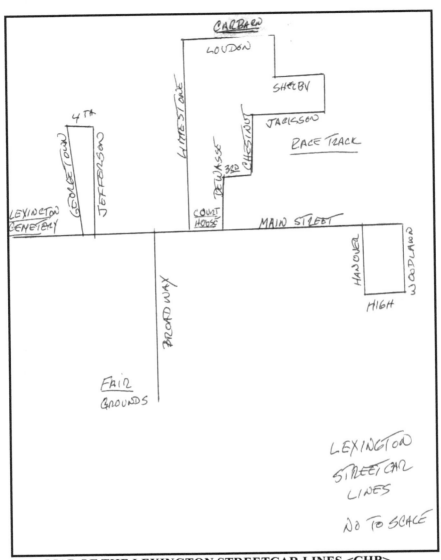

MAP OF THE LEXINGTON STREETCAR LINES <CHB>

Bird's Eye View showing West Main Street Viaduct, Lexington, Ky.

TO THE RIGHT, AN L&N PASSENGER TRAIN LEAVES THE RAILROAD DEPOT BOUND FOR LOUISVILLE. IN THE CENTER, A STREETCAR CROSSES OVER THE L&N RAIL LINE TO PARIS FOR THE LEXINGTON CEMETERY. <CHB>

Bird's Eye View, West from Phoenix Hotel. Lexington, Ky.

A CITY CAR AMBLES DOWN MAIN STREET. <CHB>

Cooling Plant at Power House,
Lexington, Ky.

ABOVE AND BELOW ARE VIEWS OF THE POWER PLANT THAT
SUPPLIED ELECTRICITY FOR THE CITY LINE. SOON SALES TO
RESIDENTIAL AND BUSINESS CUSTOMERS BECAME MORE
VALUABLE THAN THE STREETCAR FRANCHISE. <CHB>

Electric Light and Power Plant, Lexington, Ky.
Hot Water from boilers being recooled for further use.

IN THE FOREGROUND IS THE TRANSFER STATION LOCATED AT MAIN AND CHEAPSIDE. <CHB>

THE TRANSFER STATION ALONG WITH TWO STREETCARS IS SEEN LOWER CENTER. <CHB>

Bird's Eye View, East from Phoenix Hotel, Lexington, Ky.

IN THE LOWER RIGHT IS THE LEXINGTON UNION TRAIN STATION. A CITY CAR IS PREPARING TO STOP AT THE DEPOT. <CHB>

Main Street Flood - July 1928 - Lexington, KY

DURING HEAVY RAINS, TOWN BRANCH CREEK HAD A TENDENCY TO FLOOD DOWNTOWN LEXINGTON UNTIL MODERN STORM DRAINS WERE INSTALLED. IF THE WATER GETS MUCH HIGHER IT WILL SHORT OUT THE STREETCAR TRACTION MOTORS. <CS>

Main Street, looking West, at Night, Lexington, Ky.

ABOVE AND BELOW ARE VIEWS OF CITY CARS IN DOWNTOWN
LEXINGTON. <CHB>

Lexington, Ky. Main Street Looking West from Railway Station

A 17073 Main Street, Lexington, Ky. "Hello girls"

ABOVE AND BELOW ARE SEEN CITY CARS RUNNING IN DOWNTOWN LEXINGTON. <CHB>

Main Street, looking East, Lexington, Ky.

Main Street, Looking West,
Lexington, Ky.

ABOVE AND BELOW ARE SOME VIEWS OF CITY CARS OPERATING IN DOWNTOWN LEXINGTON. <CHB>

Scene on Main Street, looking West, showing
New Fayette Bank Building in distance,
Lexington, Ky.

Main Street, looking West,
Lexington, Ky.

ABOVE AND BELOW ARE VIEWS OF CITY CARS IN DOWNTOWN LEXINGTON. <CHB>

Main Street, looking East,
Lexington, Ky.

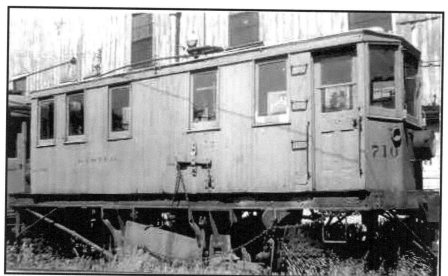

KT&T #710 WAS USED FOR SWEEPING THE STREETS AND PUSHING
LIGHT SNOW AWAY FROM THE TRACKS. <CS>

KT&T #1 IS SEEN PUSHING SNOW AWAY FROM THE RAILS TO
INSURE THAT THE STREETCARS DO NOT DERAIL BECAUSE OF
PACKED SNOW OVER THE RAILS. <WA>

A SAFETY ISLAND HAS BEEN ESTABLISHED IN THE STREET NEXT TO THE STREETCAR TRACKS TO PROTECT THOSE GETTING ON AND OFF THE STREETCAR. <CS>

EXTENDING DOWNWARD OVER THE FRONT OF THE CAR CAN BE SEEN THE SWITCH THROWER. THE MOTORMAN, UPON REACHING A SWITCH, WOULD LEAN OUT HIS WINDOW, TAKE THE SWITCH THROWER, AND THEN USE IT TO ENGAGE THE SWITCH ACTIVATOR IN THE STREET.   THIS WOULD DIRECT THE TRACK IN THE DIRECTION HE WISHED TO GO. <CS>

IT WAS COMMON TO PLACE BILLBOARDS ON THE FRONT END OF STREETCARS TO ADVERTISE SOME LOCAL HAPPENING. IN THIS CASE, IT IS THE MOVIE *HAPPY LANDINGS.* <CS>

STREETCAR SERVICE HAS ENDED. KT&T #220 RESTS AT THE CARBARN ON LOUDON AVENUE AWAITING ITS FATE. <CS>

THREE CARS AT THE LOUDON BARN PREPARE FOR THAT DAY'S RUN. <CS>

A NUMBER OF LEXINGTON STREETCARS SIT ABANDONED AT THE CARBARN. WILL THEY BE BURNED FOR SCRAP METAL OR SOLD FOR USE AS A SUMMER COTTAGE? <CS>

A KT&T TRANSFER STUB <CHB>

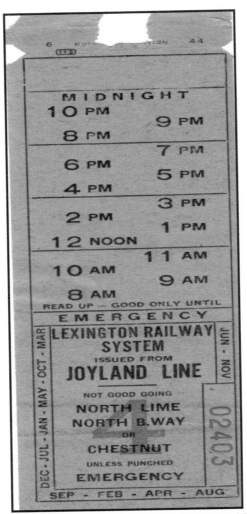

A LEXINGTON RAILWAY SYSTEM TRANSFER STUB. <CHB>

Above—Lexington Single-Truck One-Man Car Has Front and Rear Doors.
Below—Construction of Curved Side Framing

AN ADVERTISEMENT POINTING OUT THE ADVANTAGES OF LEXINGTON'S NEW LIGHTWEIGHT ONE-MAN CARS <CHB>

KT&T INTERURBAN CAR #311 SERVED AS A GASOLINE STATION FOR A NUMBER OF YEARS AT BROADWAY AND LOUDOUN. <CS>

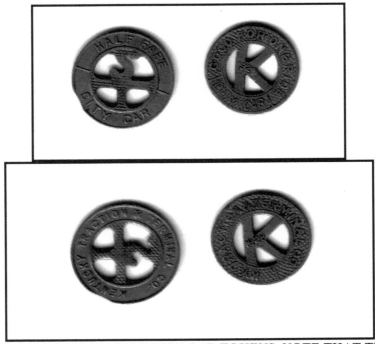

FRONT AND BACK OF KT&T CITY CAR TOKENS. NOTE THAT THE LARGER TOKEN IS MARKED HALF FARE AND ITS INTERIOR DESIGN IS A "1" OVER A "2". THIS TOKEN WAS USED BY SCHOOL CHILDREN. THE FULL FARE TOKEN IS DATED 1928. <CHB>

THE BRAKES FAILED

Downtown Lexington, Kentucky, lies roughly on an east-west orientation. It is about three city blocks wide by nine blocks long and is located in the flood plain of Town Branch Creek. This creek is generally a small stream, but at times of heavy rainfall, it can fill its former streambed with water from bank to bank. In 1832, Lexington began to build the Lexington & Ohio Railroad (L&O) eastward from Water Street & Broadway to Louisville. The L&O would get no farther west than Frankfort but would later become part of the Louisville & Nashville Railroad's (L&N) mainline between Louisville, Lexington, and Winchester.

Lexington's first railroad depot was located at Water Street and Broadway, then circa 1870, the depot was moved two blocks east, to the back of the Phoenix Hotel at Water & Mill Street. This depot served the Lexington & Eastern Railroad (Lex&E), the L&N, and the Chesapeake and Ohio Railway (C&O). The C&O track ran from Ashland via Morehead and Winchester to Lexington and then from Lexington it ran over L&N tracks to Louisville. The Lex&E ran eastward from Lexington via Winchester to Stanton and beyond. When an Lex&E, L&N, or C&O passenger train was discharging and picking up passengers at the Lexington Depot, its consist of passenger and baggage cars would extend beyond the immediate area of the depot and block traffic on cross streets.

The other railroad serving Lexington was the Cincinnati Southern, which at this time was being operated as part of the Queen and Crescent Route (Q&C), Cincinnati, Ohio, to New Orleans, Louisiana. The Q&C Depot was located one mile south of downtown Lexington on Broadway and was tied to downtown by a trolley car that ran along Broadway.

On May 9, 1907, George Wells, motorman, and George Clayton, conductor, took Car #56 out of the Lexington Railway Company's Loudoun Street Carbarn for service on the Broadway Street Line. The car's destination was the Q&C Depot. (This streetcar operation was commonly called the Train Car Run.) Upon arrival at the Q&C Depot, Conductor Clayton telephoned the street railway dispatcher, Frank Timberland, and told him that Car #56 was experiencing braking problems. Dispatcher Timberlake later testified that he instructed Conductor Clayton to "bring the car in if you can get it in." Timberlake went on to say he assumed that they would immediately return Car #56 to the streetcar barn and had not thought that they would wait at the Q&C Depot to pick up passengers deboarding from the Q&C's Royal Palm.

Instead of returning immediately for the carbarn, Conductor Clayton and Motorman Wells waited at the depot for the arrival of the Royal Palm. Upon its arrival, they picked up ten passengers for downtown Lexington, and on the way into town, they also picked up two local citizens. At approximately 11:15 AM, as Car #54 was preceding north on Broadway, C&O's Train No. 22, the *Fast Flying Virginian* (FFV), was arriving at the Lexington Depot from Louisville. Pulling the train was locomotive #153, a 4-6-2, with Engineer J. W. Smith at the throttle. Immediately behind the locomotive was a wooden combination baggage/mail/express car. Riding in this car were Julian Childers, mail clerk, M. M. Stratton, baggage master, and Mr. O'Dossett, express agent.

As C&O's FFV approached Broadway, E. Blanders, the crossing guard, entered onto Broadway to stop traffic. He, however, was on the north side of the train and did not observe Car #56 coming down Broadway Hill. FFV's locomotive, C&O #153, was at this point slowing down for a stop at the Lexington Depot platform. Smith had just cleared Broadway with his locomotive when he heard a thunderous crash and his train went into emergency.

The cars of the C&O train had just started to cross Broadway when Car #56, with Wells at the controls, started down the hill toward Water Street. As he normally did, Wells began to apply his brakes as the car descended the 10 percent grade, planning to stop short of the railroad crossing on Water Street. However, the defective brakes of Car #56 failed to engage and slow the car; instead the car accelerated as it descended Broadway Hill. The streetcar sped across Vine Street toward Water Street where it struck the FFV's baggage car, which was knocked from its wheels by the force of the crash and fell on its side, while Car #56 "was reduced to kindling."

The *Lexington Herald* would record the incident as follows: "Brake on South Broadway car fails to work on steep hill and causes worst mishap ever seen in this city. Baggage coach's side is crushed. Streetcar crumbled like an eggshell. Debris is piled high. Baggage coach thrown against telegraph pole and streetcar is collapsed like a paper bag. The crash was heard throughout downtown."

Onlookers immediately rushed to the scene to help. George Wells was found alive at the brake stand but badly crushed with a leg severed; he died shortly after being removed from the car. Conductor Clayton and the other passengers were transported to nearby hospitals. Within the C&O's baggage/mail/express car, amazingly only the mail clerk, Julian Childers, suffered injuries requiring hospitalization.

The *Lexington Leader* went on to report, "After the victims had been removed, a force of men arrived from the C&O and the Lex&E shops. Unfortunately, there was no wrecking crane at the C&O or Lex&E yards. The men worked like Trojans to clear the track. The accident closed the tracks for almost an hour. A C&O yard switcher was attached to the rear of the FFV train and pulled these cars, via the Belt Line, to the Lexington Depot. Here they picked up passengers and continued on the way to Winchester. At 12:35 PM the tracks were clear and traffic resumed."

The next day a Coroner's Jury ruled, "The said accident was caused by the negligence of the Lexington Street Railway Company in permitting said car to be run with passengers after being notified by the conductor that said car was disabled by defective brakes." Since Conductor Clayton was in the hospital, he was not called to testify before the Coroner's Jury. Thus, there is one question I would like answered that was not asked of Conductor Clayton. "Why did you pick up passengers when you knew the car was unsafe and had permission to return to the carbarn?" I would also have asked Motorman Wells a question. "Testimony at the Coroner's hearing brought out that it was not a rare occurrence for a streetcar to fail to be properly braking when coming down Broadway Hill. Many motormen stopped their cars at the top of the hill to ensure that a train was not entering the crossing. Why did you fail to stop at the top of the hill before proceeding down Broadway Hill?"

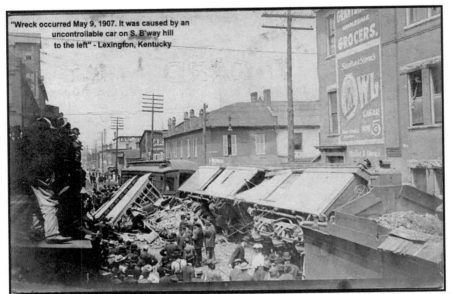

THE C&O BAGGAGE CAR LIES TILTED ON ITS SIDE WHILE THE TROLLEY CAR LIES CRUMPLED IN THE STREET. <CHB>

WHEN AROUND RAILROAD TRACK
EXPECT A TRAIN
AT ANY TIME
FROM ANY DIRECTION
AT ANY TIME

ALWAYS LOOK AND LISTEN
WHEN NEAR RAILROAD TRACKS

Index

319